NFT™

Not For Tourists Guide to
BROOKLYN

Get more on
notfortourists.com

Keep connected with:
Twitter:
twitter/notfortourists

Facebook:
facebook/notfortourists

iPhone App:
nftiphone.com

Not For Tourists, Inc   **Skyhorse Publishing**

designed by:
Not For Tourists, Inc
NFT™—Not For Tourists™ Guide to Brooklyn
www.notfortourists.com

| **Publisher** | **Managing Editor** | **Research** |
| Skyhorse Publishing | Scott Sendrow | Nalini Ramautar |

Creative Direction &   **Production Manager**   **Graphic Design and**
Information Design   Aaron Schielke   **Production**
Jane Pirone   Aaron Schielke

      Writing & Editing
Director   Sarah Enelow   **Information Systems**
Stuart Farr   Scott Sendrow   **Manager**
      Juan Molinari

Printed in China
Print ISBN: 978-1-63450-140-8 $15.99
eBook ISBN: 978-1-5107-0019-2
ISSN 2163-9035
Copyright © 2015 by Not For Tourists, Inc.
11th Edition

Every effort has been made to ensure that the information in this book is as up-to-date as possible at press time. However, many details are liable to change—as we have learned.
Not For Tourists cannot accept responsibility for any consequences arising from the use of this book.

Not For Tourists does not solicit individuals, organizations, or businesses for listings inclusion in our guides, nor do we accept payment for inclusion into the editorial portion of our book; the advertising sections, however, are exempt from this policy. We always welcome communications from anyone regarding ANYTHING having to do with our books; please visit us on our website at www. notfortourists.com for appropriate contact information.

www.skyhorsepublishing.com

10 9 8 7 6 5 4 3 2 1

Dear NFT User:

Once upon a time, there were unicorns and trolls, dog breeds were dog breeds, and guidebooks were widely agreed to be useful tools of navigation and exploration. But now that even your curmudgeonly old Uncle Max has an iDroid and Street-tooth and a tiny BlueTube delivering user ratings directly into his amygdala, why spend a hard-earned Hamilton-and-a-half to take home this old-fashioned pack of paper?

Because like a well-played game of stickball, marathon session of double dutch or hard-fought round of skully, NFT is old school: a thoughtfully assembled, well-edited collection of maps, listings, and descriptions designed to help you find the best of Brooklyn and not waste a nanosecond of your time on anything else.

That's right, friends: For the price of a Roberta's pizza—or a little less than what you'd spend for three helpings of tacos from Sunset Park's Tacos Matamoros…or for just about what you'd spend for a dozen or so pupusas at the Red Hook Ballfields—you'll have a fully updated catalog of local restaurants, bars, shops, and landmarks, plus extended coverage of parks, beaches, sports arenas, and museums. If you're nonplussed by the giant super-expensive glossy foldout map in the back, think about this: Do you really want to rely on Taxi TV to get from Greenpoint to Crown Heights?

Face it: you need us. Wrap your furry paws around this superior guide of all things Brooklyn and get ready to scout the tastiest dim sum, the artiest art, the rowdiest pubs, the prettiest parks, the quirkiest 24-hour bowling alleys, and all the rest of the borough's hidden treasures. When you come across something we missed, send us a note at www.notfortourists.com. The only thing we like more than your incalculable admiration is snappy and pointed, yet pertinent, critique.

Jane, Scott, Sarah, Aaron, et al.

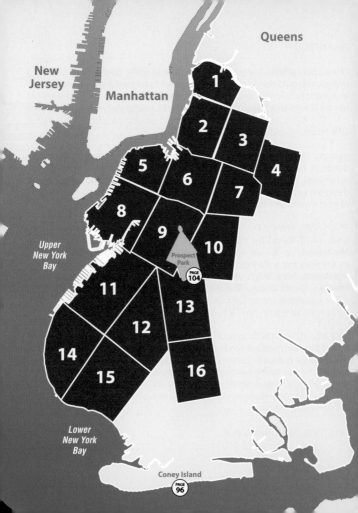

Queens

New Jersey

Manhattan

1

2

3

4

5

6

7

8

9

10

Upper New York Bay

Prospect Park

PAGE 104

11

12

13

14

15

16

Lower New York Bay

Coney Island

PAGE 96

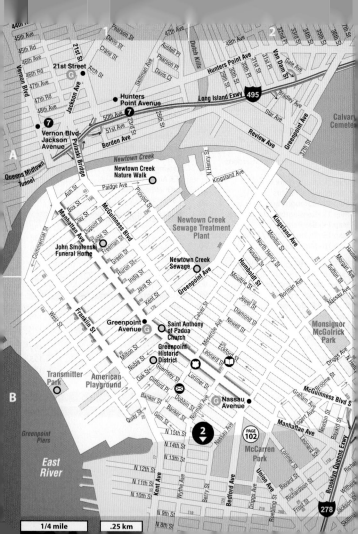

Map 1

The northernmost neighborhood in Brooklyn, Greenpoint has multiple personality disorder. It's strongly Polish (hence the mouth-watering bakeries and butcher shops) and solidly trendy. As the name suggests, parts are indeed green, but it's also home to one of America's filthiest waterways.

As longtime hub for shipping and manufacturing, Greenpoint sits at the nexus of Newtown Creek and the East River. Newtown Creek is infamous for the 1950 oil spill more than twice the size of Exxon Valdez; now an EPA Superfund site, remediation will continue for years. On a brighter note, Newtown Creek's quarter-mile **Nature Walk** is a valiant attempt to spruce things up, and the tree-lined **Greenpoint Historical District** (originally home to local industrial workers) is still in excellent shape. Greenpoint is also the proud owner of the verdant oasis known as **McGolrick Park**. Manhattan Avenue Park (at the northern dead-end of that thoroughfare) is a well-kept, tiny gem with several cool sculptures. Also check out the impressive **Eagle Street Rooftop Farm**; support their efforts by buying fresh greens (give your regards to the rabbits and chickens). And **Transmitter Park**, the former home of WNYC's radio towers at the end of Greenpoint Avenue, is a rare spot of green along the waterfront; head to the end of the zig-zagging pier for a respite from the heat of the city—it's like ten degrees cooler out in the middle of the East River.

Manhattan Avenue is the neighborhood's main artery (buses and the G train run along it). Mass is held at the stunning **Saint Anthony of Padua Church** and your everyday needs are met along the way—fruit & vegetable stands, taco restaurants, bars and the like. Franklin Street is a relaxing antidote to the grimy bustle of Manhattan Avenue, with galleries, boutiques and various high-concept entities. East of McGuinness Boulevard you'll find various cheap bars, liquor stores, restaurants, Polish bakeries and a few real, respectable coffee shops, including Hannah Horvath's employers, **Café Grumpy**.

One exciting aspect of Greenpoint (though not for locals with cars) is the frequent number of movie and television productions filmed here. It's close to Manhattan and Long Island City (where a number of studios are based) and can stand in for a green, industrial, or cozy neighborhood setting. *Flight of the Conchords* shot their French song video in McGolrick Park. *30 Rock* filmed in front of a dollar store on Manhattan Avenue. Recent productions have included *The Bounty Hunter*, *Date Night*, *Boardwalk Empire*, and *Girls*. If you keep your ears open at a bar, you may even hear someone who worked on a shoot giving the lowdown on which star is a bitch or which guy played the diva and spent the entire shoot moaning about a recent breakup. Ah, New York.

Barflies of every stripe can find something to suit their tastes, from sports bars (**Red Star**) to cocktail lounges (**Manhattan Inn**). **PencilFactory** and **Black Rabbit** are excellent standbys on Greenpoint Avenue and NFT staffers can be found at the **Palace Cafe**.

5 6 7 4
8
9 10

O Landmarks

- **Greenpoint Historic District** •
Oak St & Guernsey St
Charming rowhouses that were built for
workers of early merchants.
- **John Smolenski Funeral Home** •
1044 Manhattan Ave [Freeman St]
718-389-4170
1920s landmark with one of Greenpoint's
beautiful clocks.
- **Newtown Creek Nature Walk** •
Provost St & Paidge Ave
Great views of the sewage plant!
- **Newtown Creek Wastewater
Treatment Plant** •
Greenpoint Ave & Provost St
Take a moment to contemplate all of the
famous and beautiful peoples' crap floating
around in here.
- **Saint Anthony of Padua Church** •
862 Manhattan Ave [Milton St]
718-383-3339
Beautiful church sticking out like a healthy
thumb on congested avenue.
- **Transmitter Park** •
West St bet Kent St & Greenpoint Ave
Greenpoint's waterfront park; former home of
WNYC transmitter towers.

Coffee

- **Budin** • 114 Greenpoint Ave [Manhattan Ave]
347-844-9639
High-end Scandinavian coffee. With beer. Also,
not cheap.
- **Café Grumpy** •
193 Meserole Ave [Diamond St]
718-349-7623
The finest coffee house in Brooklyn now has its
own roastery.
- **Café Riviera** • 830 Manhattan Ave [Noble St]
718-383-8450
Delicious baked-goods and such.
- **Champion Coffee** •
1108 Manhattan Ave [Clay St]
718-383-5195
Best espresso north of Greenpoint Ave.
- **Uro Café** • 277 Driggs Ave [Leonard St]
718-599-1230
Best espresso south of Greenpoint Ave.

- **Van Leeuwen Ice Cream** •
632 Manhattan Ave [Nassau Ave]
718-701-1630
Excellent coffee to go with your coffee ice
cream.
- **Variety Coffee & Tea** •
145 Driggs Ave [Russell St]
347-689-3790

Farmers Markets

- **Eagle Street Rooftop Farm** •
44 Eagle St [West St]
Sunday, 1 p.m.–4 p.m. during growing season.

Nightlife

- **Achilles Heel** • 180 West St [Green St]
347-987-3666
Worn, hip local bar way over by the docks.
- **Bar Matchless** •
557 Manhattan Ave [Driggs Ave]
718-383-5333
Weekly music showcases, heavy metal
karaoke, and foosball.
- **Beloved** • 674 Manhattan Ave [Norman Ave]
347-457-5448
Imposing entrance but low-key inside,
excellent cocktails, charming patio.
- **Black Rabbit** • 91 Greenpoint Ave [Franklin St]
718-349-1595
Fantastic fireplace, delicious mini-burgers.
Trivia night is packed.
- **The Diamond** • 43 Franklin St [Calyer St]
718-383-5030
Wine, massive beer selection, and
shuffleboard.
- **Dirck the Norseman** • 7 N 15th St [Franklin St]
718-389-2940
Excellent brewed-on-site beer with German
food as a bonus. Great space, too.
- **Enid's** • 560 Manhattan Ave [Driggs Ave]
718-349-3859
Greenpoint's finest hipster stand-by.
- **Europa** • 98 Meserole Ave [Manhattan Ave]
917-826-1119
Strobe light extravaganza.
- **The Habitat** • 988 Manhattan Ave [Huron St]
718-383-5615
Featuring waffle fries and "zero attitude."

Map 1

A Greenpoint visit must include a meal at a cheap and hearty Polish restaurant, like **Christina's**. Afterwards, get a Polish pastry at **Café Riviera** or have some caffeine in the adorable backyard of **Champion Coffee**. One of the best brunches in the city is at **Cafecito Bogota**, so come hungry.

- **The Manhattan Inn** •
  632 Manhattan Ave [Nassau Ave]
  718-383-0885
  Dark bar, pricey but delicious food, piano man in back.
- **Northern Territory** •
  12 Franklin St [Meserole Ave]
  347-689-4065
  Leafy rooftop bar with expansive view, get the Territory's Tea.
- **One Stop Beer Shop** •
  134 Kingsland Ave [Beadel St]
  718-599-0128
  Craft beer and artisanal food, of course.
- **Palace Café** • 206 Nassau Ave [Russell St]
  718-383-9848
  Heavy jukebox and stiff drinks. Metal lives!
- **Pencil Factory Bar** •
  142 Franklin St [Greenpoint Ave]
  718-609-5858
  Great beer; great vibe. Perfectly understated.
- **Pit Stop Bar** •
  152 Meserole Ave [McGuinness Blvd]
  718-383-0981
  Buy a couple scratch-offs and experience blue-collar Brooklyn.
- **Red Star** • 37 Greenpoint Ave [West St]
  718-349-0162
  A real sports bar. 2 floors and terrific wings.
- **Shayz Lounge** • 130 Franklin St [Milton St]
  718-389-3888
  Irish pub in a sea of Polish.
- **Spritzenhaus** • 33 Nassau Ave [Dobbin St]
  347-987-4632
  Predictably packed beer garden in Greenpoint.
- **TBD Bar** • 224 Franklin St [Green St]
  718-349-6727
  Backyard "beer garden" is tops on nice days.
- **Tommy's Tavern** •
  1041 Manhattan Ave [Freeman St]
  718-383-9699
  Super-dive with live music on weekends.
- **Torst** • 615 Manhattan Ave [Nassau Ave]
  718-389-6034
  Not just a beer bar, a fancy beer bar with Danish accents.
- **Warsaw** • 261 Driggs Ave [Eckford St]
  718-387-0505
  Brooklyn's best concert venue.

🍴 Restaurants

- **Acapulco Deli & Restaurant** •
  1116 Manhattan Ave [Clay St]
  718-349-8429 • $
  Authentic Mexican includes homemade chips and telenovelas at full volume.
- **Amarin Café** •
  617 Manhattan Ave [Nassau Ave]
  718-349-2788 • $
  Good, cheap Thai food.
- **Anella** • 222 Franklin St [Green St]
  718-389-8100 • $$
  Seasonal Italian, beautifully simple, bread baked in flowerpots.
- **Ashbox** • 1154 Manhattan Ave [Ash St]
  718-389-3222 • $
  Japanese-influenced cafe fare at the mouth of Newton Creek.
- **Brooklyn Ice Cream Factory** •
  97 Commercial St [Box St]
  718-349-2506 • $
  As yummy as the DUMBO shop, without the lines.
- **Brooklyn Label** • 180 Franklin St [Java St]
  718-389-2806 • $
  Scrumptious sandwiches in the stately Astral building.
- **Cafecito Bogota** •
  1015 Manhattan Ave [Green St]
  718-569-0077 • $$
  Authentic and amazing Colombian cuisine.
- **Calexico Carne Asada** •
  645 Manhattan Ave [Bedford Ave]
  347-763-2129 • $
  Polish tacos? The tasty Mexi food truck settles down in Greenpoint.
- **Christina's** • 853 Manhattan Ave [Noble St]
  718-383-4382 • $
  Traditional Polish food, cheap breakfasts!
- **Enid's** • 560 Manhattan Ave [Driggs Ave]
  718-349-3859 • $$
  Popular brunch on weekends; also dinner weeknights.
- **Erb** • 681 Manhattan Ave [Norman Ave]
  718-349-8215 • $$
  Terrific Thai; try the curry noodles.
- **Five Leaves** • 18 Bedford Ave [Nassau Ave]
  718-383-5345 • $$$
  Heath Ledger's post-mortem restaurant is cooler than you.

- **God Bless Deli** •
818 Manhattan Ave [Calyer St]
718-349-0605 • $
The only 24-hour joint in the 'hood. Cheap
sandwiches and burgers.
- **Karczma** •
136 Greenpoint Ave [Manhattan Ave]
718-349-1744 • $$
Homestyle Polish, rightly popular among
locals, rustic interior.
- **Kestane Kebab** • 110 Nassau Ave [Eckford St]
718-349-8601 • $
Refuel your party tank around the clock for
cheap.
- **Kyoto Sushi** • 161 Nassau Ave [Diamond St]
718-383-8882 • $$
Best sushi in Greenpoint; dine in for the sake
and after-dinner Dum Dums.
- **La Taverna** • 946 Manhattan Ave [Java St]
718-383-0732 • $$
Hearty Italian for cheap? Si, per favore!
- **Lomzynianka** •
646 Manhattan Ave [Nassau Ave]
718-389-9439 • $
Get your kitschy Polish fix dirt cheap.
- **Manhattan Three Decker** •
695 Manhattan Ave [Norman Ave]
718-389-6664 • $$
Greek and American fare.
- **Ott** • 970 Manhattan Ave [India St]
718-609-2416 • $$
Another excellent Thai choice on Manhattan
Ave.
- **Paulie Gee's** • 60 Greenpoint Ave [West St]
347-987-3747 • $$
Top brick-oven 'za right by the river. Nice.
- **Peter Pan Doughnuts** •
727 Manhattan Ave [Norman Ave]
718-389-3676 • $
Polish girls in smocks serving tasty donuts.
- **Relax** • 68 Newell St [Nassau Ave]
718-389-1665 • $
Polish diner w/ good prices and excellent
soups—a neighborhood favorite.
- **Sapporo Ichiban** •
622 Manhattan Ave [Nassau Ave]
718-389-9712 • $$
Fresh sushi, friendly service.

Shopping

- **Alter Men** • 109 Franklin St [Greenpoint Ave]
718-784-8818
Nice selection of vintage and hard-to-find
labels.
- **Alter Women** •
140 Franklin St [Greenpoint Ave]
718-349-0203
Nice selection of vintage and hard-to-find
labels.
- **Bellocq Tea Atelier** • 104 West St [Kent St]
1-800-495-5416
Exquisite tea sold per ounce, look hard for
the sign.
- **Brooklyn Craft Company** •
61 Greenpoint Ave [Franklin St]
646-201-4049
Girly DIY classes to while away the
crafternoon…
- **Brouwerij Lane** •
78 Greenpoint Ave [Franklin St]
347-529-6133
For beer junkies. Global bottles or pour-your-
own growlers.
- **Charlotte Patisserie** •
596 Manhattan Ave [Driggs Ave]
718-383-8313
Polish-run dessert and coffee shop, delicious
French-style pastries.
- **Cracovia Liquors** • 150 Nassau Ave [Newell St]
718-383-2010
Easiest place to spot a bum in Greenpoint.
Open late.
- **Dandelion Wine** • 153 Franklin St [Java St]
347-689-4563
Knowledgeable staff and frequent wine
tastings—double win!
- **Eastern District** •
1053 Manhattan Ave [Freeman St]
718-384-1563
Cheese and beer shop with tons of Brooklyn
brands.
- **Fox & Fawn Vintage** •
570 Manhattan Ave [Driggs Ave]
718-349-9510
Same great vintage store, new location. Hips
(arms and legs) don't lie.

Hit the (sausage) links at **Steve's Meat Market**. Visit **Old Hollywood** for vintage; refurbished is in style at **Alter Women**. The fabulously junky second-hand shop **The Thing** is more affordable than **Luddite**. Vinyl junkies browse the bins at **Permanent Records**. Shop **Eastern District** for that which is artisanal and Brooklyn-based. **Wedel** sells imported chocolates, and **New Warsaw Bakery**, **Charlotte Patisserie**, and **Jaslowiczanka** have baked goods. **WORD**'s an English-language independent bookstore.

- **The Garden** • 921 Manhattan Ave [Kent St]
  718-389-6448
  Awe-inspiring natural foods selection.
- **Jaslowiczanka Bakery** •
  163 Nassau Ave [Diamond St]
  718-389-0263
  Polish bakery with tempting layer cakes and babkas.
- **Kill Devil Hill** • 170 Franklin St [Java St]
  347-534-3088
  Interior decorating with skeletal remains.
- **Luddite** • 201 Franklin St [Freeman St]
  718-387-3450
  Beautifully curated antiques and curios.
- **Maria's Deli** • 136 Meserole Ave [Eckford St]
  718-383-9063
  One of many Polish bodegas. Pickle soup & mayonnaise salads!
- **New Warsaw Bakery** •
  866 Lorimer St [Driggs Ave]
  718-389-4700
  Respected neighborhood supplier, buy a loaf at the back entrance.
- **Old Hollywood** • 99 Franklin St [Milton St]
  718-389-0837
  From the folks who brought you the retro gentrification of North Brooklyn.
- **The One Well** •
  165 Greenpoint Ave [Leonard St]
  347-889-6792
  Cheery, girlie gift shop, emphasis on the girlie.
- **Ovenly** • 31 Greenpoint Ave [West St]
  347-689-3608
  Growing bakery serving sweet and salty treats.
- **Pentatonic Guitars & Music** •
  139 Franklin St [Java St]
  347-599-2576
  Guitars, basses, ukuleles, banjos, mandolins, gear, and repairs.

- **Permanent Records** •
  181 Franklin St [Huron St]
  718-383-4083
  Stellar selection of new and used vinyl, friendly service.
- **Pop's Popular Clothing** •
  7 Franklin St [Meserole Ave]
  718-349-7677
  Work clothes & boots for blue-collar authenticity.
- **Rzeszowska Bakery** •
  948 Manhattan Ave [Java St]
  718-383-8142
  Authentic Polish bakery; mobbed around holidays you were unaware of.
- **Slodycze Wedel** •
  772 Manhattan Ave [Meserole Ave]
  718-349-3933
  Old School chocolate shop, straight out of Poland.
- **Steve's Meat Market** •
  104 Nassau Ave [Leonard St]
  718-383-1780
  Sausages double smoked for her pleasure.
- **Sun Hee Farm** •
  886 Manhattan Ave [Greenpoint Ave]
  718-349-5965
  Ridiculously cheap fruits and veggies.
- **The Thing** • 1001 Manhattan Ave [Huron St]
  718-349-8234
  Unusual second-hand store offers thousands of used LPs.
- **WORD** • 126 Franklin St [Milton St]
  718-383-0096
  Literary fiction, non-fiction, and kids' books.

Map 2 • **Williamsburg**

Map 2

You've probably already made up your mind about Williamsburg, but let's be honest, there is always something that brings you back to this hipsturbia on the river. Are the throngs of younguns "struggling" to make rent eight times the national median obnoxious? Sure. Is your mind blown by three-hour waits at ineffectually staffed no-reservation restaurants that sell "appetizers" like "bread and butter"? Whose isn't? But do a handful of blocks around Bedford and North 7th have enough excellent restaurants, unique shops, live music, bowling alleys, enviable parks, real bookstores, and record stores for God's sake to make the rest of us schmos salivate at what our own neighborhoods can't possibly offer? Sadly, yes. Which is when you find yourself squeezing onto the L or the B62 with everyone else who knows the same to be true.

The hulking steel towers of the **Williamsburg Bridge** (1903), long before the L came to be, connected the working class neighborhoods of Brooklyn with jobs in Manhattan. Before the bridge there was the Grand Street Ferry, which departed from the end of Grand Street. That spot is now taken up by the scrappy and pleasant **Grand Ferry Park**, which was one of the few parcels of waterfront open to the public during the area's industrial heyday.

The East River of today bears the fruit of Bloomberg-era rezoning in the form of gleaming high-rise rentals and condos and a manicured waterfront. **East River State Park**, reclaimed from the weeds and still slightly rustic around the edges, is a sunny, sometimes a little too sunny, spot along the river. On summer weekends, the park hosts all manner of fairs and events. Even after the tents and tables are gone, however, East River State Park is definitely worth a weekly trip; the picnic tables at the river's edge are one of the best spots in Brooklyn to gawk at that gorgeous skyline and a killer sunset. A few blocks away is **Brooklyn Brewery**. Brooklyn branded long before Brooklyn was a brand, only a small portion of its beer is actually brewed on site (the bottles, for example, come from Utica), though this spiritual home has anchored Williamsburg's identity since the late 1990s.

Just down the street from Brooklyn Brewery at the northern end of Williamsburg sits **McCarren Park**, with its 35 acres of ball fields, dog runs, and gardens where residents of every stripe convene when the sun is out. Although not the nicest looking park in the city, or even the neighborhood, there's an anarchic spirit to the park that's hard to resist, from the infantilizing children's games being played by aging cool hunters to the pick-up softball, basketball, and soccer on dirt patches and concrete fields to the steady stream of low-key craft-film-food-music events that fill up the weekend docket during the summer; it's a park that is well used and not fussed over, unlike some of the bigger, newer, "nicer" parks. **McCarren Pool**, shuttered for decades, reopened as an actual pool and recreation center in 2012, and as such is a state-of-the-art year-round facility.

Stretching south from McCarren Park is Bedford Avenue, Williamsburg's main thoroughfare, full of shops, bars, boutiques and activity. The Bedford Avenue L station at North 7th Street functions as a sort of millennial wave pool, casting shoals of young people into the hip thick as frequently as communications-based train control can allow. Williamsburg's excesses ease the farther south and east you move from here. Along Metropolitan Avenue to the south is **City Reliquary**, a clever little (literally little) museum filled with New York City artifacts and historical tidbits, and a great way to connect with pre-gentrified Williamsburg. The south side of Broadway, where stately **Peter Luger** has served steak since 1887, is one of the city's largest and most established Hasidic neighborhoods. During the Bloomberg era the issue of bike lanes along Bedford Avenue became controversial when members of the Hasidic community objected to the idea of supposedly scantily clad (or at least less clad than they're used to) cyclists riding through their neighborhood.

Map 2

O Landmarks

- **Bedford L Train Station** •
  Bedford St & N 6th St
  L Line
- **Brooklyn Brewery** • 79 N 11th St [Wythe Ave]
  718-486-7422
  Connect with your beer by witnessing its birth;
  free samples alone encourage closeness.
- **City Reliquary** •
  370 Metropolitan Ave [Havemeyer St]
  718-782-4842
  Artifacts from New York's vast and rich history.
- **East River State Park** • Kent Ave & N 9th St
  Swath of waterfront greenspace, Williamsburg
  style.
- **Grand Ferry Park** • Grand St & River St
  Ferry is gone. Park remains.
- **McCarren Park** • Bedford Ave & N 12th St
  Hipsters, Poles, and athletes unite!
- **McCarren Park Pool** • Lorimer St & Bayard St
  718-965-6580
  Massive WPA-era pool and recreation center.
- **Williamsburg Bridge** • Driggs St & S 5th St
  Bridge of the chosen people—Jews and well-
  off hipsters.

Coffee

- **Blue Bottle Coffee Co.** • 160 Berry St [N 4th St]
  718-387-4160
  San Francisco masters with the long lines for
  pour overs.
- **Caffe Capri** • 427 Graham Ave [Frost St]
  718-383-5744
  Classic café with incredible cannolis.
- **Gimme Coffee** • 495 Lorimer St [Powers St]
  718-388-7771
  Coffee genius from Ithaca comes to Brooklyn.
- **Oslo** • 133 Roebling St [N 4th St]
  718-782-0332
  Flagship store; coffee with attention to detail.
- **Sweetleaf** • 135 Kent Ave [N 6th St]
  347-725-4862
  LIC-based West Coast bean importers share
  space with Realtor.
- **Toby's Estate** • 125 N 6th St [Berry St]
  347-457-6160
  Australian artisanal coffee powerhouse's first
  US shop.

Farmers Markets

- **Greenpoint/McCarren Park Greenmarket** •
  Union Ave & N 12th St [Driggs Ave]
  Saturday, 8 a.m.–3 p.m., year-round.
- **Williamsburg Greenmarket** •
  Broadway & Havemeyer St
  Thursday, 8 a.m.–4 p.m., July–Nov.

Nightlife

- **The Abbey** • 536 Driggs Ave [N 8th St]
  718-599-4400
  Great jukebox and staff.
- **Alligator Lounge** •
  600 Metropolitan Ave [Lorimer St]
  718-599-4440
  Ignore the décor, and enjoy the free brick oven
  pizza with your beer.
- **Ba'sik** • 323 Graham Ave [Devoe St]
  347-889-7597
  Awesome cocktails this far East? Don't tell
  them over in 11249.
- **Barcade** • 388 Union Ave [Powers St]
  718-302-6464
  Paradise for '80s console champions and craft-
  beer guzzlers.
- **Bembe** • 81 S 6th St [Berry St]
  718-387-5389
  Hookahville.
- **Berry Park** • 4 Berry St [N 14th St]
  718-782-2829
  Williamsburg's best rooftop: great beer and
  plenty of skyline.
- **Black Bear Bar** • 70 N 6th St [Wythe Ave]
  917-538-8399
  Bar in front, music in the back.
- **Burnside** • 506 Grand St [Lorimer St]
  347-889-7793
  Midwestern-themed bar complete with brats
  and cheese curds.
- **Cameo Gallery** • 93 N 6th St [Wythe Ave]
  718-302-1180
  Claustrophobic DIY speakeasy/venue in the
  heart of Williamsburg.
- **Charleston** • 174 Bedford Ave [N 7th St]
  718-599-9599
  Still going.
- **Clem's** • 264 Grand St [Roebling St]
  718-387-9617
  Classic narrow bar + drink specials = a
  neighborhood staple.

Map 2

The legendary **Knitting Factory**, relocated from TriBeCa, symbolizes the shift away from Manhattan in the New York City music scene, joining **Music Hall** and **Pete's Candy Store** in a target-rich environment. Even **Brooklyn Bowl** has a stage. After the show, head to **Spuyten-Duyvil** or **Radegast** for beers, **The Richardson** for a proper cocktail, or **Barcade** for 8-bit goodness.

- **D.O.C.** • 83 N 7th St [Wythe Ave]
718-609-4810
All-Italian wine list with upscale finger food.
- **Daddy's** • 435 Graham St [Frost St]
718-609-6388
Friendly hipster hideaway.
- **Dram** • 177 S 4th St [Driggs Ave]
718-486-3726
NYC's best cocktails that nobody knows about.
- **Duff's Brooklyn** • 168 Marcy Ave [Broadway]
718-599-2092
Heavy metal basement dive in the J train shadow.
- **East River Bar** • 97 S 6th St [Berry St]
718-302-0511
Fun interior, patio, and live music.
- **The Gibson** • 108 Bedford Ave [N 11th St]
718-387-6296
Quiet, classy Williamsburg bar.
- **Greenpoint Tavern** •
188 Bedford Ave [N 7th St]
718-384-9539
Cheap beer in Styrofoam cups.
- **Hotel Delmano** • 82 Berry St [N 9th St]
718-387-1945
Classic cocktails. Great date spot.
- **Huckleberry Bar** • 588 Grand St [Lorimer St]
718-218-8555
Solid cocktails, nice garden out back.
- **The Ides Bar at Wythe Hotel** •
80 Wythe Ave [N 11th St]
718-460-8004
Ridiculous city views (in a good way) for a chicster crowd.
- **Iona** • 180 Grand St [Bedford Ave]
718-384-5008
Plenty of choices on tap.
- **Jr. and Son** •
575 Metropolitan Ave [Lorimer St]
Unabashedly hipster free.
- **Knitting Factory Brooklyn** •
361 Metropolitan Ave [Havemeyer St]
347-529-6696
Fifth-carbon of its former greatness.
- **Larry Lawrence Bar** •
295 Grand St [Havemeyer St]
718-218-7866
Laid-back bar with a lovely loft for smokers.
- **The Levee** • 212 Berry St [Metropolitan Ave]
718-218-8787
Formerly Cokies, now a laid-back vibe with free cheese balls.

- **Maison Premiere** •
298 Bedford Ave [Grand St]
347-335-0446
Cocktails and oysters, New Orleans style.
- **Mugs Ale House** • 125 Bedford Ave [N 10th St]
718-486-8232
Surprisingly good food, great beer selection, cheap.
- **Music Hall of Williamsburg** •
66 N 6th St [Kent Ave]
212-260-4700
Brooklyn's Bowery Ballroom; national acts.
- **Nita Nita** • 146 Wythe Ave [N 8th St]
718-388-5328
Friendly, low-key spot with better-than-average bar snacks.
- **Nitehawk Cinema** •
136 Metropolitan Ave [Berry St]
718-384-3980
Dinner, cocktails and craft beer while you watch indie flicks.
- **Pete's Candy Store** •
709 Lorimer St [Richardson St]
718-302-3770
Live music, trivia nights, awesome back room, and Scrabble.
- **R Bar** • 451 Meeker Ave [Graham Ave]
718-486-6116
Locals call it "our bar."
- **Radegast Hall & Biergarten** •
113 N 3rd St [Berry St]
718-963-3973
German beer hall with retractable roof. Only in Williamsburg.
- **The Richardson** •
451 Graham Ave [Richardson St]
718-389-0839
Proper cocktails and small plates served in the BQE's shadow.
- **The Shanty** • 79 Richardson St [Leonard St]
718-412-0874
Tasting room of local distillers, packed with all stars.
- **Spuyten Duyvil** •
359 Metropolitan Ave [Havemeyer St]
718-963-4140
Join the Belgian beer cult.
- **This n' That** • 108 N 6th St [Berry St]
718-599-5959
Lively gay bar with dancing and raunchy drag queens.
- **The Trash Bar** • 256 Grand St [Roebling St]
718-599-1000
Punk rock, PBR, and free tater tots.

Map 2

5 6 7 4
8 9 10

- **Trophy Bar** • 351 Broadway [Keap St]
347-227-8515
Cool little bar under the elevated. Beware "skanks and thieves."
- **Turkey's Nest Tavern** •
94 Bedford Ave [N 12th St]
718-384-9774
Best dive in Williamsburg.
- **Union Pool** • 484 Union Ave [Skillman Ave]
718-609-0484
Good starting point—or finishing point.
- **The Woods** • 48 S 4th St [Wythe Ave]
Spacious non-hipster bar plus burgers, bacon, and tacos in back.
- **Wythe Hotel** • 80 Wythe Ave [N 11th St]
718-460-8000
Home to rooftop bar The Ides, and hip restaurant Reynard.

🍴 Restaurants

- **Acqua Santa** • 556 Driggs Ave [N 7th St]
718-384-9695 • $$
Bistro Italian—amazing patio.
- **Anna Maria Pizza** • 179 Bedford Ave [N 7th St]
718-599-4550 • $
A must after late-night drinking.
- **Aurora** • 70 Grand St [Wythe Ave]
718-388-5100 • $$
Warm, friendly rustic Italian. Just about perfect.
- **Baci & Abbracci** • 204 Grand St [Driggs Ave]
718-599-6599 • $$
Old-world Italian in a modern setting.
- **Bakeri** • 150 Wythe Ave [N 8th St]
718-388-8037 • $
Adorably Amish decor and hipster vibe. Excellent baked goods.
- **Bamonte's** • 32 Withers St [Union Ave]
718-384-8831 • $$$
Historic Italian joint; mediocre food but a great space.
- **Bozu** • 296 Grand St [Havemeyer St]
718-384-7770 • $$
Amazing Japanese tapas and sushi bombs.

- **The Brooklyn Star** •
593 Lorimer St [Conselyea St]
718-599-9899 • $$
Lovingly-presented southern classics from a Momofuku veteran.
- **Cadaques** • 188 Grand St [Bedford Ave]
718-218-7776 • $$$
Pricey but rich Catalonian tapas, flavorful brunch.
- **The Commodore** •
366 Metropolitan Ave [Havemeyer]
718-218-7632 • $
Southern hipster cuisine. Good and cheap.
- **Counting Room** • 44 Berry St [N 11th St]
718-599-1860 • $
Gorgeous space. Great wine. Fine food.
- **DeStefano's Steak House** •
89 Conselyea St [Leonard St]
718-384-2836 • $$$$
Fun old school steakhouse.
- **Diner** • 85 Broadway [Berry St]
718-486-3077 • $$
Amazing simple food like you've never tasted—never disappoints.
- **Dokebi** • 199 Grand St [Driggs Ave]
718-782-1424 • $$$
Cook your own Korean BBQ with tabletop hibachis.
- **DuMont Burger** • 314 Bedford Ave [S 1st St]
718-384-6127 • $$
The mini burger is even better proportioned than the original.
- **Egg** • 135 N 5th St [Bedford Ave]
718-302-5151 • $$
Organic breakfast and free range burgers.
- **Evil Olive Pizza Bar** • 198 Union Ave [5th St]
718-387-0707 • $$
New York-style slices, bar in the back.
- **Fanny** • 425 Graham Ave [Withers St]
718-389-2060 • $$
Cozy French bistro.
- **Fette Sau** •
354 Metropolitan Ave [Roebling St]
718-963-3404 • $$
Enjoy pounds of meat and casks of beer in a former auto-body repair shop.

...or low-key, go for hipster fusion at **Snacky**. That said, don't miss the dressed-up American spots: **Walter Foods**, **Rye**, and the more casual **DuMont**. For brunch (and believe us, we hesitate recommending brunch to anyone), **Pates et Traditions** has mouth-watering crepes. Carnivores must pay respects to **Fette Sau** and **Peter Luger**. If Luger didn't empty your bank account, **Zenkichi** is another special dining experience.

- **Frost Restaurant** • 193 Frost St [Graham Ave]
  718-389-3347 • $$
  Piles of parm and a nightcap of 'buca.
- **Grandma Rose's** •
  457 Graham Ave [Meeker Ave]
  718-389-1908 • $$
  Top-notch pizza and Italian hiding under the BQE.
- **Jerry's Pizza** • 649 Grand St [Manhattan Ave]
  718-384-7680 • $
  Slices, heroes and garlic knots.
- **Juliette** • 135 N 5th St [Bedford Ave]
  718-388-9222 • $$
  Northside bistro with rooftop deck.
- **Kellogg's Diner** •
  518 Metropolitan Ave [Union Ave]
  718-782-4502 • $
  The ultimate diner/deli.
- **La Locanda** • 432 Graham Ave [Withers St]
  718-349-7800 • $$
  Fried calamari, chicken parm, and so forth.
- **La Piazzetta** • 442 Graham Ave [Frost St]
  718-349-1627 • $$$
  Family-style restaurant with Northern and Southern Italian dishes.
- **La Superior** • 295 Berry St [S 2nd St]
  718-388-5988 • $$
  Authentic Mexican street food.
- **Le Barricou** • 533 Grand St [Union Ave]
  718-782-7372 • $$
  Everyone's all about the bouillabaisse.
- **Lodge** • 318 Grand St [Havemeyer St]
  718-486-9400 • $$$
  Great space. The Adirondacks in Brooklyn.
- **Lorimer Market** •
  620 Lorimer St [Skillman Ave]
  718-389-2691 • $
  Boffo Italian sandwiches.
- **Mable's Smokehouse & Banquet Hall** •
  44 Berry St [N 12th St]
  718-218-6655 • $$
  Totally decent BBQ in hipster ambiance (babies at the bar!).

- **Marlow & Sons** • 81 Broadway [Berry St]
  718-384-1441 • $$
  Oysters and beer, old timey-like—go for Happy Hour
- **Mexico 2000** • 367 Broadway [Keap St]
  718-782-3797 • $
  Inner-bodega taco counter replete with Mexican soap operas.
- **Moto** • 394 Broadway [Hooper St]
  718-599-6895 • $$
  Triangular nook with horseshoe bar and comfort food.
- **Northside Bakery** •
  149 N 8th St [Bedford Ave]
  718-782-2700 • $
  Best Polish bakery this side of Greenpoint/Williamsburg. Perfect chocolate croissants.
- **Nuovo Fiore** • 284 Grand St [Roebling St]
  718-782-8222 • $$
  Rustic, delicious Italian at best-bargain-in-Williamsburg prices.
- **Pates et Traditions** •
  52 Havemeyer St [N 6th St]
  718-302-1878 • $$
  Divine savory crepes, honestly worth the wait for brunch.
- **Peter Luger Steak House** •
  178 Broadway [Driggs Ave]
  718-387-7400 • $$$$$
  Best steak, potatoes, and spinach in this solar system.
- **Pies 'N' Thighs** • 166 S 4th St [Driggs]
  347-529-6090 • $$
  Comfortably Southern style where the chicken biscuits reign supreme.
- **PT** • 331 Bedford Ave [S 3rd St]
  718-388-7438 • $$$
  D.O.C.'s sophisticated older brother.
- **Roebling Tea Room** •
  143 Roebling St [Metropolitan Ave]
  718-963-0760 • $$$
  Fancy tea eatery.
- **Rye** • 247 S 1st St [Roebling St]
  718-218-8047 • $$$
  Lush, lovely speakeasy (no sign!) that serves a mean meatloaf.

Map

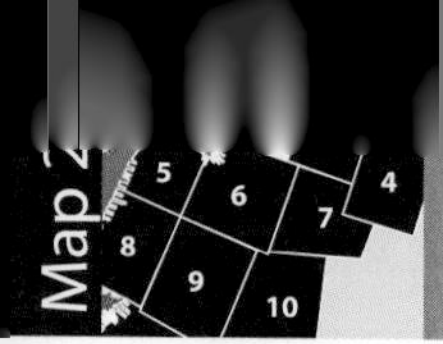

Map 2

- **Sal's Pizzeria** • 544 Lorimer St [Devoe St]
718-388-6838 • $$
Calzones, slices, heroes and pastas.
- **Sea** • 114 N 6th St [Berry St]
718-384-8850 • $$
Outshines its Manhattan counterpart.
- **Snacky** • 187 Grand St [Bedford Ave]
718-486-4848 • $
Kitschy.
- **St Anselm** •
355 Metropolitan Ave [Havemeyer St]
718-384-5054 •
We have no reservations about this sizzling
steak spot.
- **Sweetwater** • 105 N 6th St [Berry St]
718-963-0608 • $$
Just a cozy bar with nice bistro food.
- **Tabare** • 221 S 1st St [Roebling]
347-335-0187 • $$
Authentic Uruguayan food serving delicious
family recipes.
- **Taj Kabab & Curry** • 568 Grand St [Lorimer St]
718-782-1722 • $$
Cheap takeout and delivery.
- **Teddy's Bar and Grill** • 96 Berry St [N 8th St]
718-384-9787 • $
Best bar food ever. Hipster and Polish locals
unite.
- **Traif** • 229 S 4th St [Havemeyer St]
347-844-9578 • $$$
Small plates brilliance under the Williamsburg
Bridge. Go.
- **Walter Foods** • 253 Grand St [Roebling St]
718-387-8783 • $$$
Spiffed-up American classics in a warmly lit
bistro.
- **Yola's Café** •
524 Metropolitan Ave [Union Ave]
718-486-0757 • $
Terrific, authentic Mexican in a claustrophobic
atmosphere.
- **Zenkichi** • 77 N 6th St [Wythe Ave]
718-388-8985 • $$
Amazing izakaya suitable for a tryst.

🛍 Shopping

- **10 Ft. Single by Stella Dallas** •
285 N 6th St [Meeker Ave]
718-486-9482
Dress up like you're in Dazed & Confused 2.
- **A&G Merch** • 111 N 6th St [Berry St]
718-388-1779
A collection of utilitarian objects ranging from
couches to candles.
- **Academy Records Annex** •
85 Oak St [Franklin St]
718-218-8200
Bins and bins of new and used LPs.
- **Amarcord Vintage Fashion** •
223 Bedford Ave [N 4th St]
718-963-4001
Well-edited vintage goodies, many pieces
direct from Europe.
- **Artists & Fleas** • 70 N 7th St [Wythe Ave]
Market for quirky jewelry, accessories, vintage,
housewares.
- **Beacon's Closet** • 88 N 11th St [Wythe Ave]
718-486-0816
Rad resale with lots of gems.
- **Bedford Cheese Shop** •
229 Bedford Ave [N 5th St]
718-599-7588
Best cheese selection in the borough.
- **Beer Street** • 413 Graham Ave [Withers St]
347-294-0495
Rotating taps, growlers, bottles, & more at
Williamsburg's craft beer store.
- **BQE Wine & Liquors** •
504 Meeker Ave [Humboldt St]
718-389-3833
Good selection, cheap.
- **Breukelen Bier Merchants** •
182 Grand St [Bedford Ave]
347-457-6350
A beer store grows in Breukelen.
- **The Brooklyn Kitchen** •
100 Frost St [Manhattan Ave]
718-389-2982
Awesome butcher shop and gourmet cooking
supplies next to the BQE.

Map 2

Beacon's Closet and Buffalo Exchange require some stamina, but they're worth it; Amarcord's nicely edited vintage selection is the antidote. Vinyl collectors geek out within blocks of the Bedford stop at Academy, Rough Trade, and Earwax, while foodsters find gadgets at Whisk and Brooklyn Kitchen. Marlow & Daughters's locally sourced, quality (i.e., expensive) meat is paired with helpful advice.

- **Brooklyn Winery** • 213 N 8th St [Driggs Ave]
  347-763-1506
  Craft your own barrel of wine from crushing the grapes to bottling.
- **Buffalo Exchange** • 504 Driggs Ave [N 9th St]
  718-384-6901
  Recycled clothing chain's first NYC store.
- **Catbird** • 219 Bedford Ave [N 5th St]
  718-599-3457
  Unique clothing and jewelry from up-and-coming designers.
- **Crest True Value Hardware** •
  558 Metropolitan Ave [Lorimer St]
  718-388-9521
  Arty hardware store, believe it or not.
- **Desert Island** •
  540 Metropolitan Ave [Union Ave]
  718-388-5087
  Comics, visual arts books, zines, and consignment finds.
- **Earwax Records** • 167 N 9th St [Bedford Ave]
  718-486-3771
  Record store with all the indie classics.
- **Emily's Pork Store** •
  426 Graham Ave [Withers St]
  718-383-7216
  Broccoli rabe sausage is their specialty.
- **Fuego 718** • 249 Grand St [Roebling St]
  718-302-2913
  Handcrafted gifts made with passion from Mexico, Peru, Italy…
- **Golden Calf** • 319 Wythe Ave [S 2nd St]
  718-302-8800
  Eclectic retro and modern housewares.
- **Idlewild Books** • 218 Bedford Ave [N 5th St]
  212-414-8888
  Extensive foreign-language offerings and language classes.
- **KCDC Skateshop** • 252 Wythe Ave [N 3rd St]
  718-387-9006
  Shop and gallery featuring locally designed gear.
- **Marlow & Daughters** • 95 Broadway [Berry St]
  718-388-5700
  Gorgeous (yes, expensive) cuts for the discerning carnivore.
- **Mast Bros Chocolate** • 111 N 3rd St [Berry St]
  718-388-2625
  Artisan chocoholics.
- **Monk Vintage** • 496 Driggs Ave [N 9th St]
  718-384-6665
  Young and fun selection of vintage clothes, shoes, accessories.
- **Moon River Chattel** •
  62 Grand St [Wythe Ave]
  718-388-1121
  Cute store offering antiques and architectural salvage.
- **The Natural Wine Company** •
  211 N 11th St [Roebling St]
  646-397-9463
  Smart staff and excellent selection of sustainably produced, tasty wines.
- **Open Air Modern** •
  489 Lorimer St [Nassau Ave]
  718-383-6465
  Old and rare books and furniture.
- **Rough Trade** • 64 N 9th St [Kent Ave]
  718-388-4111
  NYC outpost of famous London record store; many live events.
- **Savino's Quality Pasta** •
  111 Conselyea St [Manhattan Ave]
  718-388-2038
  Homemade ravioli.
- **SlapBack** • 490 Metropolitan Ave [Rodney St]
  347-227-7133
  Indulge your inner Jayne Mansfield.
- **Smorgasburg** • N 7th St & Kent Ave
  Massive Saturday food fest. Sunglasses mandatory.
- **Spoonbill & Sugartown** •
  218 Bedford Ave [N 5th St]
  718-387-7322
  Art, architecture, design, philosophy, and literature. New and used.
- **Sprout Home** • 44 Grand St [Kent Ave]
  718-388-4440
  Contemporary home and garden store.
- **Treehouse** • 430 Graham Ave [Frost St]
  718-482-8733
  Quirky, one-of-a-kind clothing and jewelry.
- **Two Jakes** • 320 Wythe Ave [Grand St]
  718-782-7780
  Furniture: Mod, metal, misc.
- **Uva Wines & Spirits** •
  199 Bedford Ave [N 5th St]
  718-963-3939
  The staff knows and loves their small, meticulous selection.
- **Whisk** • 231 Bedford Ave [N 4th St]
  718-218-7230
  Kitchen boutique stocked with basic gear and beyond.

For anyone wondering where the old Lower East Side went, East Williamsburg might be part of the answer. Sure, new lofts dot the roads around the outlying L stops, but for the most part it's factories and bodegas, longstanding residences, and a few corners where it's best to keep your guard up. What the area lacks in Williamsburg-proper niceties, it makes up for with (relatively) cheaper rents and a genuine sense of diversity, possibility, and artistic community. All of which pales next to the real draw in this area: Awesome. Tacos.

East Williamsburg is still actively industrial. Though the hulking **Pfizer Pharmaceutical Plant** finally stopped running, the space has been reborn as a startup incubator. Surrounding blocks are filled with factories and warehouses that make everything from concrete to wontons (just follow the shifting scents in the air to find what's what). If it's history you're after, a walk south of Metropolitan will turn up plenty of shuttered giants still bearing signs of the area's past as a textile and food production hub. Along the way, check out the **Williamsburg Houses** (1937)—one of the first NYC housing projects, the massive, early modern complex has been preserved as an architectural landmark.

All of that spare factory space has helped turn this part of Brooklyn into a booming artist colony; the geography is particularly inviting for those working with large-scale installation pieces and heavy materials. Collectives offer extensive rehearsal and workspaces for rent, fostering the development and exhibition of emerging painters, photographers, woodworkers, and even aerialists (no joke). Excellent galleries also abound on the ground. In between exhibits and openings, don't forget that the best way to see street art is out on the street. Keep your eyes open for amazing **graffiti murals**—especially near Boerum Street at Graham Avenue— and Banksy-style stencil works that pop up on abandoned walls and windows.

Empty industrial areas make for plentiful art spaces (**House of Yes**), and there's always an exhibition worth checking out before finding a barstool. Local fave **duckduck** is so cozy and low-key it's like drinking on your own porch. You'll get change for a five when ordering a beer at the super-dark **King's County**. Wait at **Pine Box Rock Shop** for your table at Roberta's. For a value-added dive bar experience, head to **Don Pedro**; after dark the tiny Ecuadorian restaurant deals in stiff cocktails and underground bands.

East Williamsburg

Map 3

O Landmarks

- **Boerum Street Graffiti Mural** •
  153 Boerum St [Graham Ave]
  Cool, easy to miss street art.
- **Pfizer Pharmaceutical** •
  630 Flushing Ave [Bartlett St]
  Former Pfizer plant reborn as startup incubator.
- **Williamsburg Houses** •
  172 Maujer St [Humboldt St]
  A public housing project proclaimed a landmark in 2003.

Coffee

- **Kave** • 1087 Flushing Ave [Knickerbocker Ave]
  718-360-8685
  Outlets, wifi, patio, good coffee, homemade nut milk.
- **Little Skips** • 941 Willoughby Ave [Myrtle Ave]
  718-484-0980
  Cool little cafe with great espresso.
- **Lula Bean** • 797 Grand St [Bushwick Ave]
  718-599-5852
  Killer coffee this far down Grand St? Who knew.
- **Tar Pit** • 135 Woodpoint Rd [Withers St]
  646-469-9494
  Great cold brew, hip yet friendly staff.
- **Variety Coffee & Tea** •
  368 Graham Ave [Conselyea St]
  347-599-2351
  Good coffee, good people.

Nightlife

- **The Anchored Inn** •
  57 Waterbury St [Bushwick Ave]
  718-576-3297
  Dive for fans of cheap beer, metal, velvet paintings.
- **Boulevard Tavern** •
  579 Meeker Ave [N Henry St]
  718-389-3252
  Low-key dive with supposed ghosts in the room.
- **Brooklyn Fire Proof East** •
  119 Ingraham St [Porter Ave]
  347-223-4211
  'Schwickian cafe/bar/film and television studio/art gallery.
- **Bushwick Country Club** •
  618 Grand St [Leonard St]
  718-388-2114
  "Muffy, I've got a feeling we're not in Greenwich anymore."
- **Don Pedro** • 90 Manhattan Ave [Boerum St]
  347-689-3163
  Lively local watering hole that frequently hosts local bands.
- **The Drink** • 228 Manhattan Ave [Maujer St]
  718-782-8463
  Big hipsters, tiny cups of punch.
- **duckduck** • 153 Montrose Ave [Graham Ave]
  347-799-1449
  Badly needed neighborhood bar.
- **Harefield Road** •
  769 Metropolitan Ave [Graham Ave]
  718-388-6870
  Spacious, unpretentious spot for microbrews and hot toddies.

Map

5 6 7 4
8 9 10

Great tacos are just few minutes away on the L train: Awesome specimens can be had at **Antojitos Mexicanos**. **Grand Morelos** dishes rice and beans 24/7. Wait hours for pizza at **Roberta's** and months for a table at **Blanca**. **Carmine's** is still a local Italian institution, but an influx of Latin American immigrants created a stronghold of Salvadoran, Ecuadorian, and Mexican delights: **Bahia** makes freshly-made pupusas, and if you have a date in tow, **Mesa Coyoacan** can't be beat for atmosphere.

- **House of Yes** • 408 Jefferson St [Wyckoff Ave]
  A design & performance space for everyone from musicians to acrobats.
- **Kings County** • 286 Seigel St [White St]
  718-418-8823
  Cheap local bar for a whiskey fix.
- **Legion** • 790 Metropolitan Ave [Humboldt St]
  718-387-3797
  Williamsburgers hang where war vets used to drown their sorrows.
- **Matt Torrey's** • 46 Bushwick Ave [Devoe St]
  718-218-7646
  $5 pints, big windows, cushy booths.
- **Mother's** •
  347 Graham Ave [Metropolitan Ave]
  718-384-7778
  Beer, not too hip/crowded, what else do you need?
- **The Narrows** •
  1037 Flushing Ave [Morgan Ave]
  281-827-1800
  Cocktails, back patio, cash only, indoor space indeed quite narrow.
- **Office Ops** • 57 Thames St [Morgan Ave]
  718-418-2509
  The Rock and Rollerskate party should not be missed.
- **Pine Box Rock Shop** •
  12 Grattan St [Bogart St]
  718-366-6311
  Karaoke, trivia, vegan empanadas…liberal arts college all over again.
- **Pumps** • 1089 Grand St [Metropolitan Ave]
  718-599-2474
  Pump it up.
- **The Second Chance Saloon** •
  659 Grand St [Manhattan Ave]
  718-387-4411
  Big Buck Hunter! Drink specials! Picnic tables!
- **Tandem** •
  236 Troutman St [Knickerbocker Ave]
  718-386-2369
  Eclectic space with small plates and old-fashioned cocktails.
- **Tradesman** • 222 Bushwick Ave [Meserole St]
  718-386-5300
  Hipster local, not a union guy's hangout.

🍴 Restaurants

- **Anthony & Son Panini Shoppe** •
  433 Graham Ave [Frost St]
  718-383-7395 • $
  Italian deli, fine sandwiches, some groceries, liquor next door.
- **Antojitos Mexicanos** •
  107 Graham Ave [McKibben St]
  718-384-9076 • $
  Best Mexican food in the 'hood.
- **Bahia** • 690 Grand St [Manhattan Ave]
  718-218-9592 • $$
  Try the mouth-watering pupusas.
- **Blanca** • 261 Moore St [White St]
  646-703-2715 • $$$$
  Tasting menu by Roberta's, 12 seats, reserve months ahead.
- **Boulevard Cafe** •
  253 Bushwick Ave [Montrose Ave]
  718-381-2442 • $
  The prettiest cafe for blocks around, and good breakfast to boot.
- **Brooklyn Fire Proof** •
  119 Ingraham St [Porter Ave]
  347-223-4211 • $$
  A cafe & bar addition to the Brooklyn Fire Proof mini-empire.
- **Bushwick Pita Palace** •
  243 Bushwick Ave [Montrose Ave]
  718-456-9114 • $$
  A place for the new unadventurous hipsters.
- **Cafe Ghia** • 24 Irving Ave [Jefferson St]
  718-821-8806 • $$
  Comfortable place to eat comfort food.
- **Carmine's Pizzeria** •
  358 Graham Ave [Conselyea St]
  718-782-9659 • $
  Amazing white slices with sun-dried tomato and pesto.
- **Cobra Club** • 6 Wyckoff Ave [Jefferson Ave]
  917-719-1138 • $
  Yoga classes and coffee by day, cocktails by night.
- **Eagle Grocery and Deli** •
  317 Bushwick Ave [McKibben St]
  $
  Fat, cheap sandwiches; best of bodega.

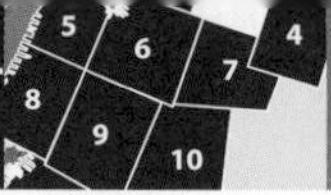

Map 5

- **Garden Grill Coffee Shop** •
318 Graham Ave [Devoe St]
718-384-8668 • $$
Classic diner grub with good donuts.
- **Grand Morelos** • 727 Grand St [Graham Ave]
718-218-9441 • $$
24-hour Mexican diner/bakery.
- **GreenStreets Salads** •
67 Irving Ave [Troutman St]
347-405-7956 • $
When you've had too many burgers and
bacon nights.
- **Gwynnett St** • 312 Graham Ave [Ainslie St]
347-889-7002 • $$$
Sous vide + locavore + friendly = foodie date
night.
- **Il Passatore** • 14 Bushwick Ave [Devoe St]
718-963-3100 • $$
Rustic, affordable pastas and pizzas for a price.
- **Lily Thai** • 615 Grand St [Leonard St]
718-218-7522 • $
Extensive menu with good lunch specials.
- **Los Primos** • 704 Grand St [Graham Ave]
718-486-8449 • $$
Authentic Latin spot with tasty seafood.
- **Mesa Coyoacan** •
372 Graham Ave [Conselyea St]
718-782-8171 • $$
Upscale "traditional" Mex.
- **Momo Sushi Shack** • 43 Bogart St [Grattan St]
718-418-6666 • $$
"Pork Betty" and fried chicken good as the
sushi "bombs."

- **Nam Nam** •
109 Montrose Ave [Manhattan Ave]
718-302-9200 • $
Cheap bánh mì joint.
- **New Mexico Place Restaurant** •
189 Graham Ave [Scholes St]
718-302-4573 • $
Cheap tacos and burritos, fast delivery.
- **Newtown** • 55 Waterbury St [Scholes St]
347-984-6215 • $
Simple hummus, falafel, soup.
- **Pacific Ocean House** •
84 Manhattan Ave [McKibben St]
718-388-3371 • $$
The only sushi in this neck of the woods.
- **Roberta's** • 261 Moore St [White St]
718-417-1118 • $$
Solid wood oven pizza in an industrial setting.
- **Sage** • 301 Graham Ave [Ainsley St]
718-218-6644 • $$
Contemporary take on Thai.
- **Taqueria El Fogon** •
1050 Flushing Ave [Morgan Ave]
718-497-7445 • $
Basic Mexican with slow but friendly service.
- **Tuffet: Cheese/Meat/Bar** •
286 Graham Ave [Grand St]
718-388-7434 • $$
Classy wine and cheese joint, seats for young
female Muffets.

For all-day shopping, the best bet is to head back toward the BQE, but there are some stops to make on the way: **Dolly G's** and **Urban Jungle** hold vintage treasures for anyone willing to put in the effort; local vendors line the **Moore Street Market**, recently saved from closure (yet again).

🛍 Shopping

- **Artist & Craftsman** •
761 Metropolitan Ave [Graham Ave]
718-782-7765
Art supplies.
- **Blue Angel Wines** • 638 Grand St [Leonard St]
718-388-2210
Excellent selection of bottles under 20 bucks.
- **Bottle Shoppe** •
353 Graham Ave [Conselyea St]
718-388-4122
Neighborhood staple for vino.
- **Brooklyn Natural** • 49 Bogart St [Grattan St]
718-381-0650
Upscale deli—check out the new late-night delivery menu.
- **Brooklyn Vintage** •
1087 Flushing Ave [Knickerbocker Ave]
917-501-9998
A cure for mid-century overkill: flawless pieces from the '30s and '40s.
- **Busura World Fashion** •
1065 Broadway [Union Ave]
Sick of sifted, high-price "thrift"? Look no further.
- **Dolly G's** • 320 Graham Ave [Ainslie St]
718-599-1044
Well-edited vintage for ladies who know quality.
- **Dun-Well Doughnuts** •
222 Montrose Ave [Bushwick Ave]
Vegan donuts tasty enough for omnivores.
- **Food Bazaar Supermarket** •
21 Manhattan Ave [Varet St]
718-532-0320
Excellent fish, produce, and beer selections.
- **Fortunato Brothers** •
289 Manhattan Ave [Devoe St]
718-387-2281
Old-school pastry and espresso shop.

- **Green Depot** • 1 Ivy Hill [Varick Ave]
718-782-2991
Al Gore would shop here if he lived in Brooklyn.
- **Huitzilli Mexican Handcraft** •
624 Metropolitan Ave [Leonard St]
718-701-3155
Mexican textiles & housewares, beats hipster gift shops selling bird art.
- **Khim's Millennium Market** •
324 Graham Ave [Devoe St]
718-302-9113
Overpriced organic and natural groceries.
- **Khim's Millennium Market** •
260 Bushwick Ave [Johnson Ave]
718-497-7068
Overpriced organic and natural groceries.
- **Leo's** • 207 Knickerbocker Ave [Troutman St]
718-456-1054
Always winning the sound battle with Alondra's across the street.
- **Moore Street Market** •
110 Moore St [Humboldt St]
718-384-1371
Latino fresh food for 50+ years (multi-vendor).
- **New Alondra Records** •
206 Knickerbocker Ave [Troutman St]
718-417-3388
Always sound-battling the other record store across the street.
- **Stella Di Sicilia Bakery** •
217 Montrose Ave [Bushwick Ave]
718-417-1849
Get a massive Cuban sandwich for five bucks.
- **Urban Jungle** •
118 Knickerbocker Ave [Flushing Ave]
Hangar-like thrift store that's ripe for the picking.
- **Zukkie's** • 279 Bushwick Ave [Johnson Ave]
718-456-0048
Some good finds amongst the junk.

Map 4 · **Bushwick**

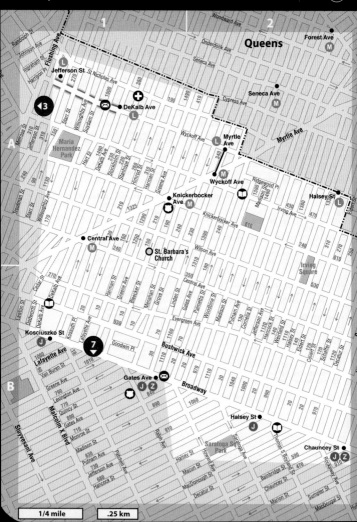

Bushwick used to be synonymous with crime and urban blight but nowadays, there's not too much anxiety on a late-night walk home. This neighborhood has been on the rise since rent in Williamsburg started sky-rocketing, and Bushwick's close location and low-rent lured over students and artists into what used to be—and, in many pockets, continues be—a family-oriented, predominantly Latino community.

Get ready for a lot of grey—much of what's considered "residential" to the Williamsburg expats of Bushwick's artist community are warehouses and factories renovated into loft spaces. But Bushwick isn't completely color-starved. Commissioned murals like the one on the corner of Central and Myrtle break up the monotony of uneven sidewalks and just-functional architecture. Get up onto any rooftop to appreciate a skyline that can move even the most jaded local. Oases like Maria Hernandez Park provide residents with much-needed green (no, not that kind).

As a residential neighborhood, Bushwick is fully functional. Youngsters out past bedtime might not be able to get their midnight skinny latte (sorry, yuppies: no Starbucks for miles), but the main thoroughfares—Wilson Avenue, Central Avenue, Knickerbocker Avenue, and Broadway—provide every service imaginable. Ninety-nine cent stores compete with music stores, pawn shops, and laundromats. ("The best" of any of these businesses is usually determined by how long it takes to walk there.) Sick of those con men across the river who charge $80 for a trim, not including tip? In Bushwick, a cut from a unisex hair salon for around $10 to $20 is right around the corner.

Bushwick shows its family roots in the mind-boggling number of churches of all different denominations scattered throughout the neighborhood, many merely humble storefronts among the milieu of bodegas and take-out Chinese. For a historic parish, visit **St. Barbara's** for beautiful, if out-of-place, architecture and a thriving religious community. But residents, beware the bells: they have a tendency to interrupt a hungover Sunday morning sleep. Folks who want to bring a piece of their faith home can visit any number of the botanicas selling *articulos religosos* around the area, stocked with candles, incense, and saint-themed aerosol sprays (really!). Besides, no Bushwick home is complete without at least one glass candle-holder depicting a Catholic saint.

Bushwick's venues are never pretentious but prepare to come out smelling like Pabst and weed. Drop by the **Bushwick Starr** to see Manhattan-caliber performance art. Bring ear-plugs for the lo-fi squeals of **Silent Barn**; give those ears a rest at an acoustic set in **Northeast Kingdom's** cozy basement lounge.

Except for stand-out **Northeast Kingdom**, people looking for Michelin stars should keep it to some other neighborhoods or boroughs. Fortunately, their cuisine is so inventive and so good that we're not really complaining. Chinese take-out and Latin American cuisine dominate the scene but check out **La Isla Cuchifritos** for Puerto Rican soul-food 24/7. Cheap gems like **Tortilleria Mexicana Los Hermanos** provide good food for the thrifty. Oh, and caffeine junkies can get their fix at the **Wyckoff Starr**.

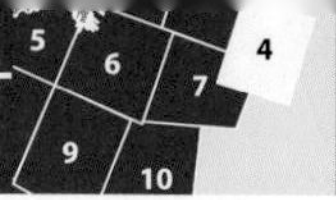

Map 4

5 6 7 4
9 10

○ Landmarks

- **St. Barbara's Roman Catholic Church** •
138 Bleecker St [Central Ave]
718-452-3660
A little piece of Europe in the middle of
Bushwick.

🖥Coffee

- **Wyckoff Starr** • 30 Wyckoff Ave [Starr St]
718-484-9766
Nice little coffee shop in desolate
surroundings.

🍸Nightlife

- **The Bushwick Starr** • 207 Starr St [Irving Ave]
Get up close with the latest art & performance
acts in the area.
- **Gotham City Lounge** •
1293 Myrtle Ave [Central Ave]
718-387-4182
A haven for grown-up geeks: booze & comic
memorabilia.
- **Northeast Kingdom** •
18 Wyckoff Ave [Troutman St]
718-386-3864
Perfectly executed downstairs bar with live
music some nights.
- **Silent Barn** • 9-15 Wyckoff Ave [Hancock St]
Raucous DIY music venue.

🍴Restaurants

- **The Bodega** •
24 St Nicholas Ave [Troutman St]
646-924-8488 • $$
Spanish and South American wines, snacks,
fun movie nights.
- **Chimu Express** • 180 Irving Ave [Stanhope St]
718-443-0787 • $
Generous portions of Peruvian food from
rotisserie chicken to skirt steak.
- **El Charro Bakery** •
1427 Myrtle Ave [Knickerbocker Ave]
718-452-1401 • $
Busy on the weekends, but some of the best
sweetbread around.
- **Fortunata's II** •
305 Knickerbocker Ave [Hart St]
718-497-8101 • $
Pizza, ice cream, and one killer meatball sub.
- **La Isla Cuchifritos** •
1439 Myrtle Ave [Knickerbocker Ave]
718-417-0668 • $
Fried dough stuffed with meat—and more
meat. Mmmm.
- **Northeast Kingdom** •
18 Wyckoff Ave [Troutman St]
718-386-3864 • $$
Cozy, hip ski lodge-style eatery in gritty nabe.
- **Shen Zhou** • 159 Wilson Ave [Hart St]
718-821-1172 • $
Cheap and greasy, no booze to be had.
- **Tortilleria Los Hermanos** •
271 Starr St [Wyckoff Ave]
718-456-3422 • $
Fantastic tacos tucked away in a tortilla
factory.
- **Wyckoff Starr** • 30 Wyckoff Ave [Starr St]
718-484-9766 •
Nice little coffee shop in desolate
surroundings.

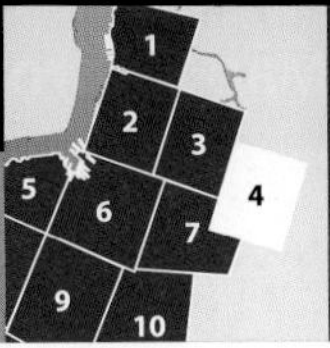

Bushwick

Associated is everyone's grocery staple but check out **Angel's Fruit Market** across the street for the freshest produce and a wide variety of Mexican sodas. **Rincon Musical** provides low-price instruments and no Bushwick home is complete without at least one glass candle-holder depicting a Catholic saint from **Botanica Santeria and Magic**.

Map 4

🛍 Shopping

- **The Angel's Fruit Market** •
272 Knickerbocker Ave [Willoughby Ave]
718-366-7664
Freshest produce and an assortment of specialty items.
- **Associated Supermarket** •
1291 Broadway [Lexington Ave]
718-443-7913
Join the Association.
- **Botanica Santeria and Magic** •
1485 Myrtle Ave [Menahan St]
718-366-6939
Articulos religiosos & other label-in-Spanish oils.
- **Bravo's Bike Repair** •
187 Wilson Ave [Dekalb Ave]
718-602-5150
Affordable repair, knowledgeable staff. Helps if usted habla espanol.
- **Bushwick Bike Shop** •
1342 Dekalb Ave [Central Ave]
347-405-7966
Fair prices and no attitude? No, you're not dreaming.
- **C-Town** • 346 Central Ave [Menahan St]
718-452-4313
No-frills market way cheaper than your local bodega.

- **C-Town** • 1781 Broadway [Pilling St]
718-453-3339
No-frills market way cheaper than your local bodega.
- **Circo Pastry Shop** •
312 Knickerbocker Ave [Hart St]
718-381-2292
Old school bakery for cannolis, ices, cookies.
- **Food Bazaar Supermarket** •
454 Wyckoff Ave [Madison St]
718-381-8338
A huge selection of fresh produce, aisles of canned goods, and a large selection of frozen foods.
- **Green Village** • 276 Starr St [St Nicholas Ave]
718-456-8844
Piles of resale items for you to spend the day rummaging through.
- **Key Food** • 1533 Broadway [Hancock St]
718-453-7000
No-frills market way cheaper than your local bodega.
- **My Dream Party** •
203 Wilson Ave [Stanhope St]
718-443-3275
Need wedding invites—and after the wedding, kid's birthday plates? Voila.
- **Rincon Musical** •
307 Knickerbocker Ave [Hart St]
Come get your cuatro guitar and bachata greatest hits CD here.

Map 3 • Brooklyn Heights/DUMBO/Downtown

Three 'nabes for the price of one! Or is that three 'nabes for the price of ten? Yes, Brooklyn Heights really is that expensive, but there's a reason: it's one of the most sublimely beautiful neighborhoods in all of New York, with jaw-dropping city views along the **Brooklyn Heights Promenade**, two friendly retail strips on Montague and Henry Streets, views of the iconic **Brooklyn Bridge**, and perhaps the city's best stock of brownstones and clapboard homes, especially around the "fruit street" area of Orange, Cranberry, and Pineapple, but even heading all the way south along Henry and Hicks Streets until the neighborhood ends at busy Atlantic Avenue.

By the time one hits Court Street heading east from Brooklyn Heights, however, you can chuck the sublime right out the window. The borough's central nervous system, Downtown Brooklyn features several courthouses (you'll learn your way around when Kings County jury duty calls), **Brooklyn Borough Hall**, **Metrotech Center** (encompassing the **New York City College of Technology**, a large Marriott hotel, **Polytechnic Institute of New York University**, and a convenient **TKTS Booth**), Brooklyn Law School, the **Fulton Street Mall**, jam-packed daily with lunchtime shoppers, and finally, a warren of subways that can take you to any other point in New York City. Speaking of which, don't miss the **New York Transit Museum**, a fascinating look at how our underground web of trains came to be—and not just for aficionados.

DUMBO ("Down Under the Manhattan Bridge Overpass," the acronym appropriated from Walt Disney since the late 1970s), the third neighborhood in this trilogy, has followed the warehouse-turned-artist-studio-turned-expensive-condo route. Like Brooklyn Heights, DUMBO features killer views of downtown Manhattan, just closer to the waterfront. Retail in DUMBO, will be forever limited, and many shops close early (by New York standards). As DUMBO truly only has one subway stop (the York Street F), it can get a little desolate, especially late at night. And while this all sounds like a quiet, idyllic little neighborhood, there's only one problem: the *constant* rumble of the B, D, N, and Q trains overhead on the **Manhattan Bridge**. Thank goodness for double-pane windows.

For true peace and quiet, you'd have to head east about five blocks from DUMBO to check out one of our favorite micro-neighborhoods, **Vinegar Hill**. Literally only three blocks wide and two blocks long, Vinegar Hill is bordered by a power plant to the north, the **Navy Yard** to the east, the Farragut Houses to the south, and DUMBO to the west. Inside its cobblestoned streets are a vestige of 19th-century Navy housing and an ex-retail strip along Hudson Street.

And then there's **Brooklyn Bridge Park**, stretching 1.3 miles along the East River waterfront from Atlantic Avenue to the south all the way past Manhattan Bridge to the north. Comprising six repurposed shipping piers, the former Empire-Fulton Ferry State Park, two Civil War-era historic buildings, and various city-owned open spaces along the waterfront, the 85-acre site combines active and passive recreation with the stunning backdrop of the Brooklyn and Manhattan Bridges, Lower Manhattan and the New York Harbor beyond.

By 8 p.m., teeming Downtown Brooklyn is a ghost town; you'll either need to head north to DUMBO or west to the Heights to wet your whistle. In DUMBO check out bustling **Galapagos Art Space** after a performance at brilliant **St. Ann's Warehouse**. In the Heights, **Henry Street Ale House** is a good complement to catching a flick at cozy **Heights Cinema**.

O Landmarks

- **Brooklyn Borough Hall** •
  209 Joralemon St [Cadman Plz W]
  718-802-3700
  Built in the 1840s, this Greek Revival landmark
  was once employed as the official City Hall of
  Brooklyn.
- **Brooklyn Bridge** • Adams St & East River
  If you haven't walked over it at least twice yet,
  you're not cool.
- **Brooklyn Bridge Park** •
  Old Fulton St & Furman St
  718-222-9939
  Waterfront park with stellar views and many
  active recreational amenities.
- **Brooklyn Heights Promenade** •
  Montague St & Pierrepont Pl
  The best place to really see Manhattan. It's the
  view that's in all the movies.
- **Brooklyn Historical Society** •
  128 Pierrepont St [Clinton St]
  718-222-4111
  Want to really learn about Brooklyn? Go here.
- **Brooklyn Ice Cream Factory** •
  1 Water St [Old Fulton St]
  718-246-3963
  Expensive, old-fashioned ice cream beneath
  the bridge.

- **The Brooklyn Tabernacle** •
  17 Smith St [Livingston St]
  718-290-2000
  Home of the award-winning Brooklyn
  Tabernacle Choir.
- **Fulton Street Mall** • Fulton St & Flatbush Ave
  The shopping experience, Brooklyn style. Hot
  sneakers can be had for a song.
- **Jetsons Building** • 110 York St [Jay St]
  View this sculptural roof from the Manhattan
  Bridge at night when it's lit with colored lights.
- **Junior's Restaurant** •
  386 Flatbush Avenue Ext [DeKalb Ave]
  718-852-5257
  For the only cheesecake worth its curds and
  whey.
- **Manhattan Bridge** •
  Flatbush Avenue Ext & Nassau St
  Connecting Brooklyn to that other borough.
- **MetroTech Center** •
  16-acre commercial/governmental/
  educational/cultural entity in Downtown
  Brooklyn.
- **New York Transit Museum** •
  130 Livingston St [Boerum St]
  718-694-1600
  Ride vintage subway cars through formerly
  abandoned tunnels? Yes, please!
- **Vinegar Hill** • Water St & Hudson Ave
  NYC's coolest micro-neighborhood. Promise.

Brooklyn Heights/DUMBO/Downtown

Our favorite places here are mostly in the "special occasion" category due to price: the Heights' cozy gastropub **Jack the Horse**, game-oriented old-school **Henry's End**, and the superb **Vinegar Hill House**. Otherwise, get great pizza at **Juliana's**, grab fast food on **Fulton Street Mall**, or hit classic **Junior's** for hangover food.

Coffee

- **Almondine Bakery** • 85 Water St [Main St]
  718-797-5026
  Grab a cup and check out the view.
- **Brooklyn Roasting Company** •
  25 Jay St [John St]
  718-855-1000
  DUMBO roasters; international focus.
- **Iris Café** • 20 Columbia Pl [Joralemon St]
  718-722-7395
  Very tiny. Very Brooklyn.

Farmers Markets

- **Brooklyn Borough Hall Greenmarket** •
  Court St & Montague St
  Tues, Thurs & Sat, 8 a.m.–6 p.m., year-round.

Nightlife

- **68 Jay Street Bar** • 68 Jay St [Front St]
  718-260-8207
  Arty local bar.
- **Henry Street Ale House** •
  62 Henry St [Cranberry St]
  718-522-4801
  Cozy, dark space with good selections on tap.
- **Jack the Horse Tavern** •
  66 Hicks St [Cranberry St]
  718-852-5084
  Outstanding upscale pub/New American cuisine, great feel.
- **O'Keefe's Bar & Grill** •
  62 Court St [Livingston St]
  718-855-8751
  Sports bar (large Mets following). Surprisingly decent food.
- **St Ann's Warehouse** • 29 Jay St [Plymouth St]
  718-254-8779
  Be careful not to cut yourself on the edginess.

Map 5

Restaurants

- **AlMar** • 111 Front St [Washington St]
718-855-5288 • $$$
Cavernous, friendly, communal-table Italian in DUMBO. Go to hang.
- **Fascati Pizza** • 80 Henry St [Orange St]
718-237-1278 • $
Excellent slice pizza.
- **Five Guys** • 138 Montague St [Henry St]
718-797-9380 • $
Burger joint with tasty fries and free peanuts while you wait.
- **Grimaldi's** • 1 Front St [Cadman Plaza W]
718-858-4300 • $
Excellent, respected, arguably among the best NYC pizza joints.
- **Hale & Hearty Soup** • 32 Court St [Remsen St]
718-596-5600 • $
Super soups.
- **Heights Café** • 84 Montague St [Hicks St]
718-625-5555 • $$$
Decent dining near the Promenade.
- **Henry's End** • 44 Henry St [Cranberry St]
718-834-1776 • $$$
Inventive, game-oriented menu.
- **Hill Country Chicken** •
345 Adams St [Willoughby St]
718-885-4609 • $
Fried chicken and BBQ goodness close to the courts.
- **Iron Chef House** • 92 Clark St [Monroe Pl]
718-858-8517 • $$
Dependable sushi and cozy atmosphere.
- **Jack the Horse Tavern** •
66 Hicks St [Cranberry St]
718-852-5084 • $$$
Outsanding upscale pub/New American cuisine, great feel.
- **Juliana's Pizza** • 19 Old Fulton St [Front St]
718-596-6700 • $$
Patsy makes his triumphant return to original Grimaldi's space.
- **Junior's Restaurant** •
386 Flatbush Avenue Ext [DeKalb Ave]
718-852-5257 • $
American with huge portions. Cheesecake.
- **Lantern Thai** • 101 Montague St [Hicks St]
718-237-2594 • $$
Mediocre Thai. The Montague curse.

- **Miso** • 40 Main St [Front St]
718-858-8388 • $$$
Japanese fusion cuisine.
- **No. 7 Sub** • 11 Water St [Brooklyn Bridge]
917-618-4399 • $$
Creative, filling sandwiches under the Brooklyn Bridge.
- **Noodle Pudding** • 38 Henry St [Middagh St]
718-625-3737 • $$
Northern Italian fare.
- **Park Plaza Restaurant** •
220 Cadman Plaza W [Clark St]
718-596-5900 • $
NFT-approved neighborhood diner.
- **Queen Restaurant** •
84 Court St [Livingston St]
718-596-5955 • $$$$
Good white-tablecloth, bow-tied waiter Italian joint.
- **The River Café** • 1 Water St [Old Fulton St]
718-522-5200 • $$$$$
Great view, but overrated.
- **Shake Shack** • 409 Fulton St [Boerum Pl]
718-307-7590 • $
The empire comes to Brooklyn.
- **Shake Shack** • 1 Old Fulton St [Water St]
347-435-2676 • $
Danny Meyer's burgers, conveniently located near Brooklyn Bridge Park.
- **Siggy's Good Food** • 76 Henry St [Orange St]
718-237-3199 • $$
Organic café.
- **Superfine** • 126 Front St [Pearl St]
718-243-9005 • $$
Mediterranean-inspired menu, bi-level bar, local art and music. NFT pick.
- **Sushi Gallery** • 71 Clark St [Henry St]
718-222-0308 • $$
Sushi Express, reasonable prices.
- **Teresa's Restaurant** •
80 Montague St [Hicks St]
718-797-3996 • $$
Polish-American comfort food. Come hungry.
- **Vinegar Hill House** •
72 Hudson Ave [Water St]
718-522-1018 • $$$
Excellent wood fired meats and veggies served in old-timey setting.

Need something, anything, quick and cheap? The **Fulton Street Mall** area is your answer, with a **Macy's** and tons of discount shops. In DUMBO, you can get great books at **powerHouse**, chocolate at **Jacques Torres**, and pastries at **Almondine**. In the Heights, browse women's clothing at **Tango** on Montague.

🛍️ Shopping

- **Almondine Bakery** • 85 Water St [Main St]
  718-797-5026
  Pastry smells waft to the street.
- **Barnes & Noble** • 106 Court St [State St]
  718-246-4996
  Chain bookstore.
- **Bridge Fresh** • 68 Jay St [Water St]
  718-488-1993
  Organic grocer.
- **Brooklyn Historical Society** •
  128 Pierrepont St [Clinton St]
  718-222-4111
  Fun gift shop with all manner of Brooklyn-themed merch.
- **Brooklyn Ice Cream Factory** •
  1 Water St [Old Fulton St]
  718-246-3963
  Get your ice cream fix on the Brooklyn waterfront.
- **Cranberry's** • 48 Henry St [Cranberry St]
  718-624-3500
  Old-time deli/grocery of rationally-priced comestibles.
- **Egg Baby** • 72 Jay St [Water St]
  347-356-4097
  Clothes for mommy and baby.
- **Grumpy Bert** • 82 Bond St [State St]
  347-855-4849
  Gift-toy-print-zine-apparel boutique.
- **Halcyon** • 57 Pearl St [Water St]
  718-260-9299
  Vinyl for DJ fanatics.
- **Half Pint Citizens** •
  41 Washington St [Water St]
  718-875-4007
  Ditch Gap Kids!
- **Heights Prime Meats** • 59 Clark St [Henry St]
  718-237-0133
  Butcher.
- **Housing Works Thrift Shop** •
  122 Montague St [Henry St]
  718-237-0521
  Our favorite thrift store.
- **Jacques Torres Chocolate** •
  66 Water St [Main St]
  718-875-1269
  The Platonic ideal of chocolate.
- **Lassen & Hennigs** •
  114 Montague St [Henry St]
  718-875-6272
  Specialty foods and deli.
- **Macy's** • 422 Fulton St [Hoyt St]
  718-875-7200
  Less crazed than Herald Square by about 1700%.
- **Modell's Sporting Goods** •
  360 Fulton Mall [Red Hook Ln]
  718-855-1921
  Sports. Sports. Sports. Get your Cyclones stuff here!
- **Montague Wine & Spirits** •
  78 Montague St [Hicks St]
  718-254-9422
  Consistently good wine store in Brooklyn Heights.
- **One Girl Cookies** • 33 Main St [Water St]
  347-338-1268
  Delicious treats via Cobble Hill.
- **Peas & Pickles** • 55 Washington St [Front St]
  718-488-8336
  DUMBO's first grocery.
- **Pomme** • 81 Washington St [York St]
  718-855-0623
  Pricey imports for baby hipsters. Haircuts, too.
- **powerHouse Arena** • 37 Main St [Water St]
  718-666-3049
  One of our favorite gallery/bookstores.
- **Recycle-A-Bicycle** • 35 Pearl St [Plymouth St]
  718-858-2972
  Bikes to the ceiling.
- **Stewart/Stand** • 141 Front St [Pearl St]
  718-875-1204
  Another very cool design shop for DUMBO.
- **Super Runners Shop** • 123 Court St [State St]
  718-858-8550
  Running sneaks and the like.
- **Tango** • 145 Montague St [Henry St]
  718-625-7518
  Jodie loves the clothes here. 'Nuff said.
- **TKTS Booth** • 1 Metrotech Ctr [Jay St]
  212-912-9770
  Shhh…don't tell anyone there's one in Brooklyn!
- **Trunk** • 68 Jay St [Front St]
  718-522-6488
  Awesome dresses and accessories, run by independent local designers.
- **Waterfront Wines & Spirits** •
  360 Furman St [Joralemon St]
  718-246-5101
  Well curated selection; stop before visiting friends for dinner.
- **West Elm** • 75 Front St [Main St]
  718-875-7757
  Cool home décor at reasonable prices.

Map 6 · **Fort Greene / Clinton Hill**

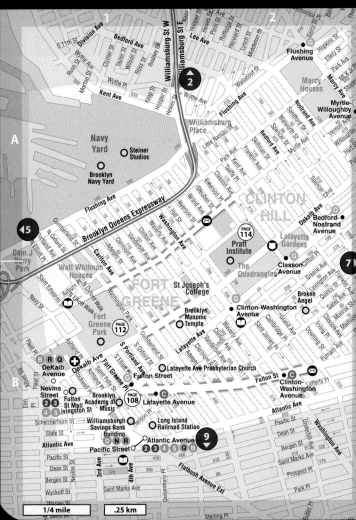

Map 6

Fort Greene could be the perfect outer borough neighborhood: the population is diverse, it's close to Manhattan, it's got a stellar park, tons of restaurants, a farmer's market, the hippest swap meet on the planet, beautiful tree- and brownstone-lined streets, historic buildings, subway and LIRR access, and a world-class performing arts center. Unfortunately, many people already know this, so rents are increasingly high, but the area still retains a homey, community vibe.

Fort Greene's landmarks run the gamut from religious to cultural to economic to civic to military. Check out the Underground Railroad murals at the **Lafayette Avenue Presbyterian Church**. In addition to templing Masons, the **Brooklyn Masonic Temple** also hosts indie concerts. The **Brooklyn Academy of Music** (BAM) has two live performance spaces, movie theaters, a cafe (which hosts free shows), plus the "Next Wave" festival of dance, opera, music, and theater. (Also, the Mark Morris Dance Center is just down the block.) The **Williamsburg Savings Bank Building** is one of the tallest structures in Brooklyn and has now been converted to condos. The **Brooklyn Navy Yard** now houses businesses as well as **Steiner Studios**. Shoppers and those who need the soul-sucking DMV flock to the hulking, commercial **Atlantic Terminal Mall**, which sits above a massive **Long Island Railroad Station**.

On weekends, hilly **Fort Greene Park** is rollicking with a **farmer's market**, playgrounds, cricket, soccer, and local community groups. Just a few blocks away, **Brooklyn Flea** is a major shopping (and eating!) destination, complete with tons of Etsy-type crafts vendors and enough food to fill up a year's worth of blog entries.

But that's only half the story, because Fort Greene's "sister" neighborhood, Clinton Hill, has a lot going for it, namely a proximity to the amenities of Fort Greene with fewer crowds. Clinton Hill hosts bucolic **St. Joseph's College** and the **Pratt Institute**, whose grounds are home to both sculpture art and a **Power Plant**. Several historic churches also dot the Clinton Hill landscape, which is filled with beautiful brownstones as well as some massive single-family homes on Washington Street.

Clinton Hill is home to an African community that has set up a number of restaurants and shops in the neighborhood, and it's also home to a whole row of artist's studios on Lexington Avenue. And film shoots—that peculiar New York City metric of neighborhood self-worth—are a regular occurrence in Clinton Hill. As if that weren't enough, you know Clinton Hill has clearly arrived when local coffee/food nexus **Choice Market** had its BLT profiled by Food Network.

Frank's, **Alibi**, and **Stonehome** are all great places to grab a drink before or after a movie at **BAM Rose Cinemas** or a performance at the **Masonic Hall**. **Hanson Dry** focuses on cocktails. Farther afield, **The Fulton Grand** is a nice option.

Map 6

O Landmarks

- **Brooklyn Academy of Music (BAM)** •
  30 Lafayette Ave [Ashland Pl]
  718-636-4100
  America's oldest continuously operating
  performing arts center. Never dull.
- **Brooklyn Masonic Temple** •
  317 Clermont Ave [Lafayette Ave]
  718-638-1256
  Its vestrymen have included Robert E. Lee and
  Thomas J. (Stonewall) Jackson.
- **Brooklyn Navy Yard** •
  Flushing Ave & Clinton Ave
  718-907-5900
  Nation's first navy yard employed 70,000
  people during WWII. Today, it houses a diverse
  range of businesses.
- **Fort Greene Park** •
  Willoughby Ave & Washington Park
  718-222-1461
  Liquor store proximity is a plus on a warm
  afternoon when you visit this welcome chunk
  of green.
- **Lafayette Avenue Presbyterian Church** •
  85 S Oxford St [Lafayette Ave]
  718-625-7515
  Nationally known church with performing
  arts; former Underground Railroad stop.
- **Long Island Rail Road – Atlantic Terminal** •
  Flatbush Ave & Hanson Pl
  718-217-5477
  A low red-brick building hosting more than 20
  million passengers annually. A total craphole.
- **Pratt Institute Steam Turbine Power Plant** •
  200 Willoughby Ave [Hall St]
  This authentic steam generator gets fired up
  a few times a year to impress the parents. Cool.
- **Prison Ship Martyrs' Monument** •
  Fort Greene Park
  Crypt holds remains of thousands of
  Revolutionary War-era prisoners.
- **Steiner Studios** •
  15 Washington Ave [Flushing Ave]
  718-858-1600
  Film studio in the Brooklyn Navy Yard.
- **Williamsburgh Savings Bank Building** •
  1 Hanson Pl [Ashland Pl]
  Still the tallest building in the borough and
  when you're lost, a sight for sore eyes.

Coffee

- **Outpost** • 1014 Fulton St [Downing St]
  718-636-1260
  Important Fulton-area coffee shop.
- **WTF Coffee Lab** •
  47 Willoughby Ave [Adelphi St]
  Third wave, expensive, etc.

Farmers Markets

- **Fort Greene Park Greenmarket** •
  Dekalb Ave & Washington Park
  Saturday, 8 a.m.–4 p.m., year-round, SE corner
  of park.

It's all here, folks: Italian (**Locanda** and **Scopello**), French (**Chez Oskar**), BBQ (**Smoke Joint**), tapas (**Olea**), hip (**General Greene** and **No. 7**), Middle Eastern (**Black Iris**), Mexican (**Castro**), burgers (**67 Burger**), and a reliable greasy spoon diner (**Mike's Coffee Shop**). Full yet?

Map 6

Nightlife

• **The Alibi** • 242 Dekalb Ave [Vanderbilt Ave]
718-783-8519
Real deal neighborhood bar.
• **Bar Olivino** • 899 Fulton St [Vanderbilt Ave]
718-857-7952
Companion wine bar to Olivino Wines.
• **Brooklyn Masonic Temple** •
317 Clermont Ave [Lafayette Ave]
718-638-1256
Masons + indie rock = smiles all around.
• **Brooklyn Public House** •
247 Dekalb Ave [Vanderbilt Ave]
347-227-8976
Lots of beers, with food, open 'till 2 am.
Perfect.
• **Der Schwarze Kolner** •
710 Fulton St [S Oxford St]
347-841-4495
German beer hall, w/ food. Ft. Greene now
almost perfect.
• **Dick & Jane's Bar** •
266 Adelphi St [Dekalb Ave]
347-227-8021
A very, very cool speakeasy hidden behind
four garage doors. Sssshhhh…

• **The Emerson** • 561 Myrtle Ave [Emerson Pl]
347-763-1310
Good pub for Pratt students and locals.
• **Frank's Cocktail Lounge** •
660 Fulton St [S Elliott Pl]
718-625-9339
When you need to get funky.
• **The Fulton Grand** •
1011 Fulton St [Grand Ave]
718-399-2240
Well appointed, good beer and whiskey
selection.
• **Hanson Dry** • 925 Fulton St [Waverly Ave]
Good cocktails.
• **One Last Shag** •
348 Franklin Ave [Lexington Ave]
718-398-2472
Great locals bar with patio, free grill, and
Guinness on tap.
• **Project Parlor** • 742 Myrtle Ave [Sanford St]
347-497-0550
Cozy bar with surprisingly huge backyard in
shabby environs.
• **Rustik Tavern** • 471 Dekalb Ave [Kent Ave]
347-406-9700
Neighborhood tap draws cozy clientele.
• **Stonehome Wine Bar** •
87 Lafayette Ave [S Portland Ave]
718-624-9443
Dark cave for serious oenophiles.

Map 6

🍴 Restaurants

- **67 Burger** • 67 Lafayette Ave [S Elliott Pl]
718-797-7150 • $$
Super-cool stop for a quick bite before your
movie at BAM.
- **Bati** • 747 Fulton St [S Portland Ave]
718-797-9696 • $$
Friendly (aren't they all?) Ft. Greene Ethiopian.
Good pre-BAM option.
- **Black Iris** • 228 Dekalb Ave [Clermont Ave]
718-852-9800 • $$
Middle Eastern; good lamb, terrible chicken,
excellent Zataar bread.
- **Black Swan** •
1048 Bedford Ave [Lafayette Ave]
718-783-4744 • $$$
Great pub, long menu, late-night bites…about
perfect.
- **Castro's** • 511 Myrtle Ave [Grand Ave]
718-398-1459 • $$
Burritos delivered con cervesas, if you like.
- **Chez Oskar** • 211 Dekalb Ave [Adelphi St]
718-852-6250 • $$$
French cuisine in a good neighborhood bistro.
- **Choice Market** •
318 Lafayette Ave [Grand Ave]
718-230-5234 • $
Excellent sandwiches, baked goods, burgers,
etc. served w/ maddening slowness.
- **Colonia Verde** • 219 Dekalb Ave [Adelphi St]
347-689-4287 • $$$$
Latin American flavors and 3 great dining
spaces. Nice.
- **Dolores Deli Grocery** •
173 Park Ave [Adelphi St]
718-246-9707 • $
Dominican delicacies (roast pork, goat, etc.) for
$3.50. Awesome.
- **Dough** • 305 Franklin Ave [Lafayette Ave]
347-533-7544 • $
The perfect coffee partner: amazing
doughnuts!
- **Five Spot Soul Food** •
459 Myrtle Ave [Washington Ave]
718-852-0202 • $$$
Hoppin' soul food joint w/ live entertainment.

- **The General Greene** •
229 Dekalb Ave [Clermont Ave]
718-222-1510 • $$
Two words: candied bacon.
- **Hoya Santa** • 250 Dekalb Ave [Vanderbilt Ave]
347-463-9460 • $$
Tasty Mexican comes to the DeKalb strip…
good, a tad pricey though.
- **Il Porto** • 37 Washington Ave [Flushing Ave]
718-624-2965 • $$
Cute Italian/pizzeria in front of the Navy Yard.
- **Joloff Restaurant** • 930 Fulton St [St James Pl]
718-636-4011 • $$
Plain rice splendorized by West African sauces.
- **Locanda Vini & Olii** •
129 Gates Ave [Cambridge Pl]
718-622-9202 • $$$$$
Rustic but pricey neighborhood Italian.
Marvelous décor.
- **Lulu & Po** • 154 Carlton Ave [Myrtle Ave]
917-435-3745 • $$$
Small-plates goodness arrives in Fort Greene.
Sweet(breads)!
- **Luz** • 177 Vanderbilt Ave [Myrtle Ave]
718-246-4000 • $$$
Yuppie interior with requisite brunch.
- **Madiba** • 195 Dekalb Ave [Carlton Ave]
718-855-9190 • $$$
South African—Bunny Chow, need we say
more? Shebeen with live music.
- **Marietta** • 285 Grand Ave [Lafayette Ave]
718-638-9500 • $$$$
Haute-Southern cuisine plus good cocktails.
- **Mike's Coffee Shop** •
328 Dekalb Ave [St James Pl]
718-857-1462 • $
Classic diner option.
- **No. 7** • 7 Greene Ave [Fulton St]
718-522-6370 • $$$
Hip killer postmodern goodness in Ft. Greene.
- **Olea** • 171 Lafayette Ave [Adelphi St]
718-643-7003 • $$
Friendly, buzzing neighborhood tapas/
Mediterranean. Get the bronzino.
- **Putnam's Pub & Cooker** •
419 Myrtle Ave [Clinton Ave]
347-799-2382 • $$$
Buzzing bar, oysters, burgers, mussels, two
levels, outdoor seating…we love it.

Hit either **Greene Grape Provisions** or **Choice Greene** for gourmet groceries to go with that nice bottle of wine from **Olivino**, **Gnarly Vines**, or **Thirst**. Pick up books at **Greenlight Books**, mid-century antiques at **Yu Interiors**, and everything else at **Target**. Watch for the occasional artsy bazaar outside of BAM.

- **Roman's** • 243 Dekalb Ave [Vanderbilt Ave]
718-622-5300 •
Postmodern Italian buzzes in Fort Greene. Recommended.
- **Scopello** • 63 Lafayette Ave [S Elliott Pl]
718-852-1100 • $$
Sicilian chic in stylish surroundings. Get the octopus.
- **The Smoke Joint** •
87 S Elliot Pl [Lafayette Ave]
718-797-1011 • $$
Spend the $16 and get the short rib. Thank us later.
- **Speedy Romeo** • 376 Classon Ave [Greene St]
718-230-0061 • $$
Bizzaro pizzas, good grilled meats, and a killer Caesar salad.
- **Umi Nom** • 433 Dekalb Ave [Classon Ave]
718-789-8806 • $$
Filipino-heavy Asian fusion done right.
- **Walter's** • 166 Dekalb Ave [Cumberland St]
718-488-7800 • $$$
Hip oysters, meats, and fish steps from Ft. Greene Park.
- **Zaytoons** • 472 Myrtle Ave [Washington Ave]
718-623-5522 • $$
Above-average Middle Eastern's second outpost. Get the chicken.

🛍 Shopping

- **Atlantic Terminal Mall** •
Atlantic Ave & Flatbush Ave
718-834-3400
And then there's Target.
- **Bicycle Station** • 171 Park Ave [Adelphi St]
718-638-0300
Laid-back store convenient to points east and west.
- **Brooklyn Flea** •
176 Lafayette Ave [Clermont Ave]
Already-famous flea market with rotating vendors & killer food.
- **Choice Greene** • 214 Greene Ave [Grand Ave]
718-230-1243
Cheese, game, produce. The gentrification of Fort Greene is complete.
- **Gnarly Vines** • 350 Myrtle Ave [Carlton Ave]
718-797-3183
Cool Myrtle wine merchant.

- **Green in BKLYN** •
432 Myrtle Ave [Clinton Ave]
718-855-4383
One-stop shop to help you live an eco-friendly lifestyle.
- **The Greene Grape** •
765 Fulton St [S Oxford St]
718-797-9463
Ft. Greene wine nexus.
- **Greene Grape Provisions** •
753 Fulton St [S Portland Ave]
718-233-2700
Excellent gourmet meat-cheese-fish trifecta.
- **Greenlight Bookstore** •
686 Fulton St [S Portland Ave]
718-246-0200
Ft. Greene's newest and immediately best bookstore.
- **Hardware 2.0** • 860 Atlantic Ave [Clinton Ave]
347-663-4603
Best music in a hardware store you'll ever hear.
- **Malchijah Hats** •
942 Atlantic Ave [St James Pl]
718-643-3269
Beautiful and unique hats.
- **Olivino Wines** • 905 Fulton St [Clinton Ave]
718-857-7952
Micro-sized wine shop.
- **Out of the Closet** •
475 Atlantic Ave [Nevins St]
718-637-2955
Thrift shop with clothing, furniture, pharmacy, and free HIV testing.
- **Target** • 139 Flatbush Ave [Atlantic Ave]
718-290-1109
The everything store. Seriously.
- **Thirst Wine Merchants** •
187 Dekalb Ave [Carlton Ave]
718-596-7643
Brilliant wine and alcohol selection, plus bar.
- **Utrecht Art Supplies** •
536 Myrtle Ave [Grand Ave]
718-789-0308
Cavernous art store servicing Pratt students & local artists.
- **Yu Interiors** • 15 Greene Ave [Cumberland St]
718-237-5878
Modern furniture, bags, and candles.

Somewhere between the tough streets immortalized in hip-hop and the hot-topic chatter of gentrification and hipster-invasion lies the real Bedford-Stuyvesant, one of North Brooklyn's largest, most storied neighborhoods. The diversity of Bed-Stuy's blocks—from brownstone to project high-rise, nail salon to wine bar—is slowly being matched by its population. Partly revitalized and yet still bearing the brunt of decades of economic struggle, today's Bed-Stuy offers an interesting mix of transition and history in one of the borough's most fascinating areas.

"Bed-Stuy" is a mash-up of what were once two separate neighborhoods: Bedford and Stuyvesant Heights. Bed-Stuy also includes the communities of Ocean Hill and Weeksville, the latter of which was one of the first free African American communities in the US. The greater Bed-Stuy demographic remains predominantly African American, and is to this day a touchstone of hip-hop culture, though Jay-Z has long since upgraded to TriBeCa from his roots in the Marcy projects.

Bed-Stuy is home to hundreds of stunning brownstone and greystone homes, typically three to four stories in height and ranging in condition from condemned to immaculately restored. Much of the Stuyvesant Heights end of the neighborhood is historically designated, including the anomalous and expansive **Akwaaba Mansion** (1860s), an Italianate home now converted into a high-end bed and breakfast. And did you know you could landmark a tree? The **Magnolia Grandiflora** in **Von King Park** is one of the city's rare examples. Visit in the springtime when its marzipan-like petals begin to explode. Don't overlook (as if you could) the amazing stature of two of the neighborhood's former armories on Marcus Garvey Boulevard at Jefferson, and on Bedford Avenue at Atlantic. They're now homeless shelters, but they look like medieval castles right in the heart of the 'hood.

Though not a nightlife destination (depending on your idea of nightlife), Bed-Stuy has cultivated several fantastic locals' spots, and while the new shining stars of Lewis Avenue's commercial strip begin to draw people just that much farther out on the A train, the real local treasures are the hole-in-the-wall Caribbean spots—get there before the doubles—chickpea curry pockets served in greasy mini roti pockets and wrapped in twisty wax paper—run out in the early afternoon.

Though the skinny jeans set sticks to the Bushwick borderlands under the J/M/Z train, Bed-Stuy offers an array of supper/nightclubs (**Sugar Hill**, **Brown Sugar**) and **Therapy Wine Bar**, with a casual by-the-glass vibe.

Bed-Stuy's evolving culinary landscape now extends well beyond Crown Fried Chicken (though there are still a few dozen outlets to choose from in the neighborhood) to Neapolitan pizza (**Saraghina**), Trinidadian roti (**Ali's**, **A&A**), and plenty of vegetarian options. **Peaches** is Southern cooking on high.

Map 7

O Landmarks

- **Akwaaba Mansion** •
  347 Macdonough St [Stuyvesant Ave]
  718-455-5958
  Restored 1860s villa that now operates as a
  beautiful B&B.
- **Herbert Von King Park** •
  Lafayette Ave & Marcy Ave
  One of the first parks in Brooklyn's history.
  BYO dog.
- **Magnolia Tree Earth Center** •
  679 Lafayette Ave [Tompkins Ave]
  718-387-2116
  One of two landmarked trees in all of NYC. Visit
  in spring when it blossoms.

Coffee

- **Common Grounds** •
  376 Tompkins Ave [Putnam Ave]
  347-533-9525
  Community-minded coffee house serving
  waffles, pastries, and panini.
- **Reconnect Cafe** •
  139 Tompkins Ave [Vernon Ave]
  347-406-9780
  Community minded cafe; healthy juices, too.
- **Sistas' Place** • 456 Nostrand Ave [Hancock St]
  718-398-1766
  Best known for its coffee, tea, and juices, but
  the crowd stays for the jazz, poetry and open
  mike nights.

Farmers Markets

- **Hattie Carthan Community Garden** •
  654 Lafayette Ave [Marcy]
  718-638-3566
  Saturday, 9 a.m.-3 p.m., July-Nov.

Nightlife

- **Brown Sugar Club** •
  433 Marcus Garvey Blvd [Macon St]
  718-919-4163
  Bar, grill, open mike, karaoke.
- **Sistas' Place** • 456 Nostrand Ave [Hancock St]
  718-398-1766
  Jazz, poetry, and open mic nights.
- **Therapy Wine Bar** • 364 Lewis Ave [Halsey St]
  718-513-0686
  Casual, chill by-the-glass boîte.
- **Tip Top Bar & Grill** •
  432 Franklin Ave [Madison St]
  718-857-9744
  Good, cheap dive.

Breukelen Cellars and **Olivino Wines** are two non-plexiglass wine & spirit stores. For basic goods, the Fulton Street retail strip has all you'll ever need. And **Tony's Country Life** is no Johnny-Come-Lately on the Bed-Stuy scene.

Restaurants

- **A&A Bake & Doubles** •
481 Nostrand Ave [Macon St]
718-230-0753 • $
A neighborhood favorite—no one leaves without their doubles.
- **Ali's Trinidad Roti Shop** •
1267 Fulton St [Arlington Pl]
718-783-0316 • $
West Indian roti.
- **Brooklyn Beso** • 370 Lewis Ave [Macon St]
347-915-2900 • $$
Latin-inspired cuisine.
- **Common Grounds** •
376 Tompkins Ave [Putnam Ave]
347-533-9525 • $
Community-minded coffee house serving waffles, pastries, and panini.
- **Do or Dine** • 1108 Bedford Ave [Quincy St]
718-684-2290 • $$$
Definitely Do it. Bizarro small plates and back garden. Killer.
- **Peaches** • 393 Lewis Ave [MacDonough St]
718-942-4162 • $$$
Southern cooking from the guys who own Smoke Joint.
- **Peaches HotHouse** •
415 Tompkins Ave [Hancock St]
718-483-9111 • $$
Delectable Nashville-style "hot chicken." Believe it.
- **Saraghina** • 435 Halsey St [Lewis Ave]
718-574-0010 • $
Bed-Stuy gets on the wood-fired 'za bandwagon.
- **Scratch Bread** •
1069 Bedford Ave [Greene Ave]
917-803-5773 • $
Fancy pants breads, pastries, and sandwiches to go.
- **Sud** • 1102 Bedford Ave [Lexington Ave]
718-484-8474 • $$$
Classy and romantic. Bon appetito!
- **Sugar Hill Supper Club** •
609 Dekalb Ave [Nostrand Ave]
718-797-1727 • $$
Downtown soul(food).

Shopping

- **Andrew Fish Market** •
1228 Fulton St [Bedford Ave]
718-623-6774
You pick it, they cook it. Fried to perfection on the spot.
- **Breukelen Cellars** •
504 Nostrand Ave [Halsey St]
347-240-5421
Boutique equal parts wine, art & olde-tyme spelling.
- **Brooklyn Kolache Co.** •
520 Dekalb Ave [Bedford Ave]
718-398-1111
Sweet and savory kolaches, not just in Texas anymore.
- **Brooklyn Weinstein Paint & Home Center** •
420 Tompkins Ave [Halsey St]
718-638-7207
Paint the town whatever color you choose.
- **Foot Locker** • 1258 Fulton St [Nostrand Ave]
718-399-6979
For all your footwear needs.
- **Little Red Boutique** •
374 Lewis Ave [Macon St]
718-443-1170
The accessory and candle racket hard at work here.
- **Olivino Wines** •
426 Marcus Garvey Blvd [Macon St]
718-249-0721
Pinot Noir, not PBR.
- **Tony's Country Life** •
1316 Fulton St [Nostrand Ave]
718-789-2040
Best health emporium in the 'hood with a friendly and helpful staff.

Map 8 • **BoCoCa** / ok

Grace Ct
Aitken Pl
Schermerhorn St
Schermerhorn St
Hoyt-
Schermerhorn
Atlantic Ave
Atlantic Ave
State St
Pacific St

COBBLE
HILL
BOERUM
HILL
Bergen
Street
Warren St
Wyckoff St
Butler St
Gowanus
Housing
Douglass St
Degraw St
Sackett St
Union St
Warren Place
Baltic St
President St
Carroll
Street
1st St
2nd St
3rd St

CARROLL
GARDENS
4th St
5th St
6th St Basin
7th St Basin
Smith-
9th Street
W 9th St
8th St
10th St
11th St Basin
Gowanus
Canal
Gowanus Expy
11th St
12th St
13th St
14th St
15th St

Hugh L. Carey Tunnel

Red Hook
Park
Red Hook
Housing

RED
HOOK
Red Hook
Ballfields
Brooklyn Clay
Retort and Fire
Brick Building
Red Hook
Recreational
Area
Reed St
Cool
House
Beard
Street
Pier
Red Hook
Grain Terminal

1/4 mile
.25 km

Map 8

Sorry for the "BoCoCa" thing, but we just can't fit "Boerum Hill / Cobble Hill / Carroll Gardens" along with "Red Hook" on the header bar. Crusty oldtimers will say "I remember when this area was just called 'South Brooklyn.'" Well, Mr. Crusty Oldtimer, this is what happens when neighborhoods age, become economically stable, and are ravaged by hungry real estate agents.

Cobble Hill is like the bastard child of Brooklyn Heights—waterfront without the Promenade, nice-but-not-stunning brownstones, and slightly less convenient subway access. That said, Cobble Hill's dining, shopping, and nightlife are far and away superior to the Heights. Plus, it has one of the quaintest small parks in all of New York—if you've ever seen **Cobble Hill Park** right after a snowfall, you'll know what we're talking about.

Boerum Hill, immortalized in Jonathan Lethem's *The Fortress of Solitude*, has an unusual floor plan in that it's much wider east-west than north-south; Boerum Hill extends east all the way to 4th Avenue, and encompasses more retail along the Atlantic Avenue corridor, as well as Smith Street's northern half. Boerum Hill has come a long way, as evidenced by Smith Street's high commercial rents (say goodbye to porn video, furniture rental, and dollar stores) and the ongoing renovation of many brownstones.

The image of Carroll Gardens is of hard-working immigrant Italian families tending to wide brownstones with those unusual garden frontages. Now many of these owners are either condo-izing or selling outright to Manhattanites who flock to Carroll Gardens for its schools, amenities, a 20-minute subway ride to Manhattan, and huge retail options on lower Court and Smith Streets. There are still old-school Italian shops and eateries that hold their own against the influx of hip restaurants on lower Court Street and the design shops of Smith Street. Somewhere east of Carroll Gardens lies/flows the **Gowanus Canal**, the notorious gonorrhea-breeding waterway/polluted vestigial nightmare that is home to various and sundry household refuse and alleged mafia dumping ground. All that aside, things are looking up for this low-lying stretch of "South Brooklyn," what with new remediation technologies and even a Whole Foods on 3rd Avenue.

And then there's Red Hook. Isolated, peppered with derelict industrial sites (re: the **Red Hook Grain Terminal**), and lacking high-quality housing, Red Hook still draws folks to the other side of the BQE. Even with the closest subway stop over a mile away, **Fairway** and **IKEA** have chosen to make Red Hook their Brooklyn home. Elsewhere, the vibrant sports-and-food-stall scene at the **Red Hook Ball Fields** during summer is not to be missed, and did we mention the view of New York Bay from **Louis J Valentino Park**? It rocks.

Map 8

O Landmarks

- **Beard Street Pier** • Van Brunt St & Reed St
  Historic 19th century warehouses, now a
  cluster of shops and offices.
- **Brooklyn Clay Retort and Fire Brick Works** •
  76 Van Dyke St [Richards St]
  Red Hook's first official Landmark building
  dates to the mid-19th century.
- **Cobble Hill Park** • Clinton St & Verandah Pl
  One of the cutest parks in all of New York.
- **Cool House** • 26 Reed St [Van Brunt St]
  One of the coolest single-family dwellings in
  the city.
- **Gowanus Canal** • Smith St & 9th St
  Brooklyn's answer to the Seine.
- **Louis Valentino Jr Park and Pier** •
  Coffey St & Ferris St
  Escape gentrification-industrial complex with
  perfect view Statue of Liberty.
- **Red Hook Ball Fields** • Clinton St & Bay St
  Watch futbol and eat Central American street
  food every Saturday from spring through fall.
- **Red Hook Grain Terminal** •
  Columbia St & Halleck St
  Visit just to wonder what it's doing there.
- **Warren Place** • Warren Pl [Warren St]
  Public housing from the 1870s.

Coffee

- **Black Gold** • 461 Court St [Luquer St]
  347-227-8227
  Coffee, records, antiques, baked goods. All
  they're missing is cheese.
- **Cafe Pedlar** • 210 Court St [Warren St]
  718-855-7129
  Stumptown Coffee is served here. That's all
  you need to know.
- **D'Amico Foods** • 309 Court St [Degraw St]
  718-875-5403
  The neighborhood spot for fresh beans.

Farmers Markets

- **Carroll Gardens** • Smith St & Carroll St
  Sunday, 8 a.m.–3 p.m., year-round.

Each of the 'nabes here has their stalwarts. In Boerum Hill, it's classic **Brooklyn Inn** or the jukebox at **The Boat**. In Cobble Hill, has several great places on Atlantic (**Floyd**, **Montero's**, **Last Exit**), or stick with old-tyme cocktails at **Henry Public**. In Carroll Gardens, it's **Gowanus Yacht Club** in summer and **Brooklyn Social** in winter, and in Red Hook, **Bait and Tackle** and **Fort Defiance** compete with classic dive **Sunny's**.

🍸 Nightlife

- **61 Local** • 61 Bergen St [Smith St]
718-875-1150
Spacious bar with a wide, local craft beer selection.
- **Abilene** • 442 Court St [3rd Pl]
718-522-6900
Cozy and unpretentious. Drink specials galore.
- **Bar Great Harry** • 280 Smith St [Sackett St]
718-222-1103
There's a blog devoted to the draft beer section.
- **Black Mountain Wine House** •
415 Union St [Hoyt St]
718-522-4340
Try the Lebanese wine!
- **Boat Bar** • 175 Smith St [Wyckoff St]
718-254-0607
Dank, dark and friendly. Nice tunes to boot.
- **Botanica** • 220 Conover St [Coffey St]
347-225-0148
Classy looking joint.
- **The Brazen Head** • 228 Atlantic Ave [Court St]
718-488-0430
Cask ale, mixed crowd.
- **The Brooklyn Inn** • 148 Hoyt St [Bergen St]
718-522-2525
When you're feeling nostalgic.
- **Brooklyn Social** • 335 Smith St [Carroll St]
718-858-7758
Old boy's lounge revamped. Cocktails still the same. NFT Pick.
- **Building on Bond** • 112 Bond St [Pacific St]
347-853-8687
Coffee by day, alcohol by night. Perfect.
- **Clover Club** • 210 Smith St [Baltic St]
718-855-7939
Charming den of cocktails and conversation.
- **Cody's American Bar & Grill** •
154 Court St [Dean St]
718-852-6115
Great sports bar. Seriously.
- **Downtown Bar & Grill** •
160 Court St [Amity St]
718-625-2835
Gets the package games. More beers than God intended for man.
- **Floyd** • 131 Atlantic Ave [Henry St]
718-858-5810
Indoor bocce ball court!

- **Fort Defiance** • 365 Van Brunt St [Dikeman St]
347-453-6672
Great cocktails, great beer, great pork chop.
- **Gowanus Yacht Club** •
323 Smith St [President St]
718-246-1321
Dogs, burgers, and beer. Love it.
- **Henry Public** • 329 Henry St [Atlantic Ave]
718-852-8630
From those that brought us Brooklyn Social.
- **home/made** • 293 Van Brunt St [Pioneer St]
347-223-4135
Wine-soaked snacking on the Red Hook waterfront.
- **The JakeWalk** • 282 Smith St [Sackett St]
347-599-0294
The important things in life: wine and whiskey.
- **Jalopy Tavern** •
315 Columbia St [Hamilton Ave]
718-395-3214
Live music from rockabilly to out jazz; banjos in the window.
- **Last Exit** • 136 Atlantic Ave [Henry St]
718-222-9198
Still trying to win trivia night. $10 pails of PBR.
- **Montero's Bar and Grill** •
73 Atlantic Ave [Hicks St]
718-624-9799
A taste of what things used to be like.
- **Other Half Brewing** •
195 Centre St [Hamilton Ave]
347-987-3527
Elegant/bold brews sold in cans or from tasting room.
- **Red Hook Bait & Tackle** •
320 Van Brunt St [Pioneer St]
718-451-4665
Kitschy, comfy pub with cheap drinks and good beers on tap.
- **Rocky Sullivan's** • 34 Van Dyke St [Dwight St]
718-246-8050
The six-point portfolio is on tap—a Red Hook must.
- **Roebling Inn** • 97 Atlantic Ave [Hicks St]
718-488-0040
Good vibe at this sister tavern of the Brooklyn Inn.
- **Sunny's** • 253 Conover St [Reed St]
718-625-8211
No longer pay-what-you-wish, but still cheap and good.
- **Waterfront Ale House** •
155 Atlantic Ave [Clinton St]
718-522-3794
Renowned burgers and sizable beer list.

Map 3

Map 8

🍴 Restaurants

- **Alma** • 187 Columbia St [Degraw St]
718-643-5400 • $$$
Top NYC Mexican with great views of lower
Manhattan.
- **Atlantic Chip Shop** •
129 Atlantic Ave [Henry St]
718-855-7775 • $$
Heart attack on a plate.
- **Bacchus** • 409 Atlantic Ave [Bond St]
718-852-1572 •
Low key neighborhood Frenchy bistro.
- **Bar Bruno** • 520 Henry St [Union St]
347-763-0850 • $$
Mexican gastropub just off the main drag in
Carroll Gardens.
- **Bar Tabac** • 128 Smith St [Dean St]
718-923-0918 • $$$
Open late; fabulous frites, burgers, et al.
- **Battersby** • 255 Smith St [Degraw St]
718-852-8321 • $$$$$
Upscale joint in tiny space. Let us know if you
get in.
- **Bedouin Tent** • 405 Atlantic Ave [Bond St]
718-852-5555 • $
Two words: lamb sandwich. No, four: best
lamb sandwich ever.
- **Bocca Lupo** • 391 Henry St [Warren St]
718-243-2522 • $$$
Postmodern panini by day and (late) night.
We love NYC.
- **Brooklyn Crab** • 24 Reed St [Van Brunt St]
718-643-2722 • $$
3 floors of delish seafood with a view of New
York Bay. We love it, except for weekends.
- **Brooklyn Farmacy & Soda Fountain** •
513 Henry St [Sackett St]
718-522-6260 •
A blast from the past. Homemade sodas and
shakes.
- **Buddy's Burrito & Taco Bar** •
260 Court St [Baltic St]
718-488-8695 • $
Fast, cheap, and out-of-control huge burritos.
- **Buttermilk Channel** •
524 Court St [Huntington St]
718-852-8490 • $$$
Oysters, sausages, fried chicken, waffles,
burgers, ahhh.
- **Café Luluc** • 214 Smith St [Butler St]
718-625-3815 • $$$
Friendly French bistro.
- **Carroll Gardens Classic Diner** •
155 Smith St [Bergen St]
718-403-9940 • $$
Good diner food with 24 hour delivery. Crucial
for survival.
- **Chance** • 223 Smith St [Butler St]
718-242-1515 • $$$$
Upscale Asian fusion—recommended.
- **Char No. 4** • 196 Smith St [Baltic St]
718-643-2106 • $$
Worship (and eat) at this temple of whisky
and bourbon.
- **Chocolate Room** • 269 Court St [Douglass St]
718-246-2600 •
Guess what's here?
- **DeFonte's Sandwich Shop** •
379 Columbia St [Luquer St]
718-625-8052 • $
Crazy-ass Italian hero shop.
- **Fatoosh** • 330 Hicks St [Atlantic Ave]
718-243-0500 • $
Nicely priced Middle Eastern Food.
- **Ferdinando's Focacceria** •
151 Union St [Hicks St]
718-855-1545 • $
Sicilian specialties you won't find anywhere
else! Get the panelle special.
- **Fragole Ristorante** • 394 Court St [Carroll St]
718-522-7133 • $$
Fresh and cozy Italian. An absolute gem.
- **Frankie's 457** • 457 Court St [Luquer St]
718-403-0033 • $$
Fantastic meatballs. Cool space. Killer brunch.

Map 3

There's more good food here than in some entire states, trust us, from Michelin-noted **Ki Sushi**, **Saul**, and **The Grocery** to brick-oven goodness at **Lucali** (we're still waiting for a table), loud Thai at **Joya**, fried chicken at **Buttermilk Channel**, seasonal Italian at **Frankies 457**, Central European comfort food at **Karloff**, Middle Eastern haven **Bedouin Tent**, late-night French at **Bar Tabac**, or rooftop Mexican at **Alma**.

- **The Good Fork** • 391 Van Brunt St [Coffey St]
718-643-6636 • $$$
Yep. It's good. VERY good.
- **The Grocery** • 288 Smith St [Sackett St]
718-596-3335 • $$$$
Magnificent. Reservations recommended.
- **Hanco's** • 135 Smith St [Dean St]
718-858-6818 • $
Bánh mì for people who won't trek to Sunset Park.
- **Hibino** • 333 Henry St [Pacific St]
718-260-8052 • $$
Highly regarded Cobble Hill sushi.
- **Hometown Bar-B-Que** •
454 Van Brunt St [Reed St]
347-294-4644 • $$
Grab some 'cue while the significant other shops for groceries at Fairway.
- **Hope & Anchor** •
347 Van Brunt St [Wolcott St]
718-237-0276 • $$
Great upscale diner.
- **Joya Thai** • 215 Court St [Warren St]
718-222-3484 • $$
Excellent, inexpensive, but super-noisy Thai.
- **Karloff** • 254 Court St [Kane St]
347-689-4279 • $$
Eastern European classics won't bust your gut, plus ice cream!
- **Ki Sushi** • 122 Smith St [Dean St]
718-935-0575 • $$
Affordable sushi in sleek surroundings; Michelin-starred.
- **Layla Jones** • 214 Court St [Warren St]
718-624-2361 • $
The best pizza delivery in the hood.
- **Le Petit Café** • 502 Court St [Nelson St]
718-596-7060 • $$
Good bistro food—check out the garden.
- **Lucali** • 575 Henry St [Carroll St]
718-858-4086 • $$
One man makes every perfect pizza by hand. Be prepared to wait.

- **Mazzat** • 208 Columbia St [Sackett St]
718-852-1652 • $$
Donut-style falafel will make you a believer.
- **Mile End** • 97 Hoyt St [Atlantic Ave]
718-852-7510 • $$
Jewish deli, Montreal-style. Two words: smoked meat.
- **Pok Pok NY** • 117 Columbia St [Kane St]
718-923-9322 • $$$
Killer Thai with spicy wings straight from the Godhead.
- **Prime Meats** • 465 Court St [Luquer St]
718-254-0327 • $$$
German delights like wurst and sauerbraten take center stage.
- **Red Gravy** • 151 Atlantic Ave [Clinton St]
718-855-0051 • $$$
Perfect Italian courtesy of Saul. We'll be back.
- **Rucola** • 190 Dean St [Bond St]
718-576-3209 • $$$
Rustic neighborhood Northern Italian. Just a great vibe.
- **Saul** • 200 Eastern Pkwy [Washington Ave]
718-935-9844 • $$$
Romantical and delicioso.
- **Strong Place** • 270 Court St [Butler St]
718-855-2105 • $$
Good beer selection and delicious duck.
- **Tripoli** • 156 Atlantic Ave [Clinton St]
718-596-5800 • $$
A Lebanese standby since 1973 is great for a party, with meze platters and BYOB
- **Yemen Café** • 176 Atlantic Ave [Clinton St]
718-834-9533 • $
More good Yemeni food, because you can never have too much lamb.
- **Yemen Cuisine** • 145 Court St [Atlantic Ave]
718-624-9325 • $$
Don't let the decor (or lack thereof) keep you out, go and eat amazing lamb.
- **Zaytoons** • 283 Smith St [Sackett St]
718-875-1880 • $$
Excellent Middle Eastern pizzas and kebabs.

Shopping

- **A Cook's Companion** •
  197 Atlantic Ave [Court St]
  718-852-6901
  A fantastic shop with everything for your kitchen (except the food).
- **Article&** • 198 Smith St [Baltic St]
  718-852-3620
  Designer duds and accessories. Who needs the LES?
- **Bien Cuit** • 120 Smith St [Pacific St]
  718-852-0200
  Stand-out breads and pastries.
- **BookCourt** • 163 Court St [Dean St]
  718-875-3677
  Classic Cobble Hill bookstore w/ great readings, selection, etc.
- **Botanica El Phoenix** •
  224 Columbia St [Union St]
  718-422-0300
  Santeria accessories, religious candles, icons, books.
- **By Brooklyn** • 261 Smith St [Degraw St]
  718-643-0606
  Dedicated to stuff made in the borough of Kings.
- **Caputo's Fine Foods** • 460 Court St [3rd Pl]
  718-855-8852
  Italian gourmet specialties. The real deal.

- **City Foundry** • 365 Atlantic Ave [Hoyt St]
  718-923-1786
  If you can afford it your place will be in a magazine.
- **Clayworks on Columbia** •
  195 Columbia St [Degraw St]
  718-694-9540
  Unique, practical pottery and classes for all levels.
- **Community Bookstore** •
  212 Court St [Warren St]
  718-834-9494
  General interest.
- **D'Amico Foods** • 309 Court St [Degraw St]
  718-875-5403
  The best coffee in the 'hood, if not the city.
- **Dig** • 479 Atlantic Ave [Nevins St]
  718-554-0207
  Garden store specializing in tricky urban environments.
- **Erie Basin** • 388 Van Brunt St [Dikeman St]
  718-554-6147
  Jewelry and stuff from the 19th and early 20th century.
- **Eva Gentry Consignment** •
  371 Atlantic Ave [Hoyt St]
  718-522-3522
  Fashionista consignment emporium.
- **Exit 9** • 127 Smith St [Dean St]
  718-422-7720
  Quirky gifts.
- **Fairway** • 480 Van Brunt St [Reed St]
  718-694-6868
  Best grocery store in Brooklyn. By far.

You can find anything on Atlantic, Smith, or Court Streets, especially food: **Sahadi's, Staubitz, D'Amico's, Caputo's, Fish Tales, Smith & Vine,** and **Stinky** are all great. Treat yourself at **Swallow** or **Article &. Clayworks on Columbia**'s housewares are made by local artists, **GRDN** has lush plants, **Idlewild Books** is the spot for travel books, and all manner of kitchenware can be found at **A Cook's Companion.**

- **Fish Tales** • 191 Court St [Wyckoff St]
  718-246-1346
  The place for expensive, but fresh, fish.
- **Flight 001** • 132 Smith St [Dean St]
  718-243-0001
  Luggage, etc, for the pampered traveler.
- **G. Esposito & Sons** •
  357 Court St [President St]
  718-875-6863
  Sopressata and sausages direct from the Godhead.
- **Gowanus Nursery** • 9 Carroll St [Van Brunt St]
  718-852-3116
  Make your garden happen in a not-so-green 'hood.
- **GRDN** • 103 Hoyt St [Pacific St]
  718-797-3628
  Great store…if you're lucky enough to have a garden.
- **Hard Soul Boutique** •
  418 Atlantic Ave [Bond St]
  718-625-2838
  Fierce jewelry, recording studio founded by Strafe ("Set It Off").
- **Heights Chateau Wines** •
  123 Atlantic Ave [Henry St]
  718-330-0963
  Consistently good store straddling Brooklyn Heights & Cobble Hill.
- **Idlewild Books** • 249 Warren St [Court St]
  718-403-9600
  Extensive foreign-language offerings and language classes.
- **IKEA** • 1 Beard St [Otsego St]
  718-246-4532
  Everything you need for your 312 sq ft apt.
- **Malko Karkanni Bros.** •
  174 Atlantic Ave [Clinton St]
  718-834-0845
  Cashew Baklava makes you believe again.
- **Mazzola Bakery** • 192 Union St [Henry St]
  718-643-1719
  Top bakery in CG. Get the lard bread.
- **One Girl Cookies** • 68 Dean St [Smith St]
  212-675-4996
  Custom cookies in Cobble Hill.
- **Red Hook Lobster Pound** •
  284 Van Brunt St [Visitation Pl]
  718-858-7650
  Mmmmm…fresh gorgeous lobsters.
- **Sahadi's** • 187 Atlantic Ave [Court St]
  718-624-4550
  Totally brilliant Middle Eastern supermarket—olives, cheese, bread, etc.
- **Smith & Vine** • 268 Smith St [Douglass St]
  718-243-2864
  If NFT owned a liquor store, this would be it.
- **Staubitz Market** • 222 Court St [Baltic St]
  718-624-0014
  Top NYC butcher.
- **Stinky** • 215 Smith St [Butler St]
  718-596-2873
  I get it! It's a cheese store!
- **Swallow** • 361 Smith St [2nd St]
  718-222-8201
  An exquisite selection of glass, jewelry, and books.
- **Trader Joe's** • 130 Court St [Court St]
  718-246-8460
  The line moves pretty fast, really.

Map 8

Flatbush Ave

State St

Atlantic Ave

Pacific St

The Co-Cathedral
of St. Joseph

Washington Ave

Grand Ave

B Q

2 3

4 5

Atlantic
Avenue

Pacific Street

D N R

Dean St

Bergen St

Bergen
Street

2 3

Dean St

Bergen St

St Mark's Ave

Carlton Ave

Vanderbilt Ave

Underhill Ave

PROSPECT
HEIGHTS

Sterling Pl

St Johns Pl

Lincoln Pl

10

B Q

7th Avenue

St Mark's Pl

Warren St

Baltic St

Butler St

Douglass St

Degraw St

Fourth Ave

Fifth Ave

Dusenbury Pl

Prospect Pl

Park Pl

Sterling Pl

St Johns Pl

Lincoln Pl

Sixth Ave

Seventh Ave

Park Ave

2 3

Grand Army
Plaza

Grand
Army
Plaza

Brooklyn
Public
Library

Puppet
Library

Grand Army Plz

Flatbush Ave

Bailey
Fountain

Eastern Pkwy

St Johns Pl

Lincoln Pl

Brooklyn
Museum

Brooklyn
Botanic
Garden

PAGE
106

Third Ave

Sackett St

Union
Street

R

Berkeley Pl

Union St

President St

Carroll St

Garfield Pl

Park Slope
Food Co-op

Eighth Ave

Polhemus Pl

Fiske Pl

Montgomery Pl

West Dr

East Dr

8

1st St Basin

4th St Basin

Whitwell Pl

Denton Pl

1st St

2nd St

3rd St

4th St

5th St

6th St

7th St

8th St

PARK
SLOPE

Eighth Ave

PAGE
104

Prospect Park W

Prospect
Park

4th Avenue-
9th Street

R

F G

10th St

11th St

12th St

13th St

14th St

15th St

16th St

Third Ave

Fourth Ave

Fifth Ave

Sixth Ave

9th St

7th Avenue

F G

Seventh Ave

Prospect
Avenue

R

15th Street-
Prospect Park

F G

Prospect Park SW

Prospect Park W

W Lake Dr

WINDSOR
TERRACE

Tenth Ave

Howard Pl

Fuller Pl

Sherman St

11th Ave

278

Hamilton Ave

Prospect Expy

11

Jackson Pl

Webster Pl

Calder Pl

Windsor Pl

Prospect Ave

17th St

18th St

27

12

17th St

18th St

Prospect Park W

Howard Pl

Fuller Pl

13

17th St

18th St

1/4 mile

.25 km

Park Slope is an easy target. Power moms use their strollers as battering rams, stylish dads use the hippest bars and bistros as daycare centers, and the children, *the children*, they are born into this vicious cycle. But you know what? The Slope isn't just a haven for wealthy breeders and toiling serfs at the **Park Slope Food Co-op**. It's also got some amazing restaurants and shops, incredible brownstones, and the only park in the city that truly rivals Central Park.

The park they're referring to at the top of the slope is **Prospect Park**, Frederick Law Olmsted and Calvert Vaux's Brooklyn masterpiece. The ultimate design was executed piecemeal in the 1860s and 1870s, delayed in part by the Civil War. People, not all of whom from Brooklyn, claim that Prospect Park was the quintessence of Olmsted and Vaux park design, eclipsing a certain little vestpocket nicety that stretches for 50-some-odd blocks in the middle of Manhattan island. Whatever the one-upmanship, the man-made landscape is a pretty nice amenity to have in your backyard. Its charms include its historic bridges and walks, the largest swath of forest in the borough, remarkable summer concerts, a zoo, and last but certainly not least, the rare opportunity to grill in a city park. The Beaux-Arts arch and neoclassical columns around **Grand Army Plaza** were added toward the end of the 19th century. Across from Grand Army Plaza is the fantastic main branch of the **Brooklyn Public Library**.

Park Slope is nineteenth-century brownstone architecture at its best. The rows of houses all have distinct touches on their stoops and facades; idyllic and photo ready. It seems every other block has a soaring limestone church, lending skyline of regal steeples. But that brings us to the modern side: The number of cool shops, restaurants, and bars on 5th Avenue, 7th Avenue, and Flatbush Avenue is simply astounding. (If you look at these three streets on a map, it forms Pi, which clearly means something.) There is so much retail on these streets that you'd think there wouldn't be room for any more, but the action has spread to 4th Avenue and now even 3rd Avenue, near the appalling **Gowanus Canal**, now an EPA Superfund site thanks to decades of factory sediment, coal-tar, heavy metals, paint, sewage, and waste-fed algae.

And the wave of development is expanding ever outward. The world-class **Barclays Center** arena is just the first phase of the fledgling and controversial redevelopment set to take place above the train tracks of the Atlantic Yards. Sports arenas aside, Vanderbilt and Washington Avenues in Prospect Heights have been bustling commercial strips for years now. And with its many lovely and relatively rare three-story brownstones, we expect at least four kids in every Prospect Heights brownstone by the end of the next decade. Meanwhile, on the southeastern end of the Slope is Windsor Terrace, a longtime Irish enclave scrunched between Prospect Park and the Prospect Expressway that has attracted a new wave of young renters who can't afford the Slope but still enjoy prime park access and a mini-retail strip along Prospect Park West. Now if they could only reroute those infernal aviation machines flying into La Guardia to, uh, somewhere else, we could actually enjoy a backyard barbecue once in a while.

Map 9

Park Slope/Prospect Heights, Windsor Terrace

O Landmarks

- **Bailey Fountain** •
  Grand Army Plaza [Flatbush Ave]
  With sculpted figures of Neptune, Triton and
  attendants (some said to represent Wisdom
  and Felicity), the power emanating from this
  fountain could supply the Justice League.
- **Barclays Center** •
  620 Atlantic Ave [Flatbush Ave]
  917-618-6700
  World-class arena in the heart of Brooklyn.
- **Brooklyn Museum** •
  200 Eastern Pkwy [Washington Ave]
  718-638-5000
  Breathtakingly beautiful building, excellent
  collection.
- **Brooklyn Public Library** •
  10 Grand Army Plaza [Grand Ave]
  718-230-2100
  Fabulous Art Deco temple to knowledge.
- **The Co-Cathedral of St. Joseph** •
  856 Pacific St [Underhill Ave]
  718-783-4500
  Check out this stunning just-renovated interior
  of this 1912 cathedral. Wow.
- **Grand Army Plaza** • Flatbush Ave & Plaza St
  Site of John H. Duncan's Soldiers' and Sailors'
  Memorial Arch.
- **New York Puppet Library** •
  Grand Army Plaza [Soliders and Sailors Arch]
  The Memorial Arch at Grand Army Plaza has a
  funky theatre at the top. A must see (Summer
  Saturdays only).
- **Park Slope Food Co-op** •
  782 Union St [7th Ave]
  718-622-0560
  These farm-fresh veggies will do for those in
  search of their peck of dirt. Rinse.
- **Prospect Park** •
  Prospect Park W & Flatbush Ave
  718-965-8951
  Olmsted & Vaux's true masterpiece.

Coffee

- **Café Grumpy** • 383 7th Ave [12th St]
  718-499-4404
  Gourmet java comes to strollerland.
- **Café Regular du Nord** •
  158 Berkeley Pl [7th Ave]
  718-783-0673
- **Colson Patisserie** • 374 9th St [6th Ave]
  718-965-6400
- **Gorilla Coffee** • 97 5th Ave [Park Pl]
  718-230-3244
  Milk, two sugars, and a shot of hipness.
- **Joyce Bakeshop** • 646 Vanderbilt Ave [Park Pl]
  718-623-7470
  Prospect Heights goodness.
- **Milk Bar** • 620 Vanderbilt Ave [Prospect Pl]
  718-230-0844
- **Sit & Wonder** •
  688 Washington Ave [St Marks Ave]
  718-622-0299

Farmers Markets

- **Bartel-Pritchard Square Greenmarket** •
  Prospect Park W & 15th St
  Wednesday, 8 a.m.–3 p.m., May–Nov.
- **Grand Army Plaza Greenmarket** •
  Flatbush Ave & Eastern Pkwy
  Saturday, 8 a.m.–4 p.m., year-round.
- **Park Slope Farmers Market** • 5th Ave & 4th St
  Sunday, 11 a.m.–5 p.m., year-round.
- **Windsor Terrace • PS 154 Greenmarket** •
  Prospect Park W & 16th St
  Sunday, 9 a.m.–3 p.m., May–Dec.

Nightlife

- **4th Avenue Pub** • 76 4th Ave [Bergen St]
  718-643-2273
  1. Toss darts. 2. Drink fine draft beer. 3. Repeat.
- **Bar Reis** • 375 5th Ave [6th St]
  718-207-7874
  Disarmingly charming when you sit on the
  terrace.
- **Bar Sepia** • 234 Underhill Ave [Lincoln Pl]
  718-399-6680
  Neighborhood fave.
- **Bar Toto** • 411 11th St [6th Ave]
  718-768-4698
  Great bar food.

Map 9

Gourmet cocktails and beers have been sprouting up everywhere at spots like **Union Hall**, or support your local dive at **Freddy's**. Since the untimely demise of Southpaw, **The Bell House** is the place for rock shows and other events (Moth StorySlams!), but **Barbes** has a fabulous mix of world music jammed into its tiny back room space.

- **Barbes** • 376 9th St [6th Ave]
  347-422-0248
  Smart-looking space with eclectic entertainment. Recommended.
- **The Bell House** • 149 7th St [3rd Ave]
  718-643-6510
  Huge Gowanus live music venue + front bar; stellar.
- **Black Horse Pub** • 568 5th St [16th St]
  718-788-1975
  Where to watch footy.
- **Brookvin** • 381 7th Ave [12th St]
  718-768-9463
  Wine. Cheese. Ambience.
- **Buttermilk Bar** • 577 5th Ave [16th St]
  718-788-6297
  A solid more-than dive.
- **Canal Bar** • 270 3rd Ave [President St]
  718-246-0011
  Dive near the Gowanus, but not into it.
- **Cherry Tree Bar** • 65 4th Ave [Bergen St]
  718-399-1353
  Rowdy Irish pub with a stately backyard.
- **Commonwealth** • 497 5th Ave [12th St]
  718-768-2040
  So many beers, so little time.
- **Double Windsor** •
  210 Prospect Park West [16th St]
  347-725-3479
  Good food. Great beer.
- **Draft Barn** • 530 3rd Ave [13th St]
  718-768-0515
  Gigantic medieval beer hall. Cool.
- **Excelsior** • 390 5th Ave [6th St]
  718-832-1599
  Decent bar with mixed gay crowd.
- **Farrell's** • 215 Prospect Park West [16th St]
  718-788-8779
  No frills neighborhood bar with styrofoam cups.
- **Freddy's Bar and Backroom** •
  627 5th Ave [18th St]
  718-768-0131
  It lives again! And with great avant-jazz bookings, too.
- **The Gate** • 321 5th Ave [3rd Ave]
  718-768-4329
  Large outdoor area. Twenty beers on tap.
- **Ginger's** • 363 5th Ave [5th St]
  718-788-0924
  Nice and casual for center Slope.
- **Hank's Saloon** • 46 3rd Ave [Atlantic Ave]
  347-227-8495
  Sweaty, hillbilly-esque.

- **littlefield** • 622 Degraw St [4th Ave]
  718-855-3388
  Eco-friendly performance space: music, film, art. Sweet.
- **Loki Lounge** • 304 5th Ave [2nd St]
  718-965-9600
  Darts and billiards tone down the classic wood bar. Good music.
- **Lucky 13 Saloon** • 273 13th St [5th Ave]
  718-499-7553
  Park Slope's only punk/metal dive bar.
- **Pacific Standard** • 82 4th Ave [St Marks Pl]
  718-858-1951
  Drinking and board games most certainly mix.
- **Park Slope Ale House** • 356 6th Ave [5th St]
  718-788-1756
  Good pub grub and beer selection.
- **The Sackett** • 661 Sackett St [4th Ave]
  718-622-0437
  Hidden on a side street. Cozy spot for a cocktail.
- **Soda Bar** • 629 Vanderbilt Ave [Prospect Pl]
  718-230-8393
  Nice summer drinkin' spot. NFT pick.
- **Tooker Alley** •
  793 Washington Ave [Lincoln Pl]
  347-955-4743
  Good cocktail spot.
- **Union Hall** • 702 Union St [5th Ave]
  718-638-4400
  Quirky spot for indie shows and stuffed birds.
- **The Vanderbilt** •
  570 Vanderbilt Ave [Bergen St]
  718-623-0570
  Specialty cocktails with free open-kitchen entertainment.
- **Washington Commons** •
  748 Washington Ave [Park Pl]
  718-230-3666
  Rotating beer selection, late happy hour, and a great outdoor space.
- **The Way Station** •
  683 Washington Ave [Prospect Pl]
  347-627-4949
  Steampunk bar w/ Dr. Who TARDIS, and screenings. Lovin' babe.
- **Weather Up** • 589 Vanderbilt Ave [Dean St]
  Pricey cocktails are justified by very cool ambience.
- **Woodwork** • 583 Vanderbilt Ave [Dean St]
  718-857-5777
  Brooklyn's World Cup headquarters.

Map 9

Park Slope/Prospect Heights/Windsor Terrace

6 7 8 9 10 11 13 12

🍴 Restaurants

- **12th Street Bar and Grill** •
1123 8th Ave [11th St]
718-965-9526 • $$$
Great New American, burgers, beers, brunch…
we can't say enough.
- **7th Avenue Donuts** • 324 7th Ave [9th St]
718-768-3410 • $
Dirt-cheap dinery goodness.
- **al di la Trattoria** • 248 5th Ave [Carroll St]
718-783-4565 • $$$
Chandelier & brick-walled Italian. Super.
- **Alchemy** • 56 5th Ave [Bergen St]
718-636-4385 • $$$
Slick pub near Barclays Center. Check
it out.
- **Amorina** • 624 Vanderbilt Ave [Prospect Pl]
718-230-3030 • $$$
Watch your perfect pizza get made with sea
salt and love.
- **Applewood** • 501 11th St [7th Ave]
718-788-1810 • $$$
Elegant, cheerful slow food.
- **Bark** • 474 Bergen St [Flatbush]
718-789-1939 •
Dogs, fries, rings, and hash browns on
weekends.
- **Beet Thai II** • 344 7th Ave [10th St]
718-832-2338 • $$$
Romantic ambiance for sumptuous Thai.
- **Blue Ribbon Brooklyn** • 280 5th Ave [1st St]
718-840-0404 • $$$$
Brooklyn outpost of brilliant late-night
Manhattan eatery.
- **Bogota Latin Bistro** •
141 5th Ave [St Johns Pl]
718-230-3805 • $$$
Stylish South- and Central-American
restaurant.
- **Bonnie's Grill** • 278 5th Ave [1st St]
718-369-9527 • $$
Habit-forming contemporary diner.

- **Café Steinhof** • 422 7th Ave [14th St]
718-369-7776 • $$
Austrian comfort food at this South Slope
mainstay.
- **Cheryl's Global Soul** •
236 Underhill Ave [Lincoln Pl]
347-529-2855 • $$
Modern, international menu emphasizing
comfort.
- **The Chocolate Room** • 82 5th Ave [Warren St]
718-783-2900 •
Chocolate-infused desserts in an inviting
location.
- **Coco Roco** • 392 5th Ave [6th St]
718-965-3376 • $$
Inexpensive Peruvian.
- **Convivium Osteria** • 68 5th Ave [St Marks Pl]
718-857-1833 • $$$$
Delicious Italian with a Portuguese influence.
Rustic, warm setting.
- **Cousin John's Café and Bakery** •
70 7th Ave [Lincoln Pl]
718-622-7333 • $
Casual breakfast and lunch.
- **Elora's** • 272 Prospect Park West [17th St]
718-788-6190 • $$
Spanish, Mexican, and margaritas, oh my!
- **Flatbush Farm** • 76 St Marks Ave [6th Ave]
718-622-3276 • $$
Local, seasonal, and delish.
- **Four & Twenty Blackbirds** •
439 3rd Ave [8th St]
718-499 2917 • $$
Seasonal pies (and other treats) baked fresh
daily. Delicious goodness!
- **Franny's** • 348 Flatbush Ave [Sterling Pl]
718-230-0221 • $$
Brilliant pizza, drop-dead fresh, NFT fave.
- **Geido** • 331 Flatbush Ave [7th Ave]
718-638-8866 • $
Get stuffed to the gills.

Park Slope/Prospect Heights/Windsor Terrace

Map 9

Where to begin? There's the Italian at **Al Di La**, slow-food at **Applewood**, Portuguese/Italian at **Convivium Osteria**, and killer pizza at **Franny's**. Branch out with Colombian at **Bogota**, Ethiopian at **Ghenet**, and Australian at **Sheep Station**. Also don't miss the warm and eclectic **Stone Park Cafe**, classic diners **Tom's** and **The Usual**, creative seasonal at **Rose Water**, and of course **Blue Ribbon**. For burgers it's **Bonnie's Grill**.

- **Gen Restaurant** •
  659 Washington Ave [St Marks Ave]
  718-398-3550 • $$$
  Delicious, fresh Japanese cuisine and laid-back service.
- **Ghenet Brooklyn** • 348 Douglass St [4th Ave]
  718-230-4475 • $$$
  Top NYC Ethiopian, hands-down.
- **Hanco's** • 350 7th Ave [10th St]
  718-499-8081 • $
  Bánh mì and bubble tea hotspot.
- **The Islands** • 803 Washington Ave [Lincoln Pl]
  718-398-3575 • $$
  Tasty Caribbean; get the jerk chicken.
- **James** • 605 Carlton Ave [St. Marks Ave]
  718-942-4255 • $$$
  Steamed Zucchini Blossoms and Peekytoe Crab, served under chandeliers.
- **Java Indonesian Rijsttafel** •
  455 7th Ave [16th St]
  718-832-4255
  Mom-and-pop Indonesian, natch!
- **Johnny Mack's** • 1114 8th Ave [11th St]
  718-832-7961 • $$
  Neighborhood bar and grill with sidewalk seating.
- **Jpan Sushi** • 287 5th Ave [1st St]
  718-788-2880 • $$$
  Excellent, inventive special rolls; weird space.
- **Kinara** • 473 5th Ave [11th St]
  718-499-3777 • $$
  Large selection of vegetarian and non-vegetarian Indian dishes.
- **Littleneck** • 288 3rd Ave [Carroll St]
  718-522-1921 • $$
  Hip oysters and seafood steps from the pastoral Gowanus.
- **Lobo** • 188 5th Ave [Sackett St]
  718-636-8886 • $$
  Guilty pleasure Tex-Mex, not Mexican, plenty of tequila.

- **Mitchell's Soul Food** •
  617 Vanderbilt Ave [St Marks Ave]
  718-789-3212 • $
  Seedy, cheap soul food.
- **Moim** • 206 Garfield Pl [7th Ave]
  718-499-8092 • $$$
  Innovative Korean in a swanky setting.
- **Nana** • 155 5th Ave [Lincoln Pl]
  718-230-3749 • $$
  Absolutely delicious pan-Asian.
- **Palo Santo** • 652 Union St [4th Ave]
  718-636-6311 • $$$
  South American elegance for date night.
- **Pino's La Forchetta** • 181 7th Ave [2nd St]
  718-965-4020 • $
  Pizza heavyweight on the Slope.
- **Rachel's Taqueria** • 408 5th Ave [7th St]
  718-788-1137 • $
  Serviceable California-style Mexican.
- **Rhythm & Booze** •
  1674 10th Ave [Prospect Ave]
  718-788-9699 • $$
  A survivor of the pre-boom 'Slope. Eat a burger.
- **Rose Water** • 787 Union St [6th Ave]
  718-783-3800 • $$$
  Intimate, airy Mediterranean.
- **Santa Fe Grill** • 62 7th Ave [Lincoln Pl]
  718-636-0279 • $$
  Dinner? Chips, salsa, and icy pinas!
- **Scalino** • 347 7th Ave [10th St]
  718-840-5738 • $$
  Fresh Italian food mama would approve of.
- **Scottadito Osteria Toscana** •
  788 Union St [7th Ave]
  718-636-4800 •
  Rustic Tuscan, with wallet-friendly prix fixe specials.
- **Shake Shack** • 170 Flatbush Ave [5th Ave]
  347-442-7711 • $$
  Danny Meyer's pitch-perfect burgers, across from Barclays Center.

Map 9

Park Slope/Prospect Heights/Windsor Terrace

- **Sheep Station** • 149 4th Ave [Douglass St]
  718-857-4337 • $$
  Australian craft beers and aussie-themed food. Mate.
- **Sidecar** • 560 5th Ave [15th St]
  718-369-0077 • $$
  Yummy comfort dining with equally comforting cocktails.
- **Smiling Pizzeria** • 323 7th Ave [9th St]
  718-788-2137 • $
  Good quick happy slices.
- **Song** • 295 5th Ave [2nd St]
  718-965-1108 • $
  Essential, tasty Thai in a pinch.
- **Sotto Voce** • 225 7th Ave [4th St]
  718-369-9322 • $$$
  Italian cuisine with better brunch options.
- **Stone Park Cafe** • 324 5th Ave [3rd St]
  718-369-0082 • $$$
  Definitely a contender for best Park Slope dining.
- **Tacos Y Burrito Grill** •
  252 Prospect Park West [Prospect Ave]
  718-768-0909 • $
  New York-style Mexican.
- **Talde** • 369 7th Ave [11th St]
  347-916-0031 • $$$$
  Fusion to die for. Worth a trip.
- **Taro Sushi** • 244 Flatbush Ave [St Marks Ave]
  718-398-5420 • $$
  Top sushi, cozy seating. Lunch specials available Monday through Saturday.
- **Tom's** • 782 Washington Ave [Sterling Pl]
  718-636-9738 • $$
  Old-school mom-and-pop diner since 1936. A cholesterol love affair.
- **Tomato N Basil** • 226 4th Ave [Union St]
  718-596-8855 • $
  Good 4th Avenue option; close to subway.
- **Tutta Pasta** • 160 7th Ave [Garfield Pl]
  718-788-9500 • $$
  Sidewalk seating, dependable penne.
- **The Usual** • 637 Vanderbilt Ave [Prospect Pl]
  718-636-0856 • $
  Diner, plain and simple, oldest restaurant on Vanderbilt below Atlantic.
- **The V-Spot** • 156 5th Ave [Degraw St]
  718-928-8778 • $
  Loads of "meat" options, good for the veggie initiate.
- **Windsor Café** •
  220 Prospect Park West [16th St]
  718-788-9700 • $$
  American diner with something for everyone.

🛍 Shopping

- **A Cheng** • 152 5th Ave [St Johns Pl]
  718-783-2826
  Modern classic women's clothing.
- **Beacon's Closet** • 92 5th Ave [Warren St]
  718-230-1630
  Rad resale with lots of gems.
- **Bergen Street Comics** •
  470 Bergen St [Flatbush Ave]
  718-230-5600
  Excellent small shop w/ events, signings, etc.
- **Bierkraft** • 191 5th Ave [Union St]
  718-230-7600
  Cheese, chocolate, and nearly 1000 varieties of beer.
- **Big Nose Full Body** • 382 7th Ave [11th St]
  718-369-4030
  Interesting, diverse rotating stock of wine.
- **Bitter & Esters** •
  700 Washington Ave [St Mark's Ave]
  917-596-7261
  Homebrew kits and supplies in Prospect Heights.
- **Bklyn Larder** • 228 Flatbush Ave [Bergen St]
  718-783-1250
  Take home a taste of Franny's every night.
- **Blue Apron Foods** • 814 Union St [7th Ave]
  718-230-3180
  Euro-style cheese, charcuterie, and imported goodies.
- **Blue Marble Ice Cream** •
  186 Underhill Ave [St Johns Pl]
  718-399-6926
  Delicious even in February.
- **Blue Sky Bakery** • 53 5th Ave [St Marks Ave]
  718-783-4123
  Moist muffins full of fresh fruit.
- **Boing Boing** • 204 6th Ave [Union St]
  718-398-0251
  Mother-child boutique plus classes, mommy groups and nursing supplies.
- **Brooklyn Homebrew** • 163 8th St [3rd Ave]
  718-832-2739
  One-stop shop for beer lovers' homebrew essentials.
- **Brooklyn Industries** • 206 5th Ave [Union St]
  718-789-2764
  Brooklyn-centric t-shirts, sweatshirts, coats, bags.
- **Brooklyn Museum** •
  200 Eastern Pkwy [Washington Ave]
  718-638-5000
  Usual art-related offerings plus fun Brooklyn-made items.

or food (and beer), try **Bierkraft**, **Bklyn Larder**, **Blue Apron**, **Blue Marble**, **Russo's**, and **United Meat**. Check out gift/jewelry stores like **The Clay Pot** and **Razor**. **Beacon's Closet** is still a clothing destination, **Dixon's** is a classic bike shop, and get your capes and lasers at **Brooklyn Superhero Supply**. If you dare enter the machine, value awaits at the fishbowl that is the **Park Slope Food Co-op**.

- **Brooklyn Superhero Supply Co.** •
  372 5th Ave [5th St]
  718-499-9884
  Capes, treasure maps, and bottled special powers. Also, McSweeney's publications.
- **The Clay Pot** • 162 7th Ave [Garfield Pl]
  718-788-6564
  Hand-crafted gifts, jewelry.
- **Community Book Store** •
  143 7th Ave [Garfield Pl]
  718-783-3075
  General books.
- **Dixon's Bicycle Shop** • 792 Union St [7th Ave]
  718-636-0067
  Classic, friendly, family-owned bike shop.
- **DUB Pies** • 211 Prospect Park W [16th St]
  718-788 2448
  Aussie/Kiwi-style meat pies.
- **Fermented Grapes Wines & Spirits** •
  651 Vanderbilt Ave [Prospect Pl]
  718-230-3216
  Diverse, affordable selection of wines & spirits in Prospect Heights.
- **Fifth Avenue Record & Tape Center** •
  439 5th Ave [9th St]
  718-499-8483
  Unassuming locale for surprising finds.
- **Flirt** • 93 5th Ave [Park Pl]
  718-783-0364
  Indie fashion, local designers, and custom bridal.
- **Gureje** • 886 Pacific St [Underhill Ave]
  718-857-2522
  West African flavored clothing, with a music club in the back!
- **Hiho Batik** • 184 5th Ave [Sackett St]
  718-622-4446
  Batik clothing and do-it-yourself classes.
- **Hooti Couture** •
  321 Flatbush Ave [Prospect Pl]
  718-857-1977
  Girlie Vintage.
- **Housing Works Thrift Shop** •
  244 5th Ave [Carroll St]
  718-636-2271
  Used books, shabby-chic home decor, and vintage designer wear.
- **JackRabbit Sports** • 151 7th Ave [Garfield Pl]
  718-636-9000
  Mecca for runners, swimmers, and cyclists.
- **Loom** • 115 7th Ave [President St]
  718-789-0061
  Irresistible gifts and housewares.

- **Midtown Florist & Greenhouse** •
  565 Atlantic Ave [Hanson Pl]
  718-237-1500
  Fully stocked with plants and gardening supplies.
- **The Pie Shop** • 211 Prospect Park W [16th St]
  718-788-2448
  Handmade meat pies from Down Under.
- **Pink Olive Boutique** • 167 5th Ave
  718-398-2016
  Whimsical gifts for kids.
- **Prospect Wine Shop** • 322 7th Ave [8th St]
  718-768-1232
  Well-edited and gets the job done.
- **Razor** • 329 5th Ave [4th St]
  718-832-0717
  Designer gear can make anyone look sharp.
- **Red, White and Bubbly** •
  211 5th Ave [Union St]
  718-636-9463
  Helpful staff with no attitude.
- **Ride Brooklyn** • 468 Bergen St [5th Ave]
  347-599-1340
  Friendly and helpful bike store.
- **Russo's Fresh Mozzarella & Pasta** •
  363 7th Ave [11th St]
  718-369-2874
  Homemade pasta and sauce. Yum.
- **Slope Cellars** • 436 7th Ave [15th St]
  718-369-7307
  Helpful staff and wine club loyalty card.
- **Sterling Grapes & Grains** •
  115 5th Ave [Sterling Pl]
  718-789-9521
  Known around the 'hood for good prices.
- **Stitch Therapy** • 138 Willoughby St [Gold St]
  718-398-2020
  Luxurious yarns. Plus knitting classes.
- **Terrace Books** •
  242 Prospect Park W [Prospect Ave]
  718-788-3475
  Used & new.
- **Trailer Park** • 77 Sterling Pl [6th Ave]
  718-623-2170
  Unique and handcrafted furnishings.
- **United Meat Market** •
  219 Prospect Park West [16th St]
  718-768-7227
  Butchered sheep flesh never tasted so good.
- **Unnameable Books** •
  600 Vanderbilt Ave [St Marks Ave]
  718-789-1534
  General new and used.

Crown Heights and Prospect-Lefferts Gardens are officially hot neighborhoods, though apartments in these limestones are still much more affordable to the average family than the ones in the brownstones on the other side of the park. And make no mistake, these are family neighborhoods, so recent changes mean more cute cafes and upmarket shops rather than an influx of cool bars. There are no cool bars.

Today's tote bags-and-Bugaboos crowd represents a return to form: the area was first developed as a bourgeois bedroom community around the turn of the twentieth century. There's plenty of great residential architecture to check out, especially around Lefferts Manor. Eastern Parkway is a tree-lined multi-lane esplanade that people both commute and relax around. Think of it as the Champs-Élysées of Brooklyn…minus the monuments and designer boutiques.

The Crown Heights Riot, three days of violence in 1991 that began after a Hasidic driver lost control of his car and killed a Guyanese child and severely injured another and led to several more injuries and two more deaths, is now a distant memory. Today there isn't much tension between the Hasidim and the Afro-Caribbean immigrants who are still the two most visible ethnic groups here, but that said, there's not too much mixing either. Outsiders are welcome to join the party at the West Indian Day Parade each September and won't feel out of place at Caribbean-owned businesses. Expect to feel more like a fish out of water visiting Judaica shops, kosher markets, or checking out Lubavitch Hasidic headquarters at 770 Eastern Parkway.

The one place where everybody comes together, along with loads of other New Yorkers and even a few intrepid tourists, is Prospect Park. While the Park Slope side has the bandshell and some fine playgrounds, here you've got the **Prospect Park Zoo**, the **Carousel**, the **Brooklyn Museum**, and the **Brooklyn Children's Museum**. But the crown jewel of Crown Heights is without a doubt the **Brooklyn Botanic Garden**, a sublime destination filled with zen calm that makes you forget the city you left behind only minutes before. Its annual Japanese cherry blossom festival, Sakura Matsuri, is a must-see in the spring.

Neighborhood haunts abound here, usually with a West Indian flavor. **Franklin Park** has a hipster/beer garden vibe.

Sit-down places like **Chavela's** are few and far between, but the takeout is amazing. Caribbean food is the name of the game. Get some roti or jerk chicken at hotspots like **Culpepper's** and **Gloria's**. On Lincoln Road, the choice is obvious: **Lincoln Park Tavern**.

Map 10

○ Landmarks

- **Brooklyn Botanic Garden** •
  990 Washington Ave [Crown St]
  718-623-7200
  A beautiful and peaceful spot inside and out.
  Cherry blossoms in spring are awe-inspiring.
- **Brooklyn Children's Museum** •
  145 Brooklyn Ave [St Marks Ave]
  718-735-4400
  Take your own kids or someone else's so you
  can get in on the fun without looking silly.
- **Prospect Park Carousel** •
  Flatbush Ave & Ocean Ave & Empire Blvd
  718-965-8951
  Carved in 1912 and restored in 1990.
- **Prospect Park Zoo** •
  450 Flatbush Ave [Empire Blvd]
  718-399-7339
  Home to approximately 400 animals.

💻 Coffee

- **Breukelen Coffee House** •
  764 Franklin Ave [St Johns Pl]
  718-789-7070
  Franklin St. godsend. Stumptown coffee,
  Balthazar treats. Sweet.
- **The Pulp & The Bean** •
  809 Franklin Ave [Lincoln Pl]
  347-425-8642
  Coffee, tables, wi-fi.

🍸 Nightlife

- **Berg'n** • 899 Bergen St [Franklin Ave]
  718-857-2337
  Massive beer hall with space for food vendors.
- **Butter & Scotch** • 818 Franklin Ave [Union St]
  347-350-8899
  Just your basic bar-bakery; stress eating to
  binge drinking.
- **Franklin Park** • 618 St Johns Pl [Franklin Ave]
  718-975-0196
  Slick beer garden with nice patio.
- **The Inkwell Cafe** • 408 Rogers Ave [Sterling]
  718-675-6145
  Drinks, jazz, comedy and karaoke…time to
  chill!
- **Wingate Field** • Brooklyn Ave & Winthrop St
  718-469-1912
  Live music every now and then.

🍴 Restaurants

- **Barboncino Pizza & Bar** •
  781 Franklin Ave [St Johns Pl]
  718-483-8834 • $$
  Real brick-oven pizza serving the new hipsters
  on Franklin.
- **Basil Pizza & Wine Bar** •
  270 Kingston Ave [Lincoln Pl]
  718-285-8777 • $$$
  Kosher Italian bistro.
- **Bombay Masala** •
  678 Franklin Ave [Prospect Pl]
  718-230-7640 • $$
  Surprisingly good Indian.
- **Brooklyn Exposure** •
  1401 Bedford Ave [St Marks Ave]
  718-783-8220 • $$$
  The classiest date place in the neighborhood.
- **Chavela's** • 736 Franklin Ave [Sterling Pl]
  718-622-3100 • $$
  Insanely popular Mexican now on Franklin.
- **Culpeppers** • 1082 Nostrand Ave [Lincoln Rd]
  718-940-4122 • $
  Deliciousness from Barbados. Get the fish over
  cou cou and a side of coconut bread.
- **The Food Sermon** •
  355 Rogers Ave [Sullivan Pl]
  718-484-7555 • $$
  Culinary school-credentialed Caribbean.
- **Gloria's West Indian Food** •
  987 Nostrand Ave [Empire Blvd]
  718-778-4852 • $
  All the locals know Gloria's roti.
- **Golden Krust** •
  1014 Nostrand Ave [Empire Blvd]
  718-604-2211 • $
  West Indian chain with a bent toward home
  cooking.
- **Golden Krust** • 568 Flatbush Ave [Maple St]
  718-282-1437 • $
  West Indian chain with a bent toward home
  cooking.
- **King of Tandoor** • 600 Flatbush Ave [Rutland]
  347-533-6811 • $$
  The king of Lefferts Indian food, definitely.

There isn't exactly a shopping mecca here, though you can find fresh fruit and West Indian sundries everywhere. Off the beaten path are Jewish stores like **Judaica World**. Get a whiff of the nearby Botanic Garden at **Barbara's**. For baked goods, hit **Allan's** or **Lily & Fig**. Wake up at **Breukelen Coffee House.**

- **Mayfield** • 688 Franklin Ave [Prospect Pl]
  347-318-3643 • $$$
  Seasonal New American from local-based industry veterans.
- **Mountain** • 903 Franklin Ave [Carroll St]
  718-771-2476 • $$
  Centered cuisine to go along with yoga classes and herbal treatments.
- **Paradise Foods** • 843 Franklin Ave [Union St]
  718-953-2270 • $$
  Tasty, inexpensive West Indian.
- **Peppa's Jerk Chicken** • 738 Flatbush Ave [Woodruff Ave]
  347-406-2515 • $
  Scrumptious and spicy.
- **Ramagi** • 594 Rogers Ave [Winthrop St]
  347-533-9490 • $$
  So much better than Papa John's.
- **Sushi Tatsu II** • 609 Franklin Ave [Dean St]
  718-398-8828 • $$
  Japanese. They deliver.
- **Sushi Tatsu III** •
  644 Flatbush Ave [Fenimore St]
  718-282-8890 • $$
  Third location is a charm.
- **Taqueria El Patron** •
  51 Lincoln Rd [Flatbush Ave] • $$
  Good salsa.
- **Trinidad Ali Roti Shop** •
  589 Flatbush Ave [Midwood St]
  718-462-1730 • $$
  Caribbean with style.

🛍 Shopping

- **65 Fen** • 65 Fenimore St [Flatbush Ave]
  347-715-6001
  Great new Lefferts wine shop; very affordable.
- **Allan's Quality Bakery** •
  1109 Nostrand Ave [Maple St]
  718-774-7892
  Lines into the night.
- **Barbara's Flowers** •
  615 Nostrand Ave [Bergen St]
  718-773-6644
  Smells as good as the Botanic Garden.

- **Brooklyn Beer & Soda** •
  507 Flatbush Ave [Lefferts Ave]
  718-622-8800
  The Epcot Center of beers.
- **Brooklyn Botanic Garden** •
  990 Washington Ave [Crown St]
  718-623-7200
  Plant-related gifts and books.
- **Elsie's Doughnuts** •
  1031 Bergen St [Rogers Ave]
  718-928-7005
  Artisanal doughnuts, aspiring to mind-blowing.
- **Ethiopian Taste** •
  985 Nostrand Ave [Empire Blvd]
  718-744-0804
  Donna buys African CDs here. So should you.
- **Judaica World** •
  329 Kingston Ave [Eastern Pkwy]
  718-604-1020
  Party time. Excellent.
- **Lily & Fig** • 727 Franklin Ave [Sterling Pl]
  718-636-0456
  It's cake time boys and girls.
- **Owl and Thistle General Store** •
  833 Franklin Ave [Union St]
  347-722-5836
  Fun local and sustainably produced gifts.
- **Pels Pie Co.** • 446 Rogers Ave [Lincoln Rd]
  Do you want wine or coffee with your pie?
- **Phat Albert's** • 495 Flatbush Ave [Lefferts Ave]
  718-469-2116
  Cheap is good.
- **Raskin's** • 320 Kingston Ave [President St]
  718-756-9521
  Worth the plunge, but hold your nose.
- **Scoops** • 624 Flatbush Ave [Fenimore St]
  718-282-5904
  Tasty ice cream.
- **Tip Of The Tongue NYC** •
  43 Lincoln Rd [Flatbush Ave]
  718-693-2253
  Off-premise catering.

Map 11 · **Sunset Park / Greenwood Heights** Ⓝ

Prospect Ave

17th St Prospect Ave →
18th St
Ⓡ

◀8

19th St
20th St
Prospect Expy

21st St
22nd St
23rd St
24th St

9

19th St

20th St

GREENWOOD
HEIGHTS

25 St
Ⓓ Ⓝ Ⓡ

26th St
27th St
28th St
29th St

PAGE
98

30th St
Ⓩ

31st St
32nd St 200
33rd St

Gowanus Expy

32nd St

Woodrow Ct

Roosevelt Ct

Green-Wood
Cemetery
Ⓞ

34th St
Ⓓ Ⓝ Ⓡ

36 St
Ⓞ

35th St

37th St →
36th St

Marginal St E

250

37th St

250
850

38th St
BMT Yard

39th St

39th St

40th St
41st St 250
42nd St
43rd St 250
44th St

440

640

Ninth Ave
Ⓓ

750
640

830
940

45th St
Ⓡ

540

44th St

Sunset
Park

740
750

12▶

Fort
Hamilton
Pkwy
Ⓓ

First Ave

46th St 440
47th St
48th St

Second Ave

SUNSET
PARK

750
640

760
830

Third Ave

Fourth Ave

49th St
50th St 250
51st St

Fifth Ave

440

540

Sixth Ave

Seventh Ave

750

830

Ninth Ave

Bush
Terminal
Warehouses

52nd St
53rd St
Ⓡ 250

53 St

540
540

640

750

53rd St

Whale Sq 74

54th St
55th St 250

✚

540

750
750

✉

830

56th St 250
57th St

540

850

Eighth Ave

58th St

540

750

59th St

640

60th St 440
61st St 250

278

59 St
Ⓝ Ⓡ

550
550

✉

640

62nd St 440
63rd St
64th St

62nd St
63rd St
64th St

550

Eighth Ave
Ⓝ

850

N Fort Hamilton
Pkwy

Tenth Ave

Fort Hamilton Pkwy

LIRR
Yard

14

1/4 mile   .25 km

65th St

66th St

Shore Road Dr

Map

Originator of the city's recent bánh mì craze, the final resting place of Basquiat, and home to one heck of a cool bowling alley, Sunset Park is a neighborhood with subtle charms hidden amidst bus depots, warehouses, and semis noisily barreling down 3rd and 4th Avenues.

The eponymous park offers breathtaking views from its central hill and an Olympic-sized public **pool** that seems to attract most of the borough during the summer months. You don't have to be into steampunk to appreciate **Green-Wood Cemetery**. Home to the highest point in Brooklyn, it offers a chance to look out over the harbor as you pass the graves of notable New Yorkers like Boss Tweed, Leonard Bernstein, and the aforementioned downtown artist. A day trip here should make your list of things to do in New York: some of the crypts are works of art in themselves, and on occasion the staff will open them for tours.

Originally settled by Irish and Dutch immigrants, Sunset Park has recently become one of the most diverse neighborhoods in New York, with Dominican, Puerto Rican, Mexican, Chinese, Malaysian, Korean, and Vietnamese communities living alongside Manhattan transplants drawn by cheaper rents. On one side of the park there's 5th Avenue, known as "Little Latin America," lined with mostly Mexican restaurants, bodegas and bakeries. In warmer months, old men play backgammon in front of their favorite delis and kids buy snow cones from street vendors who simply take a razor to a huge block of ice. South and slightly east of the park, there's 8th Avenue, "Brooklyn's Chinatown," with Buddhist temples, Asian markets, excellent Vietnamese restaurants, and dim sum spots galore. Chinese New Year is celebrated with verve here, replete with parades, confetti, and many, many dragons.

Though you'll find the respective main drags of "Brooklyn's Chinatown" and "Little Latin America" across the neighborhood from one another, everything in between is truly a melting pot. North of all this multicultural goodness is a very narrow strip of real estate sandwiched in between the river and the cemetery named Greenwood Heights, and north of *that* is a small area that's now being called "South Slope." There you'll find some nice Park Slope-ish bars, restaurants, and shops opening up, especially on 5th and 6th Avenues between the Prospect Expressway and the cemetery. But so far the only hangout around here that's well known outside the neighborhood is the delightfully old-school bowling alley **Melody Lanes**.

Melody Lanes deserves to be landmarked. **Irish Haven**, a basic pub where scenes from Scorsese's *The Departed* were filmed, has become almost as popular. In the South Slope, hit either **Korzo**, **Toby's**, or **Quarter**.

Food is Sunset Park's specialty. Bánh mì doesn't get much better than **Ba Xuyen**. Don't be discouraged by lines at dim sum spots like **Pacificana** because they're worth the wait. For sloppy late-night hangover prevention, you can't beat **Tacos Matamoros**.

Map 11

Sunset Park / Greenwood Heights

○ Landmarks

- **Green-Wood Cemetery** •
  500 25th St [5th Ave]
  718-768-7300
  Lots of winding paths and greenery good for
  contemplation.

Coffee

- **Southside Coffee** • 652 6th Ave [19th St]
  347-599-0887

Farmers Markets

- **Sunset Park Greenmarket** • 4th Ave & 59th St
  Saturday, 8 a.m.–3 p.m., July–Nov.

Nightlife

- **Brooklyn's Tiki Bar** • 885 4th Ave [33rd St]
  718-768-2797
  Ample space in this trashy tiki.
- **Irish Haven** • 5721 4th Ave [58th St]
  718-439-9893
  Good Irish dive.
- **Korzo** • 667 5th Ave [20th St]
  718-499-1199
  Bar, lounge, food, Eastern European vibe.
- **Quarter** • 676 5th Ave [20th St]
  718-788-0989
  South Slope/Greenwood bar features D.U.B.
  pies and indeterminate hours.
- **Toby's Public House** • 686 6th Ave [21st St]
  718-788-1186
  Open 'til 4 a.m. weekends. We love New York.

Restaurants

- **8th Avenue Seafood** • 4418 8th Ave [45th St]
  718-633-6366 • $$
  No brunch line!
- **Ba Xuyen** • 4222 8th Ave [42nd St]
  718-633-6601 • $
  Best bánh mì in Brooklyn.
- **Castillo Ecuatoriano** • 4020 5th Ave [40th St]
  718-437-7676 • $
  Wide range of Ecuadoran platters.
- **China #1** • 4503 8th Ave [45th St]
  718-972-8233 • $
- **El Tesoro Ecuatoriano Restaurant** •
  4015 5th Ave [40th St]
  718-972-3756 • $$
  Ecuadoran grub, great seafood.
- **George's Restaurant** • 5701 5th Ave [57th St]
  718-439-1403 • $$
  The typical florescent lights, free bread and
  big plastic menus.
- **Golden Imperial Palace** •
  618 62nd St [6th Ave]
  718-833-3777 • $$
  Massive dim sum parlor. Mandarin skills a plus.
- **International Restaurant** •
  4408 5th Ave [44th St]
  718-438-2009 • $$
  Awesome Dominican-style breakfast.
- **Johnny's Pizzeria** • 5806 5th Ave [58th St]
  718-492-9735 • $
  Classic pizza joint.
- **Kai Feng Fu** • 4801 8th Ave [48th St]
  718-437-3542 • $
  Dumplings come highly recommended.
- **Korzo** • 667 5th Ave [20th St]
  718-499-1199 • $$
  Eastern European pub grub.
- **La Gran Via Bakery** • 4516 5th Ave [46th St]
  718-954-2226 • $
  24 hour diabetes special.
- **Lanzhou Hand Pulled Noodles** •
  5924 8th Ave [59th St]
  718-492-7568 • $
  Watch the theatrical master noodle puller
  work his magic.

Sunset Park / Greenwood Heights

Map 11

Local shopping options are generally more practical (**Costco**, **Reef Aquarium**, **Sunset Beer Distributors**) than fun. The 8th Avenue branch of **Ten Ren Tea** is a great spot to buy loose tea, tea bags and bubble tea to go.

- **Lucky Eight Restaurant** •
  5204 8th Ave [52nd St]
  718-851-8862 • $$
  Michelin-starred Chinese in Sunset Park.
  Believe it.
- **Mai Thai Thai Kitchen** • 4618 8th Ave [46th St]
  718-438-3413 • $$
  Spicy-hot pad thai with cool outdoor seating.
- **Mas Que Pan** • 5401 5th Ave [54th St]
  718-492-0479 • $
  Latino bakery with killer Cuban sandwiches.
- **Nyonya** • 5323 8th Ave [53rd St]
  718-633-0808 • $$
  Hokey interior; excellent Malaysian.
- **Pacificana** • 813 55th St [8th Ave]
  718-871-2880 • $$
  Filling that dim sum-sized hole in your heart.
  Yum.
- **Piaxtla Es Mexico Deli** • 505 51st St [5th Ave]
  718-633-4816 • $
  Cheap and delicious tacos and tortas.
- **Quarter** • 676 5th Ave [20th St]
  718-788-0989 • $$
  Cheese plates and savory pies.
- **Sunset Park Empanada Cart** •
  5th Ave & 48th St • $
  Munch and stroll.
- **Sunstone Tortillas Express Restaurant** •
  5411 5th Ave [55th St]
  718-439-8434 • $
  The best and the cheapest of the Chinese-
  operated Mexican.
- **Super Pollo Latino** • 4102 5th Ave [41st St]
  718-871-5700 • $$
  Peruvian food famous for their chicken.
- **Tacos Matamoros** • 4508 5th Ave [45th St]
  718-871-7627 • $
  You can't get more Mexican than this!
- **Toby's Public House** • 686 6th Ave [21st St]
  718-788-1186 •
  4 words: Nutella and Ricotta Calzone. Trust us.
- **Wong Wong Noodle Shop** •
  5410 8th Ave [54th St]
  718-633-5633 • $
  For noodle aficionados.
- **Yun Nan Flavour Garden** •
  5121 8th Ave [52nd St]
  718-633-3090 • $
  The name says it: flavorful Chinese snacks.
  Cheap.

🛍 Shopping

- **Costco** • 976 3rd Ave [37th St]
  718-965-7603
  Where to shop if you have 4 kids and/or
  copious storage.
- **Don Paco Lopez Panaderia** •
  4703 4th Ave [47th St]
  718-492-7443
  Mexico City-style bakery with amazing
  champurrado.
- **Frankel's Discount Clothing** •
  3924 3rd Ave [40th St]
  718-768-9788
  Less about fashion, more about character.
- **Full Doe Bakery** • 5905 4th Ave [59th St]
  718-439-8880
  Inexpensive Chinese goodies.
- **The Movable Feast** •
  284 Prospect Park W [18th St]
  718-965-2900
  Catering to your every need.
- **New York Mart** • 6023 8th Ave [60th St]
  718-438-2288
  Massive Asian grocery.
- **Petland Discounts** • 5015 5th Ave [50th St]
  718-871-7699
  Crap for your stupid pet.
- **Reef Aquarium** • 5415 8th Ave [55th St]
  718-633-7850
  Large selection of fish in Brooklyn Chinatown.
- **Sunset Beer Distributors** •
  316 37th St [3rd Ave]
  718-788-8000
  For all your beer needs—kegs included.
- **Ten Ren Tea** • 5817 8th Ave [58th St]
  718-853-0660
  Lovely selection of teas.

Map 12 · **Borough Park**

Prospect Ave
17th St
Tenth Ave
11th Ave
Prospect Ave
18th St
Reeve Pl
Sherman St
Park
Grade
Flatbush Ave
Parade
Grounds
Prospect-Expwy
Buckingham Rd
Parkside Ave
Ocean Ave
E 19th St
20th St
Terrace Pl
Seeley St
Vanderbilt St
Prospect-Expwy
Park
Circle
Marlborough Rd
Rugby Rd
Argyle Rd
Westminster Rd
Stratford Rd
Beverley Rd
Q
27
Caton Pl
E 5th St
Kermit Pl
Caton Ave
Turner Pl
Hinckley Pl
Lewis Pl
Matthews Pl
Slocum Pl
Cortelyou Rd
Q
F G
Fort Hamilton Pkwy
McDonald Ave
Caton Ave
Field Pl
Coney Island Ave
Cortelyou Rd
Newkirk
Kensington Stables
Albemarle Rd
Church Ave
Beverley Rd
E 16th St
Chester Ave
E 8th St
A
Green-Wood
Cemetery
PAGE
98
Micieli Pl
Bills Pl
310
E 5th St
Ocean Pkwy
E 4th St
E 3rd St
E 2nd St
Ditmas Ave
Webster Ave
Lawrence Ave
Foster Ave
Chester Ave
Dahlma St
Clara St
Louisa St
Story St
Church Ave
F G
715
Shmura
Matzoh
Factory
35th St
Old New Utrecht Rd
1470
Minna St
Dahill Rd
13
36th St
37th St
1050
38th St
39th St
1240
1440
F
1240
Ninth Ave
40th St
1240
Ditmas Ave
D
1850
41st St
1250
1440
13th St
Fort Hamilton Pkwy
Congregation
Anshe
Lubawitz
(Temple Beth El)
42nd St
43rd St
1440
44th St
1449
1654
11
45th St
18 Ave
F
46th St
1250
1440
1642
1749
McDonald Ave
Fort
Hamilton
Pkwy
D
47th St
1120
48th St
14th Ave
1546
15th Ave
1652
17th Ave
Old New Utrecht Rd
Elmwood Ave
Dahill Rd
49th St
Bobover
Hasidic
World
Headquarters
1540
Avenue I
F
50 St
970
Tenth Ave
D
50th St
1060
51st St
1220
1640
1640
1725
18th Ave
B
950
52nd St
1440
1630
53rd St
1440
940
54th St
1540
Washington
Cemetery
830
1050
55 St
D
55th St
1440
1630
1750
New Utrecht Ave
56th St
12th St
850
940
1050
57th St
1240
1540
57th
850
58th St
1540
1750
58th
940
1050
1440
59th St
1640
16th St
Gravesend
Park
920
60th St
1550
1750
61
61st St
1220
62nd St
N
1640
N
Tabor Ct
New Utrecht Ave
63rd St
18 Ave
20 Ave
N
Fort Hamilton
Pkwy
Tenth Ave
11th Ave
62 St
D
64th St
N
N
15
1750
65th St
Durrea Ct
Ovington Ct
Cameron Ct
Wallaston Ct
66th St
1/4 mile
.25 km
67th St
67th

Williamsburg and Crown Heights have nothing on Borough Park (sometimes written Boro Park), home to the largest Orthodox Jewish enclave of Hasidim. With ever-expanding boundaries, the neighborhood keeps growing, as do the families, with an average of six children per household. It's no wonder some have been calling it the "baby-boom of Brooklyn." These religious residents might garner attention on the subways for their wigs or their peyas, but in Borough Park, it's the non-Orthodox or Hasidic Jew that's the anomaly. You will certainly feel a little out of place here if you fall into that category; best to bring along that English-to-Yiddish dictionary. Yiddish, by the way, is everywhere. Along with Hebrew and Russian, it's widely spoken in the streets and shops, printed on signs, and an option on ATM menu screens.

Borough Park is a haven of family values and religious tradition. Some of the best times to visit are during the more festive holidays—either Sukkot or Purim. But on any given day, it's not unusual to see crowds numbering in the thousands spilling into the streets as a wedding lets out at a nearby synagogue. In contrast, by sundown on Friday for the Sabbath, the shtetl is virtually empty—no people, no lights, and no cars.

To move into this neighborhood, one would have better luck marrying into the community than finding something through a broker, but a few nights in **The Avenue Plaza Hotel** will give you a good dose of Borough Park culture. Catering mostly to Israelis who have come to visit relatives, attend weddings or conferences, it's one of the few luxury hotel options in Brooklyn and testament to Borough Park's importance as a hub of Orthodox and Hasidic practices. One of the neighborhood's more important synagogues is the **Congregation Anshei Lubawitz**, a landmark neoclassical structure.

Except for banks, chains are nearly non-existent, but there are plenty of independently run shops, many catering to the religious needs of the community. Wig shops, kosher delis, and Judaica bookstores abound. Be aware that in keeping with the Sabbath, most shops are closed from sundown on Friday until sundown on Saturday. Bustling 13th Avenue is the main shopping drag, and a good base to start exploring the neighborhood—it's the picture of wholesomeness and old world mercantilism with its shoe cobblers, furniture stores and bakeries. Borough Park boasts some fine discount shopping—and not just on the gefilte fish— designer housewares, china, clothes (albeit, modest ones) and furniture are among the cheapest in the city.

Around Passover, watch the lines crowd around the **Shmura Matzoh Factory**, one of the few bakeries in the United States that makes shmura matzoh, which is matzoh that has been shepherded and blessed by a Rabbi during every stage of the process from grain to unleavened bread.

Beyond the late-night discussions that go around at the falafel shops, there is little to be done here after dark. After all, six kids per household have to happen sometime. Otherwise, try shooting pool at **60th Street Billiards**.

Nowhere, apart from maybe Israel, do you have so many kosher options. Falafel does a competitive business. There are some international offerings, too, including **China Glatt** for sloppy Chinese that's been blessed by a Rabbi.

○ Landmarks

- **Bobover Hasidic World Headquarters** •
  4909 15th Ave [15th Ave]
  718-853-7900
  So you think you can daven?
- **Congregation Anshe Lubawitz** •
  4024 12th Ave [48th St]
  Graceful, neoclassical synagogue is the area's
  first—built in 1906.
- **Kensington Stables** •
  51 Caton Ave [McDonald Ave]
  718-972-4588
  Riding horses is one of life's small pleasures.
  Combine that with subway proximity and
  you're in business.
- **Shmura Matzoh Factory** •
  1285 36th St [13th Ave]
  718-438-2006
  The real deal. Only open in the pre-Passover
  season.

Farmers Markets

- **Boro Park Greenmarket** • 14th Ave & 49th St
  Thursday, 8 a.m.–3 p.m., July–Nov.

Restaurants

- **A&J Pizzeria** •
  4412 Fort Hamilton Pkwy [New Utrecht Ave]
  718-871-5745 • $
  Extra-crunchy, extra-cheesy pie.
- **China Glatt** • 4413 13th Ave [44th St]
  718-438-2576 • $$
  Kosher Chinese. Only in New York. And Israel.
- **Glatt a la Carte** • 5123 18th Ave [51st St]
  718-438-6675 • $$
  Fancy pants kosher steakhouse.
- **Mendel's Pizza** • 4923 18th Ave [49th St]
  718-438-8493 • $
  Kosher pizza plus blintzes, falafel, and such.
- **Orchidea** • 4815 12th Ave [48th St]
  718-686-7500 • $$$
  Kosher meets fine dining.

Eichler's is the spot to get your Borough Park souvenir. Get a challah at **Kaff's Bakery** and a hat at **Kova Quality**. Otherwise, hit **Trainworld** if you're a model train buff or **Bulletproof Comics** if you're, well, a geek.

Map

12

14 15

16

🛍 Shopping

- **A Touch of Spirit Liquors •**
  4720 16th Ave [47th St]
  718-438-2409
  Kosher wine is more than just Manischewitz.
- **Bari Pork Store •** 6319 18th Ave [64th St]
  718-837-9773
  Paradise for pig products.
- **Bulletproof Comics •**
  4507 Fort Hamilton Pkwy [45th St]
  718-854-3367
  Comics. If you're into that sort of thing.
- **Circus Fruits •**
  5916 Fort Hamilton Pkwy [59th St]
  718-436-2100
  Fantastic selection and prices; some exotic stuff.
- **D. Coluccio & Sons •** 1214 60th St [12th Ave]
  718-436-6700
  Imported Italian specialties.
- **Eichler's •** 5004 13th Ave [50th St]
  718-633-1505
  Borough Park Judaica superstore.
- **Ferrara Cycle Shop •** 6304 20th Ave [63rd St]
  718-232-6716
  Sales, service and repairs.
- **Focus Electronics •** 4509 13th Ave [46th St]
  718-436-4646
  Local B&H with appliances that go off and on automatically on Shabbos.
- **Kaff's Bakery •**
  4518 Fort Hamilton Pkwy [45th St]
  718-633-2600
  Kosher bread-a-plenty.

- **Kosher Candy Man •** 4702 13th Ave [47th St]
  718-438-5419
  Yummy holiday and gift arrangements.
- **Kova Quality Hatters •**
  4317 13th Ave [44th St]
  718-871-2944
  Men's clack fedoras with a variety of brims.
- **Mostly Music •** 4815 13th Ave [49th St]
  718-438-2766
  Mostly Jewish music.
- **The Peppermill •** 5015 16th Ave [50th St]
  718-871-4022
  Upscale cookware and bakeware.
- **Scribbles •** 1308 40th St [13th Ave]
  718-435-8711
  Classroom supplies and crafts.
- **Strauss Bakery •** 5115 13th Ave [51st St]
  718-851-7728
  Amazingly fancy cakes.
- **Trainworld •** 751 McDonald Ave [Ditmas Ave]
  718-436-7072
  Wholesale prices on hundreds of model trains. A choo choo paradise.
- **Underworld Plaza •**
  1421 62nd St [New Utrecht Ave]
  718-232-6804
  Underwear city.
- **United Colors of Benetton •**
  4610 13th Ave [46th St]
  718-853-3420
  Orthodox-approved selection of modest clothes.
- **Weiss Bakery •** 5011 13th Ave [50th St]
  718-438-0407
  Wedding cakes to party-size challahs.

Map 73 Kensington/Ditmas Park

Gigantic, turreted Victorian homes, many with surprising and unique architectural details, make Ditmas Park one of the least "New York"-looking neighborhoods in New York. You'll see film crews out here regularly getting the tree-lined, moneyed-suburbia shots they'd otherwise have find in Connecticut. Stroll down some of Ditmas Park's side streets—try Malborough, Argyle or Rugby—for an eyeful of some breathtaking mansions; an overnight stay at one of the many lovely (and affordable) bed and breakfasts will tide you over until you can swing the down payment on one of them.

Cortelyou Road, the main drag, has become something of the new Park Slope—blending cosmopolitan eating and drinking establishments with a family-friendly, residential quality on the side streets. However, the neighborhood remains refreshingly diverse. Walk down Foster Avenue and you'll pass by Hasidim, Caribbean-Americans, young married couples with strollers, middle-aged guys passing the time together outside the liquor store, and perhaps a crazy cat lady giving you the stink eye as she weeds her begonia patch.

Lacking the architectural grandeur and quality dining options of Ditmas Park, adjacent Kensington has little to recommend it to those passing through. Comprised mostly of Polish groceries, Mexican restaurants, and discount stores, it is mainly a residential neighborhood and though it's a little on the boring side, residents find the safety and affordability more than enough to recommend this little slice of Brooklyn tucked just below Prospect Park. The homes here are a bit smaller than in Ditmas Park, but there's still a sense of spaciousness and suburbia here. If the backyards here weren't cause enough to make one wonder if they were still in New York, a parade of horses being groomed in the street on Caton Place nearby **Kensington Stables** certainly will. With easy park access, the barn offers trail rides through the park, lessons and boarding. Kensington's **Erasmus Hall Academy**, built in 1786, is one of the oldest high schools in the U.S.; the building was abandoned several years ago though restoration efforts are underway. The **Flatbush Dutch Reform Church**, however, is alive and well. The current building was built in 1783–98 and houses a magnificent pipe organ. Listen for the chimes on the hour.

Kensington and Ditmas Park were originally settled by the Dutch in the 1600s, remaining mostly farmland until the early twentieth century. In the late 1970s and '80s, Ditmas Park became the fashionable alternative to Long Island for wealthy Manhattan commuters before briefly falling into disrepair and neglect in some areas. Recent interest in both neighborhoods' low rents and space options have brought the attendant gentrification, though it's happening here at a much slower pace than elsewhere in New York.

The scene between Ditmas Park and Kensington couldn't be more stark. Start the evening off at the upscale pick-up bar **Sycamore** and if the evening is taking a more adventurous, late-night turn, wind up at **Shenanigans** where good ol' Brooklyn Guys sing karaoke and down whiskey shots.

Map 13

Kensington / Ditmas Park

O Landmarks

- **Brooklyn Historic Railway Association** •
  599 E 7th St [Ditmas Ave]
  718-941-3160
  Explore the world's oldest subway tunnel.
- **Erasmus Hall Academy** •
  911 Flatbush Ave [Church Ave]
  Boasts famous graduates such as Alexander
  Hamilton, Neil Diamond, and Barbara
  Streisand.
- **Flatbush Dutch Reform Church** •
  890 Flatbush Ave [Church Ave]
  Originally constructed in 1654 by order of
  Bloomberg's predecessor, Peter Stuyvesant.

Coffee

- **Cafe Madeline** • 1603 Cortelyou Rd [E 16th St]
  718-941-4020
  Coffee house with french fare.

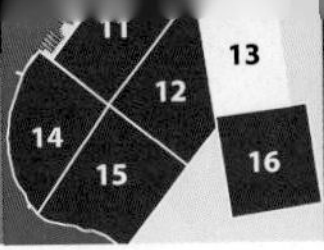

Map 1

Between these two neighborhoods, there's some exquisite, in-the-know type of fooding to be done. Cortelyou Road is bursting with fantastic, Manhattan-quality restaurants, with **The Farm on Adderley** and **The Purple Yam** leading the pack. Church Avenue is a good place to start adventuring; **Taqueria Los Poblanos** is among the best for cheap take-out.

Farmers Markets

• **Cortelyou Greenmarket** •
Cortelyou Rd & Rugby Rd
Sunday, 8 a.m.–4 p.m., year-round.
• **Kensington Youthmarket** •
Fort Hamilton Pkwy & 4th St
Saturday, 9 a.m.–4 p.m., July–Nov.

Nightlife

• **The Castello Plan** •
1213 Cortelyou Rd [Westminster Rd]
718-856-8888
Cozy wine bar and nice selection of tapas.
• **Denny's Steak Pub** •
106 Beverley Rd [Church Ave]
718-435-2156
Attracts nefarious souls with missing teeth in need of liberal pours.
• **Shenanigans Pub** • 802 Caton Ave [E 8th St]
718-633-3689
Tavern-like with a dark tropical feel.
• **Sycamore** • 1118 Cortelyou Rd [Stratford Rd]
347-240-5850
Flower shop by day, barroom by night.

Map 14

Restaurants

- **Am Thai Bistro** • 1003 Church Ave [E 10th St]
718-287-8888 • $$
Cheerful and casual with more vegetarian options than most.
- **Bahar** • 984 Coney Island Ave [Newkirk Ave]
718-434-8088 • $$
Authentic Afghan cuisine (like we'd know).
- **Bukhari** • 1095 Coney Island Ave [Foster Ave]
718-859-8044 • $
Eat like a raja for less than a cocktail.
- **Cafe Tibet** •
1510 Cortelyou Rd [Marlborough Rd]
718-941-2725 • $
Near the train station, perfect for people-watching. Excellent momos.
- **Cinco De Mayo Restaurant** •
1202 Cortelyou Rd [E 12th St]
718-693-1022 • $
Great taste, large portions.
- **Don Burrito** • 5 Newkirk Plz [E 16th St]
718-421-9525 • $
Looks like a dive, but surprisingly fresh and healthy.
- **El Gaucho Glatt Steakhouse** •
4102 18th Ave [E 4th St]
718-438-3006 • $$$$
We'll eat at any kind of steakhouse.
- **Exquisite Delight** •
2847 Church Ave [Nostrand Ave]
718-693-4643 • $
Jerk chicken for president.
- **The Farm on Adderley** •
1108 Cortelyou Rd [Stratford Rd]
718-287-3101 • $$$
An unlikely gem in a reviving 'nabe. Killer desserts and a heated garden.
- **George's** •
753 Coney Island Ave [Cortelyou Rd]
718-282-0152 • $$
Multi-cuisine—American, Greek, and Italian smorgasbord.
- **Little Bangladesh** •
483 McDonald Ave [Church Ave]
718-871-7080 • $$
Bangladeshi delight.
- **Los Mariachis** •
805 Coney Island Ave [Dorchester Rd]
718-826-3388 • $$$
Muy authentic, especially on weekends with live mariachi music.
- **Madina** • 563 Coney Island Ave [Beverley Rd]
718-469-3535 • $$
Pakistani goodness open 24 hours.
- **Mamma Lucia** • 1701 Foster Ave [E 17th St]
718-434-9858 • $$
One of the last old-school Italian joints in Brooklyn.
- **Mimi's Hummus** •
1209 Cortelyou Rd [Westminster Rd]
718-284-4444 • $$
Candlelight and a variety of Middle Eastern small plates.
- **Mirage Restaurant** •
2143 Cortelyou Rd [Flatbush Ave]
718-941-4452 • $
Tasty traditional Nigerian.
- **Ox Cart Tavern** •
1301 Newkirk Ave [Argyle Rd]
718-284-0005 • $$
As elegant as wings and fried pickles get.
- **Picket Fence** • 1310 Cortelyou Rd [Argyle Rd]
718-282-6661 • $$
Wonderful comfort food.
- **Purple Yam** • 1314 Cortelyou Rd [E 13th St]
718-940-8188 • $$
Filipino Pan Asian cuisine.
- **Qathra Cafe** • 1112 Cortelyou Rd [E 11th St]
718-484-3322 • $
Highend for the high end.
- **San Remo** • 1408 Cortelyou Rd [Rugby Rd]
718-282-4915 • $$
Try the fresh mozzarella pie.
- **Strictly Vegetarian Restaurant** •
2268 Church Ave [Flatbush Ave]
718-284-2543 • $
Vegetarian Caribbean with an every changing menu.
- **Sybil's** • 2210 Church Ave [Flatbush Ave]
718-469-9049 • $$
Delicious Caribbean bakery.
- **Taqueria Los Poblanos** •
733 Church Ave [E 8th St]
718-436-5705 • $
Killer tortas and cemitas, but the festive jukebox prevents conversation.
- **Thai Tony's** •
3019 Fort Hamilton Pkwy [E 3rd St]
718-436-6932 • $$
Nice decor and presentation in Kensington? Oh! And, the food's good too.
- **To B Thai** • 126 Beverley Rd [Church Ave]
718-435-0459 • $
Inexpensive and tasty. Try the mock duck.
- **Yen Yen** • 404 Church Ave [E 4th St]
718-633-8711 • $$
Above-average Szechuan/Hunan cuisine, with a pretty sweet bar to boot.

Golden Farm, with its 24 hours of operation and cheap food, is a reason unto itself to move to here, as is the **Flatbush Food Co-Op**. Otherwise, Kensington and Ditmas Park are pretty woefully devoid of shopping. The herbalist shop **Sacred Vibes Apothecary** easily turns into an addiction.

Shopping

- **Flatbush Food Co-op** •
  1415 Cortelyou Rd [Argyle Rd]
  718-284-9717
  The place for all your organic goods.
- **Golden Farm** • 329 Church Ave [E 4th St]
  718-871-1009
  24 hours and miraculously cheap. A reason to move to Kensington.
- **J & L Landscaping** • 702 Caton Ave [E 7th St]
  718-438-3199
  Quirky owner dispenses plant and neighborly wisdom.
- **Juice Box Wine & Spirits** •
  1289 Prospect Ave [Greenwood Ave]
  718-871-1110
  Maybe the name appeals to the parents in the area in need of their own juice.
- **MF Discount** • 309 Church Ave [E 3rd St]
  718-854-4337
  The place to get your keys copied, generic tampons and school supplies.

- **Natural Frontier Market** •
  1102 Cortelyou Rd [Stratford Rd]
  718-284-3593
  Specializing in natural and organic products.
- **Newkirk Plaza** •
  Above Newkirk Ave Subway [Foster Ave]
  Rumor has it that this was America's first mall.
- **Old Navy Outlet** •
  1009 Flatbush Ave [Tilden Ave]
  718-693-7507
  Cheaper-than-cheap wardrobe basics.
- **One Stop Market** • 626 Caton Ave [E 7th St]
  718-436-3410
  The cleanest, best-stocked deli in Kensington.
- **Sacred Vibes Apothecary** •
  376 Argyle Rd [Dorchester Rd]
  718-284-2890
  Herbs for what ails you.
- **Shakespeare & Co.** • 150 Campus Rd [Hillel Pl]
  718-434-5326
  Brooklyn outpost of Manhattan mini-chain.
- **TB Ackerson Wine Merchants** •
  1205 Cortelyou Rd [Westminster Rd]
  718-826-6600
  An unexpected selection. Use your frequent buyer's card and the 13th bottle is free.

Bay Ridge might be forever linked with *Saturday Night Fever*. Indeed, the working-class character depicted in the 1977 film survives to this day, and it remains one of the city's most affordable neighborhoods. Third Avenue's Restaurant Row is the pride of local foodies, and stores in Bay Ridge tend to be less chaotic, and less picked over than elsewhere. And would you believe that the extravagant mansions that line Colonial Road, Narrows Avenue, and Shore Road once served as summer homes for wealthy Manhattanites? It's true—though while Bay Ridge remains convenient, it's still about a 45-minute commute to Lower Manhattan.

Bay Ridge played an important role in harbor defense during the Revolutionary War and the War of 1812. **The Barkaloo Cemetery** (smallest cemetery in Brooklyn) is thought to hold the remains of many of these Revolutionary heroes. Real, live military reside at nearby **Fort Hamilton**, the only active military base in New York City. Known as the "Church of the Generals," nearby **St. John's Episcopal Church**, has been a house of worship for officers from every conflict since the Mexican War, counting Generals Robert E. Lee and Thomas J. (Stonewall) Jackson as past parishioners.

After discarding the moniker "Yellow Hook" to avoid any plague-like connotations, the neighborhood was renamed after its proximity to New York Bay and the literal "ridge" in the land left over from the last Ice Age. At the turn of the 20th century, prime water views attracted the wealthy and their extravagant taste in real estate. Notable examples still extant are **Fontbonne Hall**, the former residence of actress Lillian Russell, **The Gingerbread House**, an impressive example of Arts and Crafts architecture, and the **James F. Farrell House**, which has been at 125 95th Street since the early twentieth century. Legend has it the house plan was oriented so that its "widow's walk"—the balcony that overlooks the sea so women could watch for their husbands' ships—would no longer face the Narrows.

There are plenty of parks and promenades, especially along the the water. The **69th Street Pier-9/11 Memorial** at Shore Road and Bay Ridge Avenue is a former ferry pick-up site and a current recreation spot for sports fisherman. And did you know that Vikings discovered America? Check out the Leif Ericson Runestone in **Leif Ericson Park** if you feel the need to factcheck. Stunning views of the imposing **Verrazano-Narrows Bridge** can be had from the Belt Parkway Promenade. Completed in 1964, the behemoth is still the longest suspension bridge in the Americas.

Bay Ridge has always been known for its bar scene, but it's a bar scene of a certain clientele. Dance clubs like **Trace** attract the six-pack, spray-tanned set, while the sitters-and-talkers unwind at one of the numerous sports bars (**Salty Dog**, **Bean Post**, **Lone Star**).

O Landmarks

- **American Veterans Memorial Pier** ·
Shore Rd & Bay Ridge Ave
Once the embarkation point for the Bay
Ridge-St. George ferry, it offers a panoramic
harbor view.
- **The Barkaloo Cemetery** ·
Narrows Ave & Mackay Pl
The smallest cemetery founded in 1725 by
Dutch immigrant William Harmans Barkaloo.
- **Fontbonne Hall Academy** ·
9901 Shore Rd [99th St]
718-748-2244
Now a Catholic school, this 1890s private
residence that once belonged to actress Lillian
Russell.
- **Fort Hamilton** ·
Fort Hamilton Pkwy & 101st St
718-630-4848
Established in the 1820s as a garrison for
protecting the harbor and city against attack.
- **The Gingerbread House** ·
8220 Narrows Ave [83rd St]
The best example of Arts and Crafts
architecture in the city.
- **James F. Farrell House** ·
125 95th St [Shore Rd]
This 1849 Greek Revival house evokes the
neighborhood's days as a wealthy seaside
retreat.
- **Leif Ericson Park** · 4th Ave & 67th St
Commemorating Viking explorer who
discovered America (before what's-his-name).
- **St. John's Episcopal Church** ·
9818 Fort Hamilton Pkwy [Marine Ave]
718-745-2377
Established in 1834, the present structure
dates to 1890; its vestrymen have included
Robert E. Lee and Thomas J. (Stonewall)
Jackson.
- **Verrazano-Narrows Bridge** ·
92nd St & Gatling Pl
The longest span in North America really
puts things into perspective. Awesome views
below.

Farmers Markets

- **Bay Ridge Greenmarket** · 3rd Ave & 95th St
Saturday, 8 a.m.–3 p.m., June–Nov.

Third Avenue abounds with diverse offerings. Middle Eastern powerhouse **Tanoreen** is destination dining, but it's hardly the only place worth braving the R train for. Try **Tuscany Grill** for Italian or **Nouvelle** for Japanese. The Moroccan food at **Casablanca** comes highly recommended.

🍸Nightlife

- **Bean Post** • 7525 5th Ave [Bay Ridge Pkwy]
  718-745-9413
  Popular pub/sports bar.
- **Bullshots** • 8121 5th Ave [81st St]
  718-567-2337
  Low-key pub where the locals gather.
- **Delia's Lounge** • 9224 3rd Ave [93rd St]
  718-745-7999
  When you need to get in the mood.
- **Hall of Fame Billiards** •
  505 Ovington Ave [5th Ave]
  718-921-2694
  Large pool hall with celeb cache.
- **The Humidor** • 9212 3rd Ave [93rd St]
  718-238-2224
  Chomp a cigar with the (wise) guys.
- **JJ Bubbles** • 7912 3rd Ave [79th St]
  718-745-8790
  Comfortable dive bar.
- **Kelly's Tavern** • 9259 4th Ave [93rd St]
  718-745-9546
  Classic NY Irish bar.

- **The Kettle Black** • 8622 3rd Ave [87th St]
  718-680-7862
  Total Bayridge: beer, babes, and brawls.
- **Kitty Kiernans** • 9715 3rd Ave [97th St]
  718-921-0217
  Another Irish pub.
- **Lone Star** • 8703 5th Ave [87th St]
  718-833-5180
  Burger and a brew for under $10? We're sold!
- **The Purple Rose** • 7217 8th Ave [73rd St]
  718-680-6030
  Neighborhood nightclub. Wear stilettos.
- **Salty Dog** • 7509 3rd Ave [Bay Ridge Pkwy]
  718-238-0030
  Good food and boisterous dancing.
- **Trace** • 8814 3rd Ave [88th St]
  718-921-9500
  Lounge/restaurant serving modern Mexican bites.
- **The Wicked Monk** • 9510 3rd Ave [95th St]
  347-497-5152
  Intimate Gothic pub.

Map

14 15 12 13 16

🍴 Restaurants

• **Arirang Hibachi Steakhouse** •
8812 4th Ave [88th St]
718-238-9880 • $$$$
Japanese hibachi with a free show.

• **Bridgeview Diner** • 9011 3rd Ave [90th St]
718-680-9818 • $$
Bay Ridge's best diner.

• **Casablanca Restaurant** •
484 77th St [5th Ave]
718-748-2077 • $$
Highly recommended Moroccan.

• **Cebu Bar & Bistro** • 8801 3rd Ave [88th St]
718-492-5095 • $$$
Where locals do brunch.

• **Chadwick's** • 8822 3rd Ave [88th St]
718-833-9855 • $$$
More on the upscale side of Bay Ridge.

• **Elia** • 8611 3rd Ave [87th St]
718-748-9891 • $$$
Michelin recommended, upscale Greek.

• **Embers** • 9519 3rd Ave [95th St]
718-745-3700 • $$$
Massive steaks—try the potato potpie.

• **Gino's** • 7414 5th Ave [74th St]
718-748-1698 • $$
Classic Brooklyn Italian.

• **Grand Sichuan House** •
8701 5th Ave [87th St]
718-680-8887 • $
Food critics love this authentic Sichuan house.

• **Greenhouse Café** • 7717 3rd Ave [77th St]
718-833-8200 • $$$$
An elegant favorite for that special night.

• **Karam** • 8519 4th Ave [85th St]
718-745-5227 • $
Best of the growing Mid-Eastern.

• **Mezcal's D'Os Restaurant** •
7508 3rd Ave [Bay Ridge Pkwy]
718-748-7007 • $$
Fine Mexican fare, but we came for the tequila.

• **Mr. Tang** • 7523 3rd Ave [Bay Ridge Pkwy]
718-748-0400 • $$$
Upscale Chinese Institution.

• **MyThai Café** • 7803 3rd Ave [78th St]
718-833-1700 • $$
Slammin' Pan-Asian eats.

• **Nouvelle** • 8716 3rd Ave [88th St]
718-238-8250 • $$$$
Brooklyn's answer to Nobu; creative sushi/
Asian fusion.

• **The Pearl Room** • 8201 3rd Ave [82nd St]
718-502-6227 • $$$
Hip and modern seafood.

• **Peppino's** • 7708 3rd Ave [77th St]
718-833-3364 • $$
Brick oven goodness.

• **Petit Oven** • 276 Bay Ridge Ave [3rd Ave]
718-833-3443 • $$$
Cozy affordable French/American.

• **Pho Hoai** • 8616 4th Ave [87th St]
718-745-1640 • $
Fee Fi Pho Yum.

• **Polonica** • 7214 3rd Ave [73rd St]
718-630-5805 • $$
Cheese stuffed, bacon wrapped kielbasa,
anyone?

• **Schnitzel Haus** • 7319 5th Ave [73rd St]
718-836-5600 • $$
A multitude of meats and beers you can't
pronounce.

• **Skinflints** • 7902 5th Ave [79th St]
718-745-1116 • $$
Get the burger with bleu cheese.

• **Tanoreen** • 7704 3rd Ave [77th St]
718-748-5600 • $$
Small Middle Eastern with big flavors.

• **Tuscany Grill** • 8620 3rd Ave [86th St]
718-921-5633 • $$$
Worth going to/staying in Bay Ridge; get the
steak.

Map 1

Brand-name stores reign on 86th Street (**Century 21**, **The Gap**), but there are plenty of opportunities to support small business on 3rd and 5th Avenues. **HOM** is a neighborhood original, peddling home accents and high tea, while **Frank and Eddie's Meat Market** provides a touch of the old school.

🛍 Shopping

- **Aida Spa** • 7318 3rd Ave [74th St]
718-833-1250
Aida delivers low cost, high quality cuts. In stiletto heels.
- **Bay Ridge Bicycle World** •
8916 3rd Ave [89th St]
718-238-1118
Sales, service and repairs.
- **The BookMark Shoppe** •
8415 3rd Ave [84th St]
718-833-5115
Mostly bestsellers and children's.
- **Celtic Rose** • 8905 3rd Ave [85th St]
718-238-3355
Cead Mille Failte! Bits and pieces direct from the Emerald Isle.
- **Century 21** • 472 86th St [4th Ave]
718-748-3266
Discounted apparel, housewares, and linen—everything!
- **Choc-Oh!-Lot Plus** • 7911 5th Ave [80th St]
718-748-2100
Happy fun times with bulk candy and cake decorating supplies.
- **Frank & Eddie's Meat Market** •
302 86th St [3rd Ave]
718-836-5784
Bay Ridge butcher—an institution.
- **Frank & Eddie's Meat Market** •
7502 3rd Ave [Bay Ridge Pkwy]
718-836-4168
One of the few real butcher stores left in Brooklyn.
- **The Gap** • 423 86th St [4th Ave]
718-833-6621
Part of the brand-name 86th Street juggernaut.
- **Havin' a Party** • 8414 5th Ave [84th St]
718-836-3701
Party supplies and novelties.
- **HOM** • 8806 3rd Ave [88th St]
718-238-4466
Antiques Shopping+Homemade Cupcakes+Big Gay Sal=Fabulous!
- **Jean Danet Pastry** • 7526 5th Ave [76th St]
718-836-7566
40-year-old den of calorie-laden iniquity.
- **Kaleidoscope** • 8722 3rd Ave [88th St]
718-491-2051
Magical, unique toy shop with beautiful gift-wrapping.
- **Leske's Bakery** • 7612 5th Ave [76th St]
718-680-2323
There's only one Babka left…watch out for elbows!
- **Little Cupcake Bakeshop** •
9102 3rd Ave [91st St]
212-941-9100
Now, who doesn't just love a good cupcake?
- **Modell's Sporting Goods** •
531 86th St [5th Ave]
718-745-7900
Sports. Sports. Sports. Get your Cyclones stuff here!
- **Nordic Delicacies** •
6909 3rd Ave [Bay Ridge Ave]
718-748-1874
Norwegian carryout and grocery store.
- **Panda Ski & Sport** • 9213 5th Ave [92nd St]
718-238-4919
Full line of ski equipment. Ask about ski trips!
- **Paneantico Bakery** • 9124 3rd Ave [92nd St]
718-680-2347
Killer paninis made with just-baked Crown Bakery bread.

Map 13 · Dyker Heights / Bensonhurst

Nothing big ever happens in the Dyker Heights/Bensonhurst part of Brooklyn, but then again, that's how the mostly laid-back residents here like it. Walk east across noisy New Utrecht Avenue, however, and you've stumbled upon the full-on Eastern European area of Bensonhurst. You're in for the cold shoulder treatment here because if you can't speak at least three non-English languages fluently, they can tell you're just a "new" Brooklynite. There isn't much excitement in this neck of the woods, but the specialty food shopping remains a reason to visit.

Historically, this area of Brooklyn was created as an upscale housing development and was built as such in the late 1800s. Though much has been torn down, several of these large homes are still standing today and make for a nice walk while you're not gorging yourself at the many bakeries and bagelries around town. While you're in this part of Brooklyn, you might as well play a round of golf at one of the world's oldest courses, the **Dyker Beach Golf Course**. The world's busiest golf course in the mid-'50s, today the attached Dyker Beach Park has added facilities for tennis, handball, and bocce, as well as the usual American team sports.

Did you know that there's an amusement park in town not named Coney Island? That's right; the **Adventurer's Family Entertainment Center** (formerly Nelly Bly Amusement Park) has enough thrills, chills, and spills for anyone under the age of 10. Located along the Belt Parkway near Bay 41st Street, it's a cute park good for a family treat, but not exactly Six Flags. Around Christmastime hop on over to 84th Street between 11th and 13th Avenues, otherwise known as the epicenter for the famous **Dyker Heights Christmas Lights** spectacular. Join locals and tourists from all over the U.S. as they amble along the suburban-ish streets admiring these amazingly overdecorated mini-mansions.

During the warmer months take a stroll along Leif Ericson Park (66th & Fort Hamilton Pkwy), or step out right near the water's edge with a walk along the ocean. Sure, the highway's right on the other side of you, but at least you can feel that salty breeze.

The number of bars you won't pass here is staggering, unless you're talking about an espresso bar, in which case, go to town. Otherwise, go to town.

Who cares if the menu's not in English around here? Go for traditional Greek and souvlaki at **Meze** or pizza and upscale Italian at **Ristorante Vaccaro**, where you can still get a slice to go at the walk-up window.

Map 15

O Landmarks

- **Dyker Heights Christmas Lights** •
84th St [11th to 13th Ave]
Out-of-state visitors schlep to see these incredible lights.

Farmers Markets

- **Bensonhurst Greenmarket** •
18th Ave b/n 81st & 82nd St
Sunday, 9 a.m.–4 p.m. July–Nov.

Nightlife

- **Ocean Extreme** • 6403 11th Ave [64th St]
718-837-3136
A little bit of Chinatown in Dyker Heights.

Restaurants

- **Blue Agave** •
7201 16th Ave [New Utrecht Ave]
718-758-5822 • $$$
Promising Mexican with Japanese and French influences.
- **Columbus Deli** • 6610 18th Ave [66th St]
718-236-8623 • $
Club sandwiches to die for.
- **Hand Pull Noodle and Dumpling House** •
7201 18th Ave [72nd St]
718-232-6191 • $
The most entertaining noodles you've probably ever had.
- **Hanna Vermicelli** •
7524 18th Ave [Bay Ridge Pkwy]
718-331-9259 • $
Fab Vietnamese selection.
- **Il Colosseo** • 7704 18th Ave [77th St]
718-234-3663 • $$
Hands-down the best pizza in the 'hood.
- **La Sorrentina** • 6522 11th Ave [66th St]
718-680-9299 • $$
Upscale pizzeria with make-you-cry white pizza.
- **Meze Greek Restaurant** •
6601 13th Ave [66th St]
718-234-6393 • $$$
Traditional Greek with local crowd.
- **Outback Steakhouse** •
1475 86th St [Bay 8th St]
718-837-7200 • $$$
A little taste of suburbia.
- **Ristorante Vaccaro** •
6716 Fort Hamilton Pkwy [67th St]
718-238-9447 • $$$
Good, simple Italian.
- **Samurai Sushi** • 1709 86th St [17th Ave]
718-331-7100 •
Above-average sushi.
- **Tenzan** • 7117 18th Ave [72nd St]
718-621-3238 • $$
Japanese on pretty pillows.
- **Tommaso's** • 1464 86th St [Bay 8th St]
718-236-9883 • $$$
Good enough for the Godfather.
- **Vstrecha Restaurant** • 8421 20th Ave [84th St]
718-266-4817 • $$$
You might get a waiter who speaks some English.

Dyker Heights / Bensonhurst

Map 15

Eighteenth Avenue is a food lover's paradise and has some of the best specialty food shopping in the city—Hungarian marts, ravioli outposts, and fresh, local rabbit vendors. No joke. Stop by **B & A Pork Store** and other bakeries on 13th Avenue for great eats and a semi-local specialty called Pizza Rustica. This thick, savory pie is stuffed with prosciutto, ham, egg, cheese that's more calzone than pizza.

Shopping

- **B&A Pork Store** • 7818 13th Ave [78th St]
  718-833-9661
  Friendly service along with tasty dishes and homemade sausages.
- **Faicco's Pork Store** • 6511 11th Ave [66th St]
  718-236-0119
  Sausage that could convert the staunchest vegetarian.
- **Frank & Sal Prime Meats** •
  8008 18th Ave [80th St]
  718-331-8100
  A true Italian market with fresh and imported everything.
- **Gourmet Brands Inc.** • 7017 20th Ave [71st St]
  718-331-7325
  Fancy-schmancy good gourmet grub.
- **Great Wall Supermarket** •
  6722 Fort Hamilton Pkwy [67th St]
  718-680-2889
  Probably the best Asian grocery you've ever stepped foot in.
- **Im Mondello Fish Market** •
  6824 18th Ave [Bay Ridge Ave]
  718-236-3930
  You can stand the smell of this really fresh fish.
- **International Bookstore** •
  1914 86th Ave [19th Ave]
  718-236-1090
  Russian books.
- **Lioni Latticini** • 7819 15th Ave [78th St]
  718-232-7852
  Lots and lots of mighty fine mozzarella.
- **Maggio Music Center** •
  8403 18th Ave [New Utrecht Ave]
  718-259-4468
  Sheet music and lessons at this friendly neighborhood noisemaker.
- **Meats Supreme** • 1949 86th St [20th Ave]
  718-259-2441
  Safe for vegetarians too, a great neighborhood gourmet market.
- **Mona Lisa Bakery** • 7717 13th Ave [78th St]
  718-256-7706
  Mini pastries, giant breads, many choices.
- **New Star Cheese Co.** • 7305 20th Ave [73rd St]
  718-259-2982
  Peculiar location, but someone's gotta eat all that cheese.
- **Pastosa Ravioli** •
  7425 New Utrecht Ave [74th St]
  718-236-9615
  Pasta heaven.
- **Queen Ann Ravioli** • 7205 18th Ave [72nd St]
  718-256-1061
  18 varieties of ravioli—totally awesome.
- **Ravioli Fair** • 1484 86th Ave [15th Ave]
  718-256-5288
  You might find some ravioli among these gourmet goods.
- **Sal & Jerry's Bakery, Inc.** •
  6817 20th Ave [69th St]
  718-232-9358
  Famous for their prosciutto bread but loved for their cookies.
- **Sas Italian Records** • 7113 18th Ave [71st St]
  718-331-0539
  Italian music, games, beauty products, and soccer paraphernalia.
- **Sea Breeze** • 8500 18th Ave [85th St]
  718-259-9693
  Fresh fish at great prices.
- **Three Guys From Brooklyn** •
  6502 Fort Hamilton Pkwy [65th St]
  718-748-5486
  Fresh produce from nice guys.
- **Villabate Alba** • 7001 18th Ave [70th St]
  718-331-8430
  This place is da bomb!!! Don't go on an empty stomach.

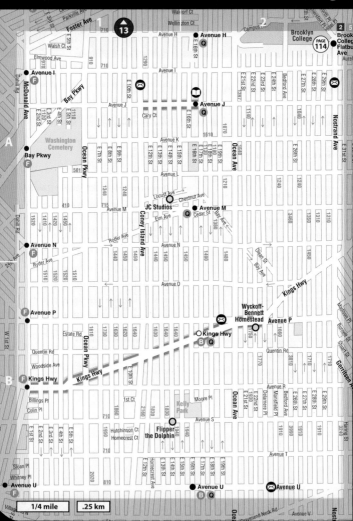

Map 16 · **Midwood**

N

Parkville Ave
Waldorf Ct
Wellington Ct

Foster Ave
710
13

Avenue H
Q

Campus Rd
2

Brooklyn
College
PAGE
114

2 5
Brook
Colleg
Flatbu
Ave
Aurel

Walsh Ct
E 5th St
910
1290

Avenue H
Q

E 16th St
E 21st St
E 22nd St
E 23rd St
E 24th St
Bedford Ave
E 26th St
E 27th St
E 28th St
E 29th St

Elmwood Ave

Avenue I
F
McDonald Ave
Dahill Rd

Bay Pkwy

Avenue I
1290

E 10th St

Avenue J
1382
1140
1040

E 31st St
Nostrand Ave

Walsh Ct
Avenue J
Q

Cary Ct
E 16th St
E 17th St

1610

Avenue K
1670
1110
1248
1340
410
715
1640
1210
1240
1240
1310
1310

A

E 3rd St
E 4th St
E 2nd St

Washington
Cemetery
Ocean Pkwy
501

E 7th St
E 8th St
E 9th St
E 12th St
E 13th St
E 14th St
E 15th St
E 16th St
E 18th St
E 19th St
Ocean Ave
E 26th St

Bay Pkwy
F

Avenue L

Locust Ave
Chestnut Ave

JC Studios
Avenue M
Q
Cedar St
Elm Ave

Ave C

1380

3480
1380
1310
1310

Avenue M

Coney Island Ave
1348
1440
1450
1440
1450
1450
1490
1480
1210
1240

Avenue N
F
Ryder Ave
1510
1520
1450
1440
1450

Avenue N

Ocean St
Bay Ave

Dean St

1450

Ryder Ave
1510
1520
1510

Avenue O

Kings Hwy

2nd Ave
E 1st St

Avenue P
F
Ocean Pkwy
1610
1630
1620
1640
1630
1640

Wyckoff-
Bennett
Homestead
Avenue P
Madison Pl
Burnett St
Stuart St

Estate Rd
1730
1640
1750
1660

Quentin Rd
Kings Hwy
B
Q
Quentin Rd
1710
1710
1710

Woodside Ave
Kings Hwy
Kings Hwy
1770
3810

B
Kings Hwy
F

Billings Pl
Colin Pl

710
1660
2160
1830

Avenue R
E 22nd St
Delamere Pl
Mansfield Pl
E 21st St
Bedford Ave
E 26th St
E 27th St
E 29th St

1930
1910
3990
1910

1st Ct
Moore Pl

Kelly
Park
Avenue S

E 1st St
E 2nd St
E 3rd St
E 5th St

Hutchinson Ct
Homecrest Ct

1590
1940
Flipper
the Dolphin

Ocean Ave
1940
1910
1910
1910
1910

Haring St
3240

Sloan Pl
Whitney Pl

710
2020
810

Avenue T

Avenue U
F

E 12th St
E 13th St
E 17th St
E 18th St
E 19th St

Avenue U
B
Q
Avenue U

Ocean Ave
Gerritsen Ave
Nost

1/4 mile
.25 km

Smack dab in the middle of Brooklyn, Midwood is one of the few melting pots—in the true sense of the word—left in New York. Russians, Pakistanis, Italians, among other nationalities, call the neighborhood home. Midwood has the feel of a small town where not much happens, and for the most part that's true, but Edward R. Murrow High School—where the late Beastie Boy Adam Yauch attended—boasts one of the best chess teams in the country, and has become something of legend and source of local pride.

In recent years the neighborhood has seen an influx of Orthodox Jewish families, with homes being expanded and built out into downright domestic palaces. That said, the neighborhood remains more liberal and diverse than neighboring Borough Park. Still, this is a quiet, family-oriented place, and the side-streets are of the tree-lined, quaint, suburban variety. Aside from Avenue J—where you'll find Jewish bakeries and decent discount shopping—and Avenue M—a mostly Russian scene with some excellent eating—there's scant hustle and bustle, especially during the Sabbath.

For decades the neighborhood has been on the radar of pizza snobs thanks to **Di Fara Pizza**, an old-school, old-fashioned pizzeria that's been touted as some of New York's best since the 1960s. Lines snake down the block and Yelp reviews long ago topped 1,000, even after a spate of less-than-stellar health inspections (67 points? yikes!). But don't stop at Avenue J: Stumbling onto a mind-blowing bowl of borscht at one of the myriad hole-in-the-wall Russian delis is also part of the fun.

On a quiet stretch of East 22nd Street is the **Wyckoff-Bennett Homestead**, believed to have been built before the American Revolution. Declared a National Historic Landmark in 1976, the house was owned by the Wyckoff Family until the mid-19th century, and then the Bennett family until the 1980s (thus, the name) until it passed to its current owners. The City has been trying to buy the house, although those plans are currently up in the air.

At one point in time, Midwood had a corner on the film and television industry. Two prominent studios, known today as **JC Studios**, were erected in 1903 and housed the sets of shows such as *The Cosby Show*, *As the World Turns*, *Saturday Night Live* (very briefly), and the *Sammy Davis Jr. Show*. Perhaps most famously, the studio was home to the *Esther Williams Show*, and the site of the memorable *Esther Williams Aqua Spectacle*; the swimming pool used for the event is still there.

The nightlife here is nearly nonexistent, unless you count neighborhood dive bars like **Nitecaps**.

Visit **Di Fara** for pizza to write on blogs about, **Tbilisi** for Georgian (the country, not the state) and **Taci's Beyti** for fresh, tasty Turkish.

14 12
15 16

○ Landmarks

- **Flipper the Dolphin** • Avenue S & E 14th St
Meet Flipper the Dolphin, the statue.
- **JC Studios** • 1268 E 14th St [Locust Ave]
718-780-6463
Where Cosby Show and As The World Turns
were filmed.
- **Wyckoff-Bennett Homestead** •
1669 E 22nd St [Ave P]
What things used to look like. Not open to
the public.

▼ Nightlife

- **Nitecaps** • 1164 Coney Island Ave [Ave H]
718-434-9685
Dive bar not for beginners.

⑪ Restaurants

- **Aksaray Turkish Café Restaurant** •
1618 E 16th St [Ave P]
718-375-9237 • $
24-hour gyro haunt that is mind-blowing and
dirt cheap.
- **Anna's Cafe** • 2925 Ave I [Nostrand Ave]
718-951-7617 • $
Counter service.
- **Buckley's** • 2926 Ave S [Nostrand Ave]
718-998-4222 • $$
Neighborhood tavern & steakhouse with great
Sunday brunch
- **Carlos and Gabby's Glatt
Kosher Mexican Grill** •
1376 Coney Island Ave [Ave J]
718-337-8226 • $
A kosher Mexican restaurant. Juan Epstein
would be proud.
- **Di Fara** • 1424 Ave J [E 14th St]
718-258-1367 • $
Meticulously crafted by hand since 1965.
- **Estihana** • 1217 Ave J [E 15th St]
718-677-1515 • $$
Kosher Asian bistro restaurant.
- **La Villita** • 1249 Ave U [Homecrest Ave]
718-998-0222 • $
Authentic, hearty Mexican.
- **Lotus Thai** • 1924 Coney Island Ave [Ave P]
718-513-6686 • $$$
Dark, mysterious, sexy. Club meets Thai
restaurant.

- **Mabat** • 1809 E 7th St [Kings Hwy]
718-339-3300 • $$
Hole-in-the-wall with tasty Moroccan dishes.
- **McDonald Avenue Diner** •
1111 McDonald Ave [Elmwood Ave]
718-951-8475 • $
Come for the characters, be drunk for the food.
- **Michael's** • 2929 Ave R [Nostrand Ave]
718-998-7851 • $$$$
Sprawling menu…everything from rack of
lamb to pasta.
- **Nagoya** • 1907 Kings Hwy [Billings Pl]
718-366-3688 • $$
Nicely presented sushi at good prices.
- **Napoli Pizza** • 2270 Nostrand Ave [Ave I]
718-338-0328 • $$
If you can't get over to DiFara's.
- **Obzhora** • 1715 Kings Hwy [E 18th St]
718-627-5005 • $$$
Russian home-style cooking. Pig out and drink
up, good comrade.
- **Olympic Pita** • 1419 Coney Island Ave [Ave K]
718-258-6222 • $
Heaven in a pita. Fantastic sauces—try the
zhoug.
- **Pizza Time** • 1324 Ave J [E 13th St]
718-252-8801 • $
Kosher Italian.
- **Salud** • 1308 Ave H [Argyle Rd]
347-295-1191 • $
Beautifully designed serving organic Mexican
tortas, soups, and smoothies.
- **Schnitzi** • 1299 Coney Island Ave [Ave J]
718-338-4015 • $$
Lots and lots of schnizel.
- **Sunflower Café** • 1223 Quentin Rd [E 12th St]
718-336-1340 • $
Surprising selection of foo-foo Kosher,
including pizza.
- **Sushi Tokyo** • 1360 Coney Island Ave [Ave O]
718-434-2444 • $$
Rabbi approved sushi? Now that's kosher.
Better for take-out.
- **Taci's Beyti** • 1955 Coney Island Ave [Ave P]
718-627-5750 • $$
Really fresh, really tasty Turkish cuisine.
- **Tbilisi** • 811 Kings Hwy [E 8th St]
718-382-6485 • $$
Good Georgian food—we're not talking pecan
pie, we're talking former Soviet chicken hearts.

Pop into **Ostrovitsky Bakery** for kosher pastries that you'll smell from a block away. Shop **Fox's** for designer gear with a considerable discount. King's Highway is lined with decent discount stores. The grocery store **Pomegranate** (think kosher Whole Foods) is a reason to make the trip.

🛍 Shopping

- **Chiffon Bakery** • 430 Ave P [E 2nd St]
  718-258-8822
  Holla at the challah, kid.
- **Chuckies** • 1304 Kings Hwy [E 13th St]
  718-376-1003
  Possibly the best shoe store in Brooklyn. We're talking Manolos and Jimmy Choos.
- **Downtown** • 2502 Ave U [Bedford Ave]
  718-934-8280
  Trendy in a junior high sorta way. But (hollah!) they do midnight madness sales.
- **Eichler's** • 1401 Coney Island Ave [Ave J]
  718-258-7643
  "The World's Judaica Store" brings joy, also "oy!"
- **Floral Kingdom** •
  1444 Coney Island Ave [Ave K]
  718-677-9797
  You have NOT seen flowers till you've been here.
- **Fox's** • 923 Kings Hwy [E 10th St]
  718-645-3620
  Brand name everything, discounted sweetly. Century 21's arch enemy.
- **Here's a Book Store** •
  1964 Coney Island Ave [Ave P]
  718-645-6675
  Quaint and impressive, rare finds, new and used, knowledgeable staff.
- **Kiev Bakery** • 1627 E 18th St [Kings Hwy]
  718-627-5438
  Elegant pastries and indulgent cakes. A Russian staple in NY.

- **Manhattan Lights** •
  1941 Coney Island Ave [Ave P]
  718-998-1111
  Any lighting you've ever dreamt up, is located here—seriously.
- **Mansoura** • 515 Kings Hwy [E 3rd St]
  718-645-7977
  Amazing bakery with Jewish specialties. Best baklava on the planet.
- **Ostrovitsky Bakery** • 1124 Ave J [E 12th St]
  718-951-7924
  You can smell the deliciousness before you open the door.
- **Pickle Guys** • 1364 Coney Island Ave [Ave J]
  718-677-0639
  Pickled pickles, tomatoes, carrots, everything pickled, everything yummy!
- **Pomegranate** • 1507 Coney Island Ave [Ave L]
  718-951-7112
  Glitzy kosher supermarket. Be prepared, you won't leave empty-handed.
- **Studio 19 Salon & Spa** •
  1610 E 19th St [Ave P]
  718-336-7373
  A spa, a salon, a favorite for many years, darling.
- **Tsakiris Mallas** • 1206 Kings Hwy [E 13th St]
  718-998-3090
  Beautiful European shoes that'll make you a real woman.
- **Wig Showcase** • 820 Kings Hwy [E 8th St]
  718-339-8300
  Lots of oddly coiffed mannequin heads.
- **Zelda's Art World** • 2291 Nostrand Ave [Ave I]
  718-377-7779
  Art supplies. F. Scott rarely around.

Overview

Nearly every community of Eastern Brooklyn is surrounded by water, and while you wouldn't exactly get an "Aye, matey" vibe from its inhabitants, this section of the borough is home to over a dozen boating and yacht clubs. In the summer, inlets along Sheepshead Bay, Plum Beach, and Paerdegat Basin become packed with jet skiers, windsurfers, and the occasional million-dollar schooner. Some neighborhoods such as Canarsie and Marine Park exude an almost suburban tranquility, while seriously affluent areas like Mill Basin and Manhattan Beach cater to an exclusive crowd. Densely populated East New York and Brownsville are packed with drab public housing, though remnants of a former Art Deco glory can be found along Pitkin Avenue. The population is a mixed bag, and with Brooklyn's seaside real estate once again on the rise, the nabe can only improve with time.

Transportation

Although the subway extends all the way out to East New York (J, Z, A, C) and Canarsie (L), there are many neighborhoods that can be accessed only by bus or car (notably Marine Park, Mill Basin, Bergen Beach, parts of East Flatbush, and the Flatlands).

Communities

Brooklyn is a borough of individual neighborhoods. The main communities that make up Eastern Brooklyn are:

Bergen Beach
Flatlands
Brownsville
Gerritsen Beach
Canarsie
Gravesend
Cypress Hills
Marine Park
East Flatbush
Mill Basin
East New York
Sheepshead Bay

Nature

What Eastern Brooklyn lacks in trendiness, it makes up for in scenery. The Eastern Brooklyn shore is lined with more than 3,000 acres of amazing parks that offer a plethora of activities: Nature trails, golf courses, horseback riding, camping, fishing, bird watching, boating, and organized athletics. When you need a break from it all, Marine Park, Floyd Bennett Field, the Jamaica Riding Academy, and Canarsie Beach Park provide a nice diversion from city life.

○ Landmarks

• **Lady Moody House** •
  27 Gravesend Neck Rd [McDonald Ave]
• **Old Gravesend Cemetery** •
  McDonald Ave & Gravesend Neck Rd

Restaurants

• **Del'Rio Diner** • 166 Kings Hwy [W 12th St]
• **Frank's Pizza** •
  2134 Flatbush Ave [Quentin Rd]
• **Joe's of Avenue U** • 287 Ave U [McDonald Ave]
• **John's Deli** • 2033 Stillwell Ave [Bay 50th St]
• **Jordan's Lobster Dock** •
  2771 Knapp St [Harkness Ave]
• **King's Buffet** • 2637 86th St [Ave U]
• **L&B Spumoni Gardens** •
  2725 86th St [W 10th St]
• **La Palina** • 159 Ave O [W 5th St]
• **Liman** • 2710 Emmons Ave [E 27th St]
• **Mill Basin Kosher Delicatessen** •
  5823 Ave T [E 58th St]
• **Peter Pizza** • 2358 80th St [Ave U]
• **Randazzo's** • 2017 Emmons Ave [Ocean Ave]
• **Roll-n-Roaster** • 2901 Emmons Ave [E 29th St]
• **Sahara** • 2337 Coney Island Ave [Ave T]
• **Sweik** •
  2027 Emmons Ave [Ocean Ave]
• **XO Creperie** • 2027 Emmons Ave [Ocean Ave]

Shopping

• **Calligaris Shop by AKO** •
  2184 McDonald Ave [Ave T]
• **Dairy Maid Ravioli** • 216 Ave U [W 4th St]
• **Enterprize** •
  1601 Sheepshead Bay Rd [E 16th St]
• **Le Monti** • 2074 McDonald Ave [Ave S]
• **Mini Centro** •
  1659 Sheepshead Bay Rd [Voohies Ave]
• **Omni Health** • 265 Ave U [Lake St]
• **Pisa Pork Store** • 306 Kings Hwy [W 6th St]
• **Sheepshead Bay Fruits &
  Vegetables Market** •
  1717 Ave Z [E 17th St]

Coney Island

For years observers have wrung their hands over the much-feared "transformation" of Coney Island. So far, however, the bold initiative to remake the area as a year-round destination has resulted in incremental development and relatively minor changes. Yes, Shoot the Freak may be gone, but **Ruby's** is still around and a boardwalk outpost of beloved Prospect Heights diner **Tom's** arrived just in time to see the Astro Tower dismantled.

Getting there:
Subway: take the D, F, N, or Q train to Coney Island/Stillwell Avenue. For the Aquarium, take the F or Q to W 8th Street/NY Aquarium.
Buses: B36, B64 and B68 all go to Coney Island.

Coney Island, USA

Address: 1208 Surf Ave (near W 12th St)
Phone: 718-372-5159
Website: www.coneyisland.com or @coneyislandusa

Coney Island, USA is the not-for-profit arts organization responsible for maintaining the Coney Island Museum, producing Sideshows by the Seashore, and organizing the annual Mermaid Parade.

The **Coney Island Museum** is open Wed–Sun from 1 p.m. to 6 p.m. during the summer and is $5 ($3 for residents of zip code 11224). Try the distortion mirrors and view other artifacts from the sideshow heyday. The gift shop has capitalized on pretty much every exploitable image available and it's a great spot to pick up some jumbo postcards.

Sideshows by the Seashore remains the only 10-in-1 circus sideshow in the USA. Sip a cold beer at the Freak Bar in the lobby and get ready to enjoy the various sword swallowers, fire eaters, contortionists and human blockheads. Performances run 45 minutes. Tickets cost $10 for adults and $5 for kids 12 and under.

The annual Mermaid Parade takes place on the first Saturday after the Summer Solstice. Rain or shine, more freaks than you knew existed strut their stuff down the main drag dressed as...mermaids! Seeing is believing and this is a don't-miss event.

For some of the best thin-crust pizza in Brooklyn go to **Totonno Pizzeria Napolitano**, 1524 Neptune Ave, 718-372-8606.

New York Aquarium

Address: Surf Ave & W 8th St
Phone: 718-265-FISH
Website: www.nyaquarium.com

In sobering contrast to the natural environs just steps away, the New York Aquarium has a colorful collection of sea life swimming happily in clean tanks. The exhibits strike a nice balance between interesting and educational. Superstorm Sandy hit the aquarium very hard, closing the facility for many months and wiping out many exhibits. The aquarium is undergoing a lengthy rebuilding process, culminating in a massive new shark exhibit set to open in 2016. While the work takes place the aquarium remains open daily year-round, for a reduced admission.

MCU Park/Brooklyn Cyclones

Location: Surf Ave b/w W 16th St & W 19th St
Phone: 718-449-8497
Website: www.brooklyncyclones.com or @BKCyclones

After a 44-year absence, professional baseball returned to Brooklyn in 2001 in the shape of the class-A minor league Brooklyn Cyclones (affiliate of the NY Mets). MCU's location couldn't be better, allowing any trip to the ballpark to double as a day at the beach or a great first date screaming your brains out and clutching hands on the Cyclones' namesake. On top of that, the team is actually pretty good. Seats start at less than a Shake Shack meal at Citi Field. You can purchase tickets either on their website or by calling 718-507-TIXX. Go 'Clones!. As a bonus, MCU also functions as a pretty decent concert venue.

Luna Park

Address: 1000 Surf Ave
Phone: 718-373-5862
Website: www.lunaparknyc.com or @LunaParkNYC

Keep your mind off impending doom while in line for the Cyclone by contemplating the historical ride you are about to take. One of the last remaining wooden roller coasters in existence, the Cyclone is the place to be at Luna Park. There are special unlimited-ride wristbands and "Luna Cards" that offer bonus credits for the more you spend. Open every day during the summer and on weekends through the cooler months. Keep in mind, there isn't any high-tech DisneyWorld or Six Flags fare here...these are the original rides (with perhaps some of the original carnies still attached). The next day you may feel like you were in a bar fight, but the memories are worth it.

Deno's Wonder Wheel Park

Address: 3059 Denos Vourderis Pl (W 12th St)
Phone: 718-372-2592 or 718-449-8836
Website: www.wonderwheel.com or @WonderWheelPark

Built in 1920, the Wheel of Wonder is still a major draw to Coney Island and offers a romantic moment well worth the $7 each for the stationary cars. Those looking to have their lives flash before their eyes can wait in a separate line for the "moving cars" and believe us, those things really move. Admission to the park is free and $25 buys 10 kid rides or 4 adult rides.

Brighton Beach

Slightly less frenetic than the Coney Island beach and boardwalk (but only slightly) is nearby Brighton Beach. Named for a resort town on the English Channel, this area is now often referred to as "little Odessa." Russian food, Russian vodka, and Russian-style bathing suits are the name of the game on this sandy stretch. The restaurants on the boardwalk are a tad overpriced—pack a lunch and skip the hassle. And a word to the wise—despite shirtless vendors parading up and down the beach hocking ice cold Coronas with lime—there are also cops on ATV's ready to hand out open container violations, so drink at your own risk! Bear in mind however that this is no white-sandy national park, but still the best beach Brooklyn has to offer. Had enough sun? Nice yourself up and head to the famed restaurant and cabaret, **National** (273 Brighton Beach Ave, 718-646-1225) whose doors whisk you off the street and into Moscow. To access Brighton Beach by subway, take the B (weekdays only) or the Q to the Brighton Beach stop.

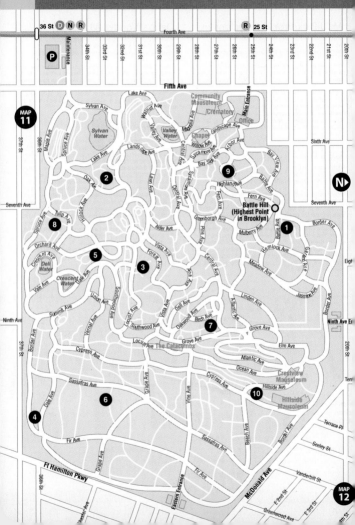

General Information

NFT Maps: 11 & 12
Main Entrance: Fifth Ave & 25th St
Phone: 718-768-7300
Website: www.green-wood.com or @GreenWoodHF
Subway: R to 25th St; D to Ninth Ave; F to Ft Hamilton Pkwy

Overview

When Green-Wood Cemetery opened in 1838, it was the largest outdoor park in all of New York City. With its winding paths, rolling hills, Victorian sculpture, and man-made lakes, this lush 478-acre cemetery inspired a contest to create a park in Manhattan—Central Park. The winning design, by Frederick Law Olmsted and Calvert Vaux, was based on Green-Wood. Today the picturesque grounds are dotted with the mausoleums and tombstones of nearly 600,000 people and counting, including several famous figures (see below). As a member of the Audubon Cooperative, this cemetery is a wildlife sanctuary and a haven for bird-watching. Green-Wood is also home to 220-foot Battle Hill, the highest point in all of Brooklyn. During the Revolutionary War, 400 Maryland soldiers held off the British Army here, allowing the rest of George Washington's troops to survive and fight another day. There are memorials to Revolutionary and Civil War dead at the summit that afford incredible views of lower Manhattan and New York Harbor. If you're craving some peace and solitude in the outdoors, this is the perfect retreat. The creepy beauty of the cemetery is now starting to be noticed by film crews and hipsters; check out Pitchfork's "Cemetery Gates" series to get a sneak-preview of the stained glass magic of the cemetery's chapel.

Visiting

The administrative offices are open Monday through Friday 8 a.m.–4 p.m. and Saturdays 8 a.m.–3:30 p.m. The cemetery itself is open to the public every day and can be accessed from various points:

• Main Entrance (Fifth Avenue & 25th Street): Open seven days a week 7:45 am–5 pm
• Fourth Avenue and 35th Street Entrance: Open seven days a week 8 am–4 pm
• Prospect Park West Entrance (Prospect Park West & 20th Street): Open 8 am–4 pm on weekends only
• Eastern Entrance (Fort Hamilton Parkway & Chester Avenue): Open 8 am–4 pm on weekends only

For the most impressive entry into the cemetery, we recommend walking through the main entrance gate. Designed by Richard Upjohn in 1860, this brownstone Gothic revival gate is embellished with four carved panels portraying scenes of death and resurrection—a great way to kick off a trip to the cemetery.

Tours and Events

Green-Wood offers various tours on the architecture and history of the cemetery and its interred. Check the website for schedules. Tours usually last about 2 hours and cost $15 per person. We highly recommend the popular Halloween tours, which include local ghost stories and tales of murder and mayhem. All tours fill up quickly, so plan in advance. In addition, the cemetery hosts other, er, live events, including concerts and cocktail nights; the setting is stunning and it's a great way to commune with Brooklyn's past.

Famous Graves

1. Leonard Bernstein—composer, conductor
2. Horace Greeley—founder of *The New Yorker* and the *New-York Tribune*
3. William M. "Boss" Tweed—the original corrupt politician
4. Susan Smith McKinney-Steward—first black female doctor in New York
5. Samuel F.B. Morse—inventor of the telegraph
6. John Michel Basquiat—graffiti artist and painter
7. Peter Cooper—founder of Cooper Union; inventor of Jell-O
8. Joey "Crazy Joe" Gallo—mobster killed in Umberto's Clam House
9. DeWitt Clinton—US Senator, NYS Governor and brain behind the Erie Canal
10. Henry Ward Beecher—abolitionist

East River

Brooklyn Bridge

Manhattan Bridge

Main Street Playground

Empire Fulton Ferry

Jane's Carousel

Tobacco Warehouse

Empire Stores

Plym

Washington St

Water St

Main St

Adams St

Front St

DUMBO

East River Ferry and Water Taxi

278 Brooklyn Queens E

Pier 1

Bridge View Lawn

Doughty St

Vine St

Old Fulton St

Poplar St

Granite Prospect

Harbor View Lawn

Squibb Park and Bridge

Middagh St

Cranberry St

Cadman Pl E

Pop-Up Pool

Kayak Dock

Boathouse

Orange St

MAP 5

Pineapple St

A C High Street

Brooklyn Heights Promenade

Columbia Heights

Clark St

2 3 Clark Street

Pier 2

Willow St

College Pl

Monroe Pl

Cadman Pl W

Tillary St

Pier 3

PAGE 112

Pierrepont St

Love Ln

Johnson St

Furman St

Montague St

BROOKLYN HEIGHTS

Clinton St

Remsen St

R Court Street

Fishing Station

Pier 5

Sports Fields

Play Area

Picnic Peninsula

Grace Ct

Grace Ct Alley

Hunts Ln

Joralemon St

2 Boro Hall

4

Court St

Pier 6

Sand Volleyball

Marsh Garden

Water Lab

Dog Run

Sandbox Village

Slide Mountain

Swing Valley

Ferry to Governors Island

Columbia Pl

Willow Pl

Hicks St

Garden Pl

Henry St

Sidney Pl

Aitken Pl

Livingston St

Schermerhorn St

State St

278

Atlantic Ave

Columbia St

Pacific St

COBBLE HILL

Amity St

General Information

NFT Map: 5
Main Entrance: Pier 1 at Old Fulton St and Furman St
Phone: 718-222-9939
Website: www.brooklynbridgepark.org or @BklynBrdgPark
Transportation: A, C to High Street, F to York Street,
2, 3 to Clark Street or the B25 bus to Fulton Ferry Landing

Overview

Stretching 1.3 miles along the East River, Brooklyn Bridge Park comprises six repurposed shipping piers, the former Empire-Fulton Ferry State Park, two Civil War-era historic buildings, and various city-owned open spaces along the waterfront. The 85-acre site combines active and passive recreation with the stunning backdrop of the Brooklyn and Manhattan Bridges, Lower Manhattan and the New York Harbor beyond.

By the 1980s shipping along this part of the waterfront slowed to a point where authorities began thinking about selling the land. Planning for a public open space began in earnest in the 2000s, culminating in a City-State plan to create Brooklyn Bridge Park. Funding for the park is unusual in that the park is mandated to be self sustaining, and reliant on several private developments within the park's boundaries. The park's granite comes from the reconstruction of the Roosevelt Island Bridge and the old Willis Avenue Bridge. The hills on Pier 1 use fill taken from the Eastside Access project connecting the Long Island Rail Road with Grand Central Terminal.

Begin your visit to the park at **Fulton Ferry Landing**, one of a handful of parcels that predates the larger site. As the name suggests, it was once the Brooklyn terminus for ferry service to Manhattan, popularized in Walt Whitman's "Crossing Brooklyn Ferry," scenes of which are immortalized in the railings. More often than not you'll come across a bridal party taking pictures with the bridge and Lower Manhattan in the background. Fulton Ferry Landing is home to the Brooklyn Ice Cream Factory and the long-running Bargemusic boat.

Pier 1 is the first of the former shipping piers, numbered from north to south (the Red Hook piers continue the numbering system). The chunky steps of the Granite Prospect and the Harbor View Lawn provide a mesmerizing panoramic view of Lower Manhattan and the harbor beyond. Pier 1 also features a boat launch, concessions, a playground and bicycle rentals. You could easily spend an afternoon here simply lazing about. Pier 1 is also accessible via the bouncy **Squibb Park Bridge**, an ADA-compliant link connecting Brooklyn Heights above with the park below.

A greenway connects Pier 1 with the other five piers to the south. **Pier 2** retains the skeletal framework of the pier's original structures, and is earmarked for active recreation. **Piers 3 and 4** are designed for passive recreation and are set off from the sound and tumult of the BQE by a 800-foot-long, 30-foot-high earth berm. **Pier 5** offers 200,000 square feet of sports fields, a fishing area, play areas for children of various ages and a picnic peninsula with grills—a rarity in a New York City public park. **Pier 6** has sand volleyball courts, a dog run and swing sets, a sandbox village and a popular water lab for children. Pier 6 is accessible to Atlantic Avenue and is a natural entrance point from Cobble Hill and points south. Seasonal ferry service to Governor's Island departs from Pier 6.

The **Empire Fulton Ferry** site links the piers to the south with the parcels to the north. Formerly a state park, this spot features a nice lawn right in the shadow of the Brooklyn Bridge, the glass-enclosed vintage Jane's Carousel, and two historic buildings, the Empire Stores and the Tobacco Warehouse. Just to the east of Empire Fulton Ferry is a parcel almost directly underneath the Manhattan Bridge, which features another lawn area and more great views of the Brooklyn Bridge.

General Information

NFT Maps: 1 & 2
Location: N 12 St, Lorimer St, Manhattan Ave bet Bayard St and Berry St-Nassau Ave
Website: www.nycgovparks.org/parks/mccarrenpark

Overview

McCarren Park is not easy on the eyes, but it's getting easier. Serving Greenpoint and Williamsburg, this 35-acre park reflects both the industrial and increasingly condo-ified surroundings of the neighborhood. However, McCarren Park is all about function, not form. When the sun is shining, the park is packed with a wide cross-section of people enjoying this rare open space. It is a much-needed sports and social hub in a part of Brooklyn that has very little parkland. Besides, where else can you play kickball in the shadow of the Empire State Building while still being within walking distance of the local dive bar selling cheap beer in styrofoam cups?

How to Get There

The easiest way to access the park is by walking, biking, or taking the subway. Take the train to the Bedford Avenue stop or the train to the Nassau Avenue stop. The bus also runs right through the park along Bedford Avenue. Parking can usually be found fairly easily in the surrounding blocks.

Activities

Public space is a limited commodity for folks in Greenpoint and Williamsburg, so the locals take full advantage of McCarren Park. There are several facilities for sports, including seven tennis courts, a soccer field, five ball fields (although two "fields" are made of asphalt), and a running track. There are also handball, basketball, and two nice bocce courts. The Vincent V. Abate Playground is a great place to take the kids and includes animal-shaped fountains for summer cooling. Other activities include sunbathing, picnicking, and people-watching from the numerous benches. On Sunday afternoons you'll find Billyburg hipsters in ironically designed uniforms hanging out and playing kickball. A small poured-concrete skate park next to the restored McCarren Pool complex features banks and lips where you can grind to your heart's content. There is a decent year-round farmers market on Union Avenue between Driggs and N 12th Street every Saturday from 8 a.m. to 3 p.m. The park stays open until 1 a.m., and it is a fine place to check out the view of the Manhattan skyline on a summer evening.

The McCarren Pool

What began as a state-of-the-art pool facility before devolving into a dilapidated, graffiti-laden, urban-gothic temple to the quasi-racist gods of pre-gentrified 1980s Brooklyn, McCarren Pool is now once again a world-class recreational amenity in the heart of the hipster north. The Art Deco landmark opened in 1936, one of eleven WPA-built pools to open across the city that summer. Accommodating an astounding 6,800 swimmers, it quickly became a popular destination for all of Brooklyn. After a long decline and decades of deferred maintenance, the pool closed in the 1980s after neighborhood residents convinced city planners that a restored facility was not worth the hassle of dealing with the various outside elements who patronized the pool. The thinly veiled racism was a source of contention as the pool sat unused for over 20 years until the summer of 2005 when Noemi LaFrance's dance company reimagined the massive pool basin as a dance stage. Subsequent summers saw the site become a hugely popular music venue. These "Pool Parties" were forced to move to the Williamsburg waterfront in 2009 when long-debated plans to renovate the pool to return it to its original use finally got underway. The $50 million renovation, which includes multiple recreation spaces, was completed in 2012. Although the dimensions of the restored pool are smaller than the original (for a maximum of 1,500 bathers), there is now a year-round health and fitness facility located on the premises and parks planners have left open the possibility that the facility will one day be able to be converted an ice skating rink during the winter.

MAP 9

MAP 10

Berkeley Pl
Union St
President St
Carroll St
Montgomery Pl
Garfield Pl
1st St
2nd St
3rd St
4th St
5th St
6th St
7th St
8th St
9th St
10th St
11th St
12th St

Grand Army Plaza
Memorial Arch
Brooklyn Public Library
Eastern Parkway
Brooklyn Museum
Eastern Pkwy
Franklin Ave
The Brooklyn Museum
Botanic Garden

St Johns Pl
Lincoln Pl
Sterling Pl

Sixth Ave
Seventh Ave
Polhemus Pl
Fiske Pl
Prospect Park W
West Dr

F G 7th Avenue

Eighth Ave
Prospect Park W

Endale Arch
Meadowport Arch
9/11 Grove
Vale of Cashmere
Rose Garden
Mt Prospect Park
Herb Garden
Osborne Garden
Native Flora Garden
Brooklyn Botanic Garden
Cranford Rose Garden
Cherry Esplanade

Flatbush Ave

PAGE 106

Washington Ave

Magnolia Plaza/Visitor Center Entrance
Steinhardt Conservatory

President St
Carroll St
Montgomery St

3

Nelly's Lawn
Litchfield Villa
P

Prospect Park

1

Rock Garden
Butterfly Children's Garden
P Prospect Park

Crown

Franklin Ave

2
Park Maintenance Area
Boulder Bridge
Payne Hill
Ravine
Tennis House

5
Carousel
Discovery Garden
B S
Empire

East Dr

West Dr

7

The Pools (Swanboat)
Nethermead Arches
Littlemead
Midwood
East Wood Arch

Music Pagoda
Pagoda Swamp
Willink Hill

Sterling
Lefferts

F G 15th Street-Prospect Park
Bartel Pritchard Circle

Ballfields

Quaker Hill

3

Lullwater Bridge
Cleft Ridge Span

8

Map

Center Dr

Friends Cemetery

Terrace Bridge
Tullwater
Hill Dr

Oriental Pavilion

East Lake Dr

Ocean Ave

Midw
Rutla

Prospect Park SW
16th St
Windsor Pl
Sherman St
17th St
18th St
19th St

Butterfly Meadow
Lookout Hill
Well House Dr
Well House

Peninsula

4
P
Parkside Avenue

Q Parkside Avenue

Fenin
Hawtho

Prospect Expy

Terrace Pl
Seeley St
Vanderbilt St
Reeve Pl
Greenwood Ave

West Lake Dr

Prospect Lake

6

Duck Island
Three Sisters
West Island

9

Parks

Lenc

Prospect Park SW
Prospect Ave

South Lake Dr
Parkside Ave

Peristyle

Flatbush Ave

St Pauls Pl

10
MAP 13

Parade Ground

Caton Ave

General Information

NFT Maps: 9, 10, 13
Location: Prospect Park W, Parkside Ave bet Flatbush Ave,
Ocean Ave and Prospect Park SW
Phone: 718-965-8951
Events: 718-965-8999
Prospect Park Alliance: www.prospectpark.org or
@prospect_park

Overview

Visit Prospect Park on a sunny Saturday and you'll witness
thousands of people grilling, biking, fishing, sunbathing, flying
kites, and playing ball games. Designed by famed landscape
architects Frederick Law Olmstead and Calvert Vaux (better
known as the team behind Central Park in Manhattan), the park
is the 585-acre home to Long Meadow, Brooklyn's only forest,
and the relatively enormous Prospect Lake. In winter, smart
locals know to eschew Manhattan's overcrowded and overpriced
Rockefeller Center and ice skate at Wollman Rink for less than
half the price. Prospect Park is also proud to have the first urban
Audubon Center, opened in 2002.

Getting There

Depending on where in the park you're visiting, subway lines 2, 3,
4, 5, B, Q, F and G stop around the perimeter. If you drive, there is
limited parking available in the park at the Wollman Center (use
the Parkside/Ocean Avenue entrance), Bartel-Pritchard Circle,
and Litchfield Villa (enter at 3rd Street).

1. Prospect Park Zoo/Wildlife Center

Address: 450 Flatbush Ave
Phone: 718-399-7339
Website: www.prospectparkzoo.com
Subway: B, Q, S to Prospect Park

The Prospect Park Zoo boasts more than 80 different species of
animals in environments mirroring their natural habitats. Open
365 days a year, the zoo opens at 10 a.m. and closes at 5 p.m.
on weekdays, 5:30 pm on weekends from April to October.
November to March, the Zoo is open from 10 a.m. to 4:30 p.m.
daily. Admission is $8 for adults, $5 for kids ages 3-12, and $6 for
seniors. Free parking is available on Flatbush Avenue and the
park is handicapped accessible. Eating options are limited to
vending machines, but there are plenty of outdoor picnic tables
for those who take their own lunch. Purchases at the gift shop
contribute to the maintenance of the park.

2. Picnic House

The Picnic House is available for rent to the public (718-287-
6215) and, in addition to its magnificent view of the Long
Meadow, features an open interior of 3600 square-feet, a raised
stage, fireplace, piano, and restrooms. To reach it, enter the park
at 3rd Street and Prospect Park West and head southeast toward
the Long Meadow.

3. Long Meadow and Nethermead

The two largest open areas of the park, Long Meadow and
Nethermead, play host to group picnics, ball-playing, Frisbee-
throwing, kite-flying, strolling, lazing about, and everything else
people do in big green spaces.

4. Wollman Center and Rink

The $74 million Lakeside project, the largest capital project
since the park itself, is an effort to bring year-round activities
to this part of the park, and features ice skating in the winter,
and roller skating and paddle boats in warmer months. For more
information visit lakesidebrooklyn.com or @lakesideBKLYN.

5. Lefferts Historic House

Lefferts Historic House is located on Flatbush, near Empire
Boulevard between the zoo and the Carousel (open April to
October, $2 per ride). The house is used primarily as a children's
museum and aims to impart knowledge about America's history
through crafts, workshops, storytelling, displays, and a variety of
hands-on activities, like candle-making and butter-churning. The
house is open to the public April–November, Thursday through
Sunday 12 p.m.–5 p.m. (extended summer hours), December–
March 12 p.m.–4 p.m. on weekends and school holidays only; $3
suggested donation.

6. Prospect Lake

In addition to pedal boat rides, the Lake also accommodates
anglers, but don't expect to catch your evening's dinner—there
is a catch-and-release rule that helps to ensure the healthiness
of the fish population. Macy's holds a fishing contest every
July for kids 14 and under at the rustic shelter located near the
Wollman Rink.

7. The Bandshell

Each summer, the Bandshell hosts the Celebrate Brooklyn!
Performing Arts Festival, which organizes performances in
music, dance, film, and spoken word from June through August.
For a $3 suggested donation, this is an inexpensive way to enjoy
the Brooklyn arts in the summer months. Check the website for
performance details at bricartsmedia.org/cb or @CelebrateBklyn.

8. The Boathouse and Camperdown Elm

One of New York's first landmarks, this majestic building houses
the nation's first urban Audubon Center. In addition to exhibits,
hands-on activities, and an environmental reference library, the
Audubon Center also provides nature trail maps so you can take
a self-guided tour of some of the most beautiful areas of the
park. The space is also available for rental (718-287-3400).

If you decide against the self-guided tour, at least check out
the Camperdown Elm (the result of grafting a Scotch Elm onto
an American Elm), a prime example of the exquisite European
trees in Prospect Park. You can find it on the southeast side of
the Boathouse.

9. Drum Circle

Totally cool, and regularly scheduled—every Sunday from 2 p.m.
to dusk, April–October. Bring your bongos!

10. Parade Grounds

Across Parkside Avenue on the southeast corner of the park, the
Parade Grounds offer playing fields and a year-round tennis
center, complete with pro shop, clubhouse, locker rooms, a café,
and even tennis lessons. The tennis center (718-436-2500) is
open daily from 7 a.m. until 11 p.m.

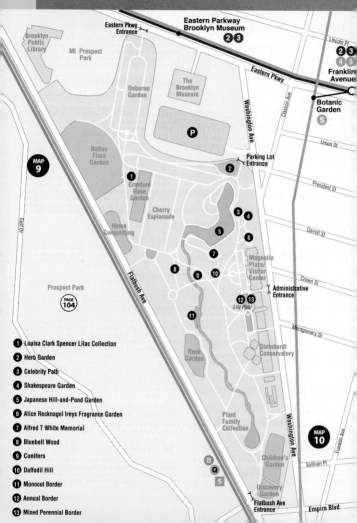

Brooklyn Museum & Botanic Garden

Eastern Pkwy Entrance

Eastern Parkway
Brooklyn Museum
2 **3**

Lincoln Pl

2 **3**
4 **5**

Franklin
Avenue

Eastern Pkwy

Botanic
Garden
S

Brooklyn
Public
Library

Mt Prospect
Park

Osborne
Garden

The Brooklyn
Museum

Washington Ave

Classon Ave

Union St

P

Parking Lot
Entrance

Native
Flora
Garden

1
Cranford
Rose
Garden

President St

2

Cherry
Esplanade

Home
Composting

3 **4**

Carroll St

5

6

7

Magnolia
Plaza/
Visitor
Center

Crown St

Administrative
Entrance

8

9 **10**

12 **13**
Lily Pool

Prospect Park

MAP
9

East Dr

MAP
**PAGE
104**

11

Rock
Garden

Steinhardt
Conservatory

Montgomery St

Flatbush Ave

Plant
Family
Collection

MAP
10

Franklin Ave

B

Q

S

Childrens
Garden

Washington Ave

Sullivan Pl

Discovery
Garden

Flatbush Ave
Entrance

Empire Blvd

1 Louisa Clark Spencer Lilac Collection

2 Herb Garden

3 Celebrity Path

4 Shakespeare Garden

5 Japanese Hill-and-Pond Garden

6 Alice Recknagel Ireys Fragrance Garden

7 Alfred T White Memorial

8 Bluebell Wood

9 Conifers

10 Daffodil Hill

11 Monocot Border

12 Annual Border

13 Mixed Perennial Border

Brooklyn Botanic Garden

NFT Maps: 9 & 10
Address: 150 Eastern Pkwy/990 Washington Ave
Phone: 718-623-7200
Website: www.bbg.org or @bklynbotanic
Subway: B, Q to Prospect Park; 2, 3 to Eastern Pkwy/Brooklyn Museum

Literally rising from the ashes (it was built on the site of a late 1800s ash dump), the Brooklyn Botanic Garden houses a number of diverse gardens, including the Plant Family Collection, Japanese Hill-and-Pond Garden, the Cranford Rose Garden, the Native Flora Garden, as well as the extraordinary Steinhardt Conservatory. Special events include the lovely Sakura Matsuri (Cherry Blossom Festival) in the spring, a lush, Asian flower market and indoor festival celebrating the Lunar New Year, plus plant sales, lectures, and changing exhibits. There is also a charming Children's Garden, offering tours and events just for kids. A welcome oasis in the bustling city, the garden is open to the public Tuesday to Sunday (also some holiday Mondays), from 8 a.m. on weekdays and 10 a.m. on weekends. The gardens close at 4:30 p.m. from November to March, and at 6 p.m. from April to October.

Admission is free on Saturdays 10 a.m. to 12 p.m. and on weekdays from mid-November to the end of February. Otherwise, entrance fees are $10 per adult, $5 for seniors and students (seniors are free on Fridays, and zilch if you're under 12 years of age).

While you're there, be sure to check out the Terrace Cafe, serving gourmet lunches and drinks outdoors in the warmer months and in the Conservatory in the winter months.

Brooklyn Museum

NFT Map: 9
Address: 200 Eastern Pkwy
Phone: 718-638-5000
Website: www.brooklynmuseum.org or @brooklynmuseum
Subway: 2, 3 to Eastern Pkwy/Brooklyn Museum

It's often noted that if Brooklyn were its own city, it would be the fourth largest in the country. By the same token, if it weren't for certain world-class institutions on the Upper East Side, the Brooklyn Museum would get a lot more attention than it does. Thus, a lot of conversations about the Brooklyn Museum start with something along the lines of, "In any other city..." and usually circle around to something along the lines of how hard it is to lure visitors from Manhattan.

That aside, we would be remiss not to remind everyone just how big and beefy the Brooklyn Museum is, and that in any other city it would probably draw millions every year. At 560,000 square feet, it's one of the larger art museums in the country. The museum's permanent collection of Egyptian artifacts is one of world's most extensive. Its recent track record of challenging exhibits and subject matter has positioned it on the cutting edge of the city's large art institutions—back in the day, Rudy Giuliani found a cause in a dung-depiction of the Virgin Mary, and more recently, the Elizabeth A. Sackler Center for Feminist Art acquired Judy Chicago's *The Dinner Party*.

In its early days the museum was, along with BAM, the Botanic Garden and the Brooklyn Children's Museum, part of the Brooklyn Institute of Arts and Sciences. In 2004 the museum underwent a $63 million renovation that added an ultramodern glass entrance and water feature that deinstitutionalized the imposing Beaux-Arts facade, and matched the more inviting look with a more pop aesthetic that took advantage of the borough's emerging cache. In addition to a Michelin-starred restaurant on site, the museum also features a fun museum shop offering an appealing mix of Brooklyn-focused wares.

Suggested donation for adults is $12, $8 for students and seniors, and free for members and kids under 12. The museum, cafe, and shops are closed on Monday and Tuesday, open Wednesday to Sunday 11 a.m.–6 p.m., and Thursdays until 10 p.m. Museum libraries and archives are open by appointment only. If you're up for a double dose of culture and nature, you can buy a combination "Art & Garden Ticket" for the museum and Botanic Garden. Tickets can be purchased only at the museum and cost $20 for adults and $11 for students and seniors. Getting to the museum is easy via its dedicated subway stop, and there is also a pay parking lot on site.

The "First Saturday" series is a popular program of free art and entertainment held during the evening of the first Saturday of every month. These Target-sponsored events feature live music, performance art, lectures, and dance parties set in the elegant Beaux-Arts Court with a cash bar and cafe. On "First Saturdays," the museum closes at 11 p.m. The museum also offers free "Arty Facts" workshops and activities for kids ages 4–7 and the Gallery/Studio program provides a variety of cool art classes for children and adults, including free work-study courses for teens.

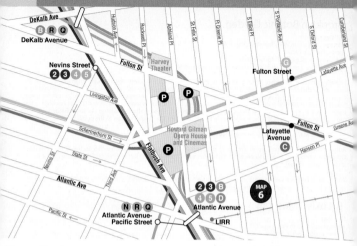

Harvey Theater

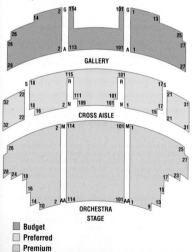

Howard Gilman Opera House

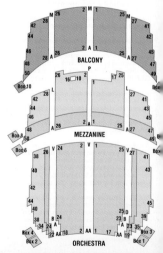

General Information

NFT Map: 6
Gilman Opera House: 30 Lafayette Ave
Harvey Theater: 651 Fulton St
Box Office Phone: 718-636-4100
Website: www.bam.org or @BAM_Brooklyn
Subway to Opera House: 2, 3, 4, 5, D, N, R, Q to Atlantic Avenue
Subway to Harvey Theater: 2, 3, 4, 5 to Nevins Street

Overview

Historic Fort Greene is home to the world-famous Brooklyn Academy of Music, better known as BAM. A thriving urban arts center dating back to 1861, BAM brings domestic and international performing arts and film to Brooklyn by way of two large theaters (the Harvey Theater and Howard Gilman Opera House), the BAM Rose Cinemas, the BAMcafe, and two smaller spaces in the Richard B. Fisher Building.

BAM presents two main seasons annually—the Spring Season and the Next Wave Festival—both of which are three-month celebrations of cutting-edge dance, theater, music, and opera. The Spring Season is geared toward major national and international artists and companies while the Next Wave focuses on groundbreaking and contemporary. Live performances at the BAMcafe happen year-round, as do BAMcinematek presentations at the BAM Rose Cinemas. Visit the BAM website for a comprehensive calendar of events and ticket information.

Seeing Stuff at BAM

It's rarely boring at BAM—we definitely recommend going at least a few times to check out the scene. One great way to get your feet wet is at the BAMcinematek series. The public spaces are cool and the stripped-down Harvey Theater is a must-see (a word of warning: If you're buying tickets for performances at the Harvey, be prepared to either spend a little extra on decent seats, or take a cushion with you to prevent fanny fatigue in the cheap seats!).

Here are the main spaces of BAM:
The Howard Gilman Opera House—The main space. A beautiful setting for music, dance, and just about anything else. Recommended.
The Harvey Theater—As we mentioned, horrific seating upstairs, but a great stripped-to-the-bones renovation makes it look utterly cool. The site of many of BAM's theater performances.
The Richard B. Fisher Building—Comprises the Fishman Space, an intimate 250-seat performance venue and Hillman Studio, a rehearsal and performance space.
The BAM Rose Cinemas—Great first-run movies, excellent documentaries, revivals, and festivals, good seating, and munchies like everywhere else.
Lepercq Space/BAMcafe—More than just for noshing, the cafe's "Eat, Drink & Be Literary" series features a buffet meal and a writer talking about his or her creative process. Cafe features free music on many nights.

How to Get Tickets

Buy individual tickets through the BAM website or by calling the box office. Memberships start at $75 and benefits include priority notice of upcoming shows and events, and free BAMfans parties for members in their 20s & 30s.

General Information

NFT Map: 5
Address: 12 MetroTech Ctr/330 Jay St
Website: www.metrotechbid.org
Subway: A, C, F, R to Jay St MetroTech; 2, 3 to Hoyt Street

Overview

The MetroTech Center is a 16-acre commercial/governmental/educational/cultural/yuppie pedestrian entity adjacent to Borough Hall in Downtown Brooklyn. Built on what was one of the earliest settled ambits in Brooklyn, the factories, frame houses, and shops that used to occupy the ten-block neighborhood were leveled to make way for the MetroTech project in the '70s. Envisioned as a center of research and technology to rival California's Silicon Valley, New York's Polytechnic University signed on as the project's sponsor and remains an integral focus of MetroTech's continued expansion. Needless to say, it is but a faint shadow of Silicon Valley.

Today, the MetroTech Commons—located between Jay Street and Duffield Street—provides the area with a necessary verdant refuge from the surrounding cement, exhibiting proof of the urban center's successful development. The complex is home to offices of JP Morgan Chase, National Grid, and Empire Blue Cross Blue Shield. The public tenants that also reside within the hyper-sterile universe include the New York City Fire Department's central data processing center, the MTA, and the city's Department of Information and Telecommunications Technology, as well as the New York State Supreme Court and Kings County Family Court.

Several scholastic institutions including Polytechnic University, the New York City College of Technology, Brooklyn Friends School, St. Joseph High School, and the Helen Keller Services for the Blind are all located within the campus. There's even a hotel (New York Marriott Brooklyn Hotel) and a church (St. Boniface Church). Empire Blue Cross and Blue Shield is housed at 9 MetroTech Center South, a 19-story edifice that was the first commercial office building constructed in New York City after September 11th, 2001.

In 1990, four historic houses were moved from their Johnson Street homes to now-permanent residences on nearby Duffield Street. Along with Brooklyn's Old Fire Department Headquarters on Jay Street, Poly's Student Center (a renovated Episcopal Church originally built in 1847) right on the Commons, and the beautiful Old American Telegraph & Telephone building on Willoughby Street, the transplanted buildings are part of MetroTech's effort to preserve the community's historic architecture.

In an effort to support local emerging artists, the Commons features rotating outdoor art exhibitions as part of the Public Art Fund. Participants are encouraged to respond to the exhibition space and the surrounding downtown area in their work. The Commons also hosts to several cultural events throughout the year, including the BAM Rhythm & Blues Festival.

Perhaps our favorite little-known fact about MetroTech Center is the presence of one of the city's three TKTS booths, right on Jay Street between Tech Place and Willoughby. You should still get there early (15 minutes before it opens at 11 am is perfect), but it's better than fighting the crowds in Times Square, hands-down.

1. Brooklyn Bridge

NFT Map: 5
At the time of its construction in 1883, this was the world's longest suspension bridge. Today, it is still widely celebrated for its structural functionality and beauty, and crossing the Brooklyn Bridge remains a quintessential New York experience. We recommend you stroll across by foot from Manhattan and reward yourself with lunch at Grimaldi's upon arrival.

2. Brooklyn Heights Promenade

NFT Map: 5
This 1,826-foot promenade undoubtedly boasts the best views of lower Manhattan (unless you live in one of the houses behind it). In addition to the skyline, the path offers spectacular vistas of the Statue of Liberty, the Brooklyn Bridge, and the boat traffic in New York Harbor. There are also plenty of benches on which to rest your weary bones and take it all in. The serenity of the path is an engineering triumph considering it's right above the BQE.

3. Dyker Beach Golf Course

Okay, so it's not the best course you've ever played, but considering its location and price, the DBGC is an attractive choice for urban golfers. The course has a good mix of difficult and easy holes and great views of the Verrazano Bridge. For more information, call 718-836-9722.

4. Floyd Bennett Field

Formerly marshland, this plot of land has been used for a variety of purposes: Garbage dump, glue factory, municipal airport, and naval base. Today Floyd Bennett Field is part of the Gateway National Recreation Area. At 1,500 acres, this park is hardly ever crowded and contains nature trails, two public campgrounds, a wildlife refuge and grassland bioreserve, and breathtaking views of the bay. FBF is quite expansive, so be sure to take some form of wheels to explore the grounds.

5. Marine Park

Marine Park, connected to Floyd Bennett Field, is another great getaway in Eastern Brooklyn. This 798-acre park offers nature trails through the salt marshes, fishing, a running track, the Marine Park Golf Course (the largest in Brooklyn), and organized athletics (most notably baseball). Marine Park is also a haven for bird-watching enthusiasts—over one hundred species of birds have been spotted in this area.

6. Fort Greene Park

NFT Map: 6
The oldest park in Brooklyn, this hilly park is a sanctuary for the residents of Fort Greene. During the summer, Fort Greene Park hosts a series of outdoor films and free concerts. The park also offers a farmers market every Saturday on the corner of Washington Park and DeKalb Avenue. www.fortgreenepark.org.

7. Brooklyn Brewery

NFT Map: 2
Since 1987 this independent brewery has been cranking out top-notch beers. On weekend afternoons the brewery hosts free tours of its Williamsburg digs. And did we mention the free samples at tour's end? The brewery also offers a happy hour every Friday night 6 p.m.–11 p.m. (take your own eats!). 718-486-7422; www. brooklynbrewery.com or @BrooklynBrewery.

8. Piers in Red Hook

NFT Map: 8
Two points of interest here. For gawking purposes only—head over to Red Hook's Brooklyn Cruise Terminal to catch The Queen Mary 2, the largest ocean liner doing the transatlantic run these days. If "The Mary" is there, you don't really need an address, you'll see 'er. Secondly, and worth more than just a stare—check out Louis Valentino Jr. Park and Pier, located at the western end of Coffey Street in Red Hook. This pier is great to check out at dusk for a romantic stroll. And if it ever does actually happen, this will be THE place to see The Statue of Liberty come alive and attack Manhattan (i.e. great views).

Brooklyn College at CUNY

NFT Maps: 13 & 16
Address: 2900 Bedford Ave
Phone: 718-951-5000
Website: www.brooklyn.cuny.edu
Subway: 2, 5 to Brooklyn College/Flatbush Ave

Founded in 1930, Brooklyn College is a part of the City University of New York, the nation's leading public urban university. Situated on a charming campus in Midwood, Brooklyn College educates over 17,000 students in five separate schools, including the School of Business, School of Education, School of Humanities and Social Sciences, School of Natural and Behavioral Sciences, and School of Visual, Media and Performing Arts.

Brooklyn Law School

NFT Map: 5
Address: 250 Joralemon St
Phone: 718-625-2200
Website: www.brooklaw.edu
Subway: 2, 3, 4, 5 to Borough Hall; R to Court St; A, C, F to Jay St

Brooklyn Law School first opened its doors in 1901 with 18 students. Today, the school has an enrollment of over 1,400. It is headquartered at 250 Joralemon Street and One Boerum Place, the intersection of the landmark Brooklyn Heights Historic District, the Brooklyn Civic Center, and Downtown Brooklyn.

Long Island University—Brooklyn Campus

NFT Map: 5
Address: 1 University Plz
Phone: 718-488-1011
Website: www.liu.edu/brooklyn
Subway: 2, 3, 4, 5 to Nevins St; R to DeKalb Ave; A, C, G to Hoyt-Schermerhorn

LIU-Brooklyn offers more than 160 programs of study to undergraduate and graduate students within the Conolly College of Liberal Arts and Sciences, School of Business, Public Administration and Information Sciences, School of Education, School of Health Professions, School of Nursing, and the Arnold & Marie Schwartz College of Pharmacy and Health Sciences.

NYU Polytechnic School of Engineering

NFT Map: 5
Address: 6 MetroTech Ctr
Phone: 718-260-3600
Website: engineering.nyu.edu
Subway: A, C, F, R to Jay St MetroTech; 2, 3, 4, 5 to Borough Hall; B, Q to DeKalb Ave

Founded in 1854, Polytechnic University is New York City's leading educational resource in science and technology education and research. After acquiring New York University's engineering school in the 1970s, the institution was reunited with NYU in 2008 and in 2014 fully merged with NYU, becoming another school in the NYU empire. Departments include Applied Physics, Chemical and Biomolecular Engineering, Civil and Urban Engineering, Computer Science, Electrical and Computer Engineering, and Finance and Risk Engineering.

Pratt Institute

NFT Map: 6
Address: 200 Willoughby Ave
Phone: 718-636-3600
Website: www.pratt.edu
Subway: G to Clinton-Washington

Founded in 1887, Pratt Institute is an undergraduate and graduate institution that includes the School of Architecture, School of Art and Design, School of Information and Library Science, School of Liberal Arts and Sciences, and Center for Continuing Education and Professional Studies. Its 4,600 undergraduate and graduate students are educated at two campuses in New York City. The Brooklyn campus is home to the schools of art and design, architecture, and liberal arts and sciences. Pratt's Brooklyn grounds are endlessly fascinating and beautifully landscaped, and feature a nice collection of outdoor sculpture.

SUNY Downstate Medical Center

NFT Map: 10
Address: 450 Clarkson Ave
Phone: 718-270-1000
Website: www.downstate.edu
Subway: 2, 5 to Winthrop St

The original school of medicine at SUNY Downstate Medical Center was founded as the Long Island College Hospital in 1860. SUNY Downstate comprises Colleges of Medicine, Nursing and Health Related Professions, Schools of Graduate Studies and Public Health, and the University Hospital of SUNY Downstate.

Golf

Driving Range	Address	Phone	Fees	Map
Brooklyn Golf Center	3200 Flatbush Ave	718-253-6816	$9 for 65 balls, $12 for 285 balls	n/a

Golf Courses	Address	Phone	Fees	Map
Dyker Beach Golf Course	7th Ave & 86th St	718-836-9722	Weekend fees $17/early, twilight/$38 morning and afternoon; weekday fees $16–$27, non-residents add $8	15

Swimming

McCarren Park Pool	Lorimer St & Bayard St	718-965-6580	June–Labor Day	Outdoor	2
Metropolitan Rec Center	261 Bedford Ave	718-599-5707	Year-round	Indoor	2
Bushwick Houses	Flushing Ave & Humboldt St	718-452-2116	June–Labor Day	Outdoor	3
Commodore Barry Swimming Pool	Park Ave & Navy St	718-243-2593	June–Labor Day	Outdoor	5
Douglass and Degraw Pool	3rd Ave & Nevins St	718-625-3268	June–Labor Day	Outdoor	6
PS 20 Playground	225 Adelphi St	718-625-6101	June–Labor Day	Outdoor	6
JHS 57/ HS 26	117 Stuyvesant Ave	718-452-0519	June–Labor Day	Outdoor	7
Kosciusko Pool	Kosciusko St & Marcy Ave	718-622-5271	June–Labor Day	Outdoor	7
Red Hook Pool	155 Bay St	718-722-3211	June–Labor Day	Outdoor	8
Sunset Swimming Pool	7th Ave & 43rd St	718-965-6578	July–Labor Day	Outdoor	11
Betsy Head Swimming Pool	697 Thomas S. Boyland St	718-965-6581			n/a
Brownsville Rec Center	155 Linden Blvd	718-485-4633	Year-round	Indoor	n/a
David Fox/PS 251	Ave H & E 54 St	718-531-2437	June–Labor Day	Outdoor	n/a
Glenwood Playground	Ralph Ave & Farragut Rd	718-531-2480	June–Labor Day	Outdoor	n/a
Howard Playground	Glenmore Ave & Mother Gaston Blvd	718-385-1023	June–Labor Day	Outdoor	n/a
Lindower Park	E 60th St & Strickland Ave	718-531-4852	June–August	Outdoor	n/a
St. John's Rec Center	1251 Prospect Pl	718-771-2787	Year-round	Indoor	n/a

General Information

Parks Permit Office: 212-360-8131
Website: www.nycgovparks.org/permits/tennis-permits
Permit Locations (Manhattan): The Arsenal, 830 Fifth Ave & 64th St; Paragon Sporting Goods Store, 867 Broadway & 18th St

Overview

There are a decent number of courts in Brooklyn, but they vary greatly in quality. If you're anal (like us), always carry some rope with you so you can strap down the center of the net to a reasonable height—it's usually the first thing to go (with the net itself being second) on non-maintained courts. Juxtaposed with all this is one of the crown jewels of NYC tennis, the **Prospect Park Tennis Center (Map 13)**, on the corner of Parkside Avenue and Coney Island Avenue in the Parade Grounds just across the street from Prospect Park itself. The center has a bunch of well-maintained Har-Tru (green clay for you bashers) courts as well as two hard courts. You can reserve courts in advance with a credit card, take lessons, play competitively, and chill out at the café. In winter the center puts a bubble over the courts so you can play year-round—and permits aren't required for the winter season, so just bring your credit card. Check out www.prospectpark.org for more information on rates, lessons, etc.

Getting a Permit

The Parks tennis season starts on the first Saturday of April and ends on the Sunday before Thanksgiving. Permits are good for use until the end of the season at all public courts in all boroughs, and are good for one hour of singles or two hours of doubles play. Fees are: Adults (18–61 yrs), $200; Juniors (17 yrs and under), $10; Senior Citizen (62 yrs and over), $20; Single-play tickets $15. Permits can be acquired in person at the Parks Department headquarters Central Park or Paragon Sporting Goods or online via the Parks website or by mail (applications can be found online). Renewals are accepted in person, by mail or via the website, except if originally purchased at Paragon.

Tennis

	Address	Phone	Type	Map
McCarren Park Tennis Courts	N 13th St & Bedford Ave	718-963-0830	Outdoor, 7 courts, hard surface, lessons offered	2
Ft Greene Park	DeKalb Ave & S Portland Ave	718-722-3218	Outdoor, 6 courts, hard surface	6
Decatur Playground	Lewis Ave & Decatur St	718-493-7612	Outdoor, 1 court, hard surface	7
Jackie Robinson Park	Malcolm X Blvd & Chauncey St	718-439-4298	Outdoor, 4 courts, hard surface	7
One Van Voohrhes Park	Hicks St & Pacific St	718-722-3213	Outdoor, 2 courts, hard surface	8
Gravesend Playground	18th Ave & 56th St	718-965-6502	Outdoor, 8 courts, hard surface	12
Prospect Park Tennis Center	95 Prospect Park W	718-436-2500	Indoor, lessons offered	13
Ft Hamilton Athletic Field School Playground	Colonial Rd & 83rd St	718-439-4295	Outdoor, 4 courts, hard surface	14
John J Carty Park	Fort Hamilton Pkwy & 95th St	718-439-4298	Outdoor, 10 courts, hard surface, lessons offered	14
Leif Ericsson Park	Eighth Ave & 66th St	718-259-4016	Outdoor, 9 courts, hard surface, lessons offered	14
McKinley Park	7th Ave & 75th St	718-259-4016	Outdoor, 8 courts, hard surface	14
Shore Road Playground	Shore Rd & 95th St	718-259-4016	Outdoor, 4 courts, hard surface	14
Lucille Ferrera Tennis Courts	Cropsey Ave & Bay 8th St	718-259-4016	Outdoor, 9 courts, hard surface, lessons offered	15
Friends Field	Ave L & E 4th St	718-965-6502	Outdoor, 2 courts, hard surface	16
Kelly Playground	Ave S & E 14th St	718-946-1373	Outdoor, 7 courts, hard surface	16
McDonald Avenue Playground	McDonald Ave & Ave S	718-946-1373	Outdoor, 7 courts, hard surface	16
Bensonhurst Park	Cropsey Ave & Bay Pkwy	718-946-5048	Outdoor, 8 hardcourts	n/a
Bridgeview Racquet Club	9000 Bay Pkwy	718-372-6878	Outdoor, 8 hardcourts	n/a
Joseph T McGuire Park	Bergen Ave & Avenue W		Outdoor, 3 hardcourts	n/a
Kaiser Playground	Neptune Ave & W 25th St	718-946-1350	Outdoor, 12 hardcourts, lessons	n/a
Lincoln Terrace Park	Portal St & Rochester Ave	718-804-7077	Outdoor, 8 hardcourts, lighted	n/a
Linden Playground	Linden Blvd & Vermont St	718-927-2059	Outdoor, 8 hardcourts	n/a
Manhattan Beach Park	Oriental Blvd b/n Ocean Ave & Mackenzie St	718-946-1373	Outdoor, 7 hardcourts	n/a
Marine Park	Fillmore Ave & Stuart St	718-376-1675	Outdoor, 15 hardcourts	n/a
Mill Basin Health & Tennis	2350 E 69th St	718-444-3600	Private, 6 hardcourts	n/a
Pacplex	1500 Paerdegat Ave N	718-209-1010	Outdoor, 1 hardcourt	n/a

Overview

In most cities, bowling is an affordable way for people of all ages to have fun, but in New York (even in Brooklyn), it'll burn a hole through your wallet. You don't have to be rich, but you might want to start saving now, and when you're ready, you have options. A North Brooklyn bowling duel was set off in 2009 with the grand opening of **Brooklyn Bowl (Map 2)**, the world's first LEED-certified bowling facility complete with 16 lanes, a very active concert stage, local beers, and delicious food from Blue Ribbon. It's smaller, slightly older rival **The Gutter (Map 2)** is a vintage style bowling alley with great brews and fixtures so retro you don't even mind when they mess up your score. **Melody Lanes (Map 11)** will provide everything you could hope for in an old-school bowling experience.

Bowling	Address	Phone	Fees	Map
Brooklyn Bowl	61 Wythe Ave	718-963-3369	$25 per lane per 1/2 hour, $3.50 for shoes.	2
The Gutter	200 N 14th St	718-387-3585	$6-$7, $2 shoe rental	2
Melody Lanes	461 37th St	718-832-2695	$5.50–$7.00 per game, $3.50 for shoe rental	11
Shell Lanes	1 Bouck Ct	718-336-6700	$3.25–$5.25 per game, $3.50 for shoe rental	n/a
Strike 10 Lanes	6161 Strickland Ave	718-763-6800	$6.00-$8.00 per game $4.25 for shoe rental	n/a

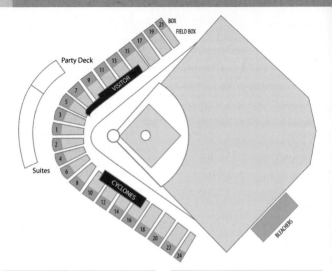

General Information

Website: www.brooklyncyclones.com or @BKCyclones
Location: 1904 Surf Ave
Phone: 718-37-BKLYN

Overview

Since 2001, MCU Park has been the home of the Brooklyn Cyclones, a Class-A minor league affiliate of the New York Mets. With tickets for games as low as $10, you can take your whole family, stuff them full of hot dogs, beer, and pretzels, and still pay less than half of what you'd pay at Citi Field. The crowd at MCU (given its location) couldn't be anything but colorful, and the 'Clones keep things lively and competitive, having clinched several division championships since their inception. Mascots Sandy the Seagull and PeeWee (the Seagull) will keep kids and adults alike enamored with their crazy antics. Imagine the crack of the bat, the roar of the crowd, the holy toots of the calliope mixed with screams from the Cyclone's namesake mere blocks away, all this cowering in the shadow of the Parachute Drop. This is American baseball—enough to make Ken Burns weep or bring to mind the immortal words of Roy Hobbs: "My dad...I love baseball."

MCU is also a major concert venue hosting sold-out shows by the likes of Bjork, Phish, Daft Punk, and Snoop Dogg.

How to Get There—Driving

The Belt Parkway to Ocean Parkway is the quickest route. Stay on Ocean Parkway to Surf Avenue. The stadium is on the south side of Surf Avenue between W 17th and W 19th streets. Parking for all Cyclones games is available in a lot right next to the park. If you're allergic to the Belt, you can take Ocean Avenue from the Prospect Park Expressway all the way to Surf Avenue, but we guarantee it won't be quicker, just different.

How to Get There—Mass Transit

Take the D, F, N, or Q train down to the Coney Island/Stillwell Avenue stop, or ride the 36, 64, 68, or 74 bus to Stillwell Avenue and Surf Avenue. MCU Park is just a few blocks west along Surf Avenue using either one.

How to Get Tickets

You can order individual or season tickets for Cyclones games online through the website, in person at the box office, or over the phone.

General Information

Address: 620 Atlantic Avenue, Brooklyn NY 11217
Website: barclayscenter.com or @barclayscenter
Nets: www.nba.com/nets or @BrooklynNets
Islanders: www.newyorkislanders.com or @NYIslanders
Tickets: 877-77-BKTIX

Overview

Barclays Center, the home of the Brooklyn Nets and New York Islanders, opened in 2012 as part of the controversial $4.9 billion Atlantic Yards redevelopment project that decked over LIRR tracks and focused everyone's attention on controversial eminent domain issues, for a while there at least, until Barbra, Jay-Z, and Deron Williams redirected it again.

The original architectural design was created by Frank Gehry, the king of urban revitalization, but it was horrendously expensive, especially following the 2008 financial collapse, so the firm of Ellerbe Becket took over. The scaled-down plans proved to be horrendously uninspiring, eliciting negative comparisons to an airplane hangar and/or the downtown Indianapolis arena where the NBA's Pacers play (also designed by Ellerbe Becket). In the end, expectations were lowered just enough to make the final product look kind of cool: the brown weathered steel exterior evokes the site's industrial past and pays slight tribute to the brownstone materials in the surrounding neighborhoods. In addition, the height is not overwhelming; the structure almost fits snugly into the Flatbush Avenue streetscape. The triangular public space at the intersection of Flatbush and Atlantic is visually appealing: the new subway entrance features a living planted roof and the arena's exterior structure, along with its oculus sky opening (don't worry, we had to look up that word, too) and mesmerizing LED screen is—yikes—almost kind of elegant. As arenas go, it's pretty nice looking. And it's about 59 times more appealing looking than the Atlantic Center Mall, if you want to know the truth.

The Brooklyn Nets began playing at the arena for the 2012–13 season after moving from New Jersey. The NHL's New York Islanders began skating at Barclays Center for the 2015-16 season after leaving Nassau Coliseum (elsewhere on Long Island) where they had played since their founding in 1972. The arena has hosted college basketball almost since it opened, including the Barclays Center Classic, an early season eight-team tournament. For those who don't dig basketball, the concerts (accommodating 19,000 fans) have been big time: Barbra Streisand, Jay-Z (who owned a small stake in the Nets before becoming a sports agent), Billy Joel, not to mention the MTV Video Music Awards, which were broadcast from Barclays Center.

How to Get There—Driving

Parking is so limited that Barclays Center practically demands that you use public transport, but if you must, you can reserve a spot at the center (should there be any available, being a suiteholder helps), find a nearby garage, or scour for street parking.

How to Get There—Mass Transit

Part of the draw of Barclays Center is its proximity to Brooklyn's largest transportation hub. The 2, 3, 4, 5, B, D, N, Q and R trains all service the arena, and you can also take the to Lafayette Avenue or the to Fulton Street. The LIRR stops at Atlantic Terminal, just across the street from the arena. In addition, eleven bus lines stop right outside or nearby.

How to Get Tickets

To avoid exorbitant Ticketmaster charges, the American Express Box Office (yes, even the freakin' box office has naming rights attached to it) is open Monday–Saturday 12 pm–6 pm (Saturday 4 pm). Despite being a box office, they will not sell tickets to events on the first day tickets are offered to the public.

General Information

Mailing Address: 2 Broadway, New York NY 10004
Call 511 for all Subway, Rail and Bus Information
From Outside New York State: 877-690-5116
International Callers: 212-878-7000
MTA Police: 212-878-1001
New York Transit Museum: 718-694-1600
New York City Paratransit Information: 877-337-2017
Website: www.mta.info
Twitter: @MTA or @NYCTSubwayScoop

Overview

Sometimes—often at rush hour, and especially if there is a murky "police investigation" or "train traffic ahead" or a "sick passenger" or even just some numbnut fellow straphanger clipping his nails—the New York City subway can unite people of all ethnicities, backgrounds and cultural heritages in a way not even Michael Jackson could dream of: We all hate the damn thing. And yet, as soon as we get to wherever it is we're trying to go and we leave the station and exhale a deep sigh of relief (or depending on the clientele and time of year, simply exhale), we thank our lucky stars that New York City has the best subway, bus and commuter rail lines in the world. Which is to say, suck it up, cheese, and come celebrate with us this massive urban achievement.

For starters, trains run 24 hours a day, though some lines only operate during rush hours (look for the "express" diamond on the map). The system has 468 stations, and will soon have more when the Second Avenue Subway eventually comes on line. The bus system is also good, and downright essential in many outerborough neighborhoods. Although there are a handful of dedicated bus lanes on major thoroughfares, Manhattan buses are only as fast as traffic allows, and are perhaps best left to the elderly and infirm, especially during rush hour. Select Bus Service on certain routes, where riders pay fares at on-street machines before getting on (and receive receipts that are spot-checked), has sped up what for so long had been such a long and tedious journey up, down or across town.

Since the subway runs 24 hours a day—and let's be clear, very few places provide 24-hour service—that means maintenance work must happen while riders are using the system. That also means you should be wary of track work and schedule changes, particularly late at night and on weekends. The MTA's website, www.mta.info, always displays the current status of each line, and has a weekend planner (with a fancy retro-map look) that will help you navigate service changes; you can also subscribe to email and text alerts about specific lines. Look for posted signs and whiteboard scribblings at subway stations for changes, and for Pete's sake, don't hesitate to ask if you're unsure: you have only yourself to blame if you meant to get off at Fulton Street and somehow ended up at Jay Street.

Folk wisdom dictates that a single subway fare costs roughly the same as a slice of pizza; depends where you get pizza, I guess. When considering raising fares, the MTA's board walks a fine line balancing everything. The tyranny of the pizza index (and the headlines generated) mean that often money comes from raising fares in other areas: the prices of monthly or weekly passes, the types of passes available (not so long ago there were one-day passes), and even the cost of the MetroCards themselves ($1, just so you're clear). Service cuts also prevent fare hikes; every so often the board will reveal a slew of draconian service cuts seemingly meant to soften the blow for wider acceptance of fare hikes; sometimes cuts even happen, such as reduced late-night service, certain trains or buses being cut altogether, and so on.

In recent years, the Authority has been making substantial gains in making the system more user friendly. For one, stations have been receiving significant upgrades to make the 100-plus year-old system ADA compliant—itself a massive undertaking. Other smaller yet important features include countdown clocks in stations, so you don't have to read tea leaves to figure out when your train is coming or whether you should take the local arriving or wait for an express.

If you find yourself hankering for the old Lionel train set in your parents' basement, or if the hair on the back of your neck stands up when you hear the sound of an old steam whistle, or if you just are interested in subway history, consider checking out the New York Transit Museum. Housed in a historic 1936 IND subway station in Brooklyn Heights, and easily accessible by subway, the museum is the largest museum in the United States devoted to urban public transportation history, and one of the premier institutions of its kind in the world. The museum explores the development of the greater New York metropolitan region through the presentation of exhibitions, tours, educational programs and workshops dealing with the cultural, social and technological history of public transportation. Go to www.mta.info for details of current exhibits and programs, or to shop the Museum's online store.

Fares

There's a single $2.75 fare for riding the subway and most buses as far as you want. Some buses are "express," meaning they make fewer stops and get you where you're going faster for $6.50. The MetroCard, a magnetic farecard, is the method for paying the subway fare and the primary method for paying the public bus fare (buses also accept coins but not paper bills). MetroCards may be purchased at many locations and used at all subway stations and on all public buses within New York City, with a 11 percent pay-per-ride bonus for amounts over $5.50. MetroCard vending machines that accept cash and credit and debit cards can be found at most subway stations. If you use a MetroCard, you can transfer for free within two hours between subway and bus, bus and subway, and bus to bus. Seven- and 30-day unlimited ride MetroCards are also available. Under the current pricing plan (including the pay-per-ride bonus), seven-day unlimited ride cards are worth it if you enter the subway more than 12 times a week. The cost-effective cutoff for 30-day unlimited cards is 48 rides, meaning to and from work five days a week and then a handful of trips in addition to regular commuting. In other words, if you use the subway each day, then it's usually worth it (especially if you get a transit benefit through work). The MetroCards themselves now cost $1, but are able to handle both unlimited-ride and pay-per-ride options.

There are half-price reduced fare cards available for customers 65 years and over and people with a qualified disability. You must apply for, and be approved to receive it; applications and further information can be found at the MTA's website. Up to three children under 44 inches tall may ride for free with a fare-paying adult on subways and on local buses.

Some handy hints on how to use your MetroCard: A steady, even swiping motion is best. If you're told to swipe your card again in the same turnstile, do it, or you will lose your fare (or be forced to find a booth agent to let you in). The turnstiles are programmed not to let you use an unlimited MetroCard twice in less than 18 minutes at the same station (even at different entrances). When going through the tall gated turnstiles, it's not necessary to wait until the person ahead of you is completely through to swipe your card—it will be read as long as they have started to push through.

A free copy of the subway map is available at any subway station booth, and although it should go without saying, we feel compelled to say that while the maps and all this information in general is current as of press time, everything is subject to change; current maps and information are always available at the MTA's website, www.mta.info.

Transfers

You can transfer from a downtown to an uptown train on the same line at all express stations, major junctions, and some local stations. Any trains that roll into the same station, or into stations that are connected on the map by a black line, allow free transfers. Free transfers are also allowed between the train and bus, bus and train, and bus and bus, as long as you make the transfer within 2 hours of paying your fare. If you use coins to pay for the bus, ask the driver for a transfer card (valid only on other buses).

Lines

As a result of most of the system being built by three competing companies in the 40 or so years after 1904, the coverage isn't exactly logical or complete. Going north-south is pretty easy, as almost all of the lines do this. Getting cross town and to the edges of the map is difficult—whole neighborhoods in the outer boroughs are completely ignored. The Straphangers Campaign rates the lines in a variety of categories every year, including regularity of service, chance of getting a seat, and cleanliness. They post their results on their website at www.straphangers.org. According to unscientific "research" by NFT staff, the A-C-E trains take forever to arrive, the 4-5-6 are always clean but crowded, the 1 has pretty frequent train arrivals, hardly anyone rides the J-M, and you can finish *War and Peace* while waiting for the G.

Rules (written and unwritten)

Subway rules:
• If you're standing next to the door when it gets to the station, try to get out of the way as much as possible.
• Don't hug, lean on, practice your exotic dance moves, or do anything except hold onto the poles.
• Never pull the emergency brake unless the train's going to run someone over.
• No one living in NY calls them the "blue train" or the "red train." Use the numbers or letters, and group them if necessary ("I took the N-R to get here.").
• Wait 'til everyone leaves the train before you start moving in. Of course, many people ignore this rule. Feel free to practice your football moves if you're still trying to exit the train.
• You're allowed to take your bike on the train, but do it at non-rush hour times and towards the less-crowded front and back of the train. Use the service gate to enter and exit the station—don't use any of the turnstiles or high gates. The lettered trains are easier to fit a bike onto because they have roomier cars.
• Don't lean against the door. (Apparently that's a rule.)
• Don't walk between trains. (Try to put up with the urine smell or the off-key do-wop group until the next stop.)
• Don't hold the door. (Hold it if your friend is actually running to catch the train, not when they're still getting their MetroCard or can't figure out how to swipe it.)
• Even if the train is empty, you can still get ticketed by undercover subway police for putting your bags or feet on an empty seat.
• Everybody does it, but you can get ticketed for eating or drinking on the train. (But, apparently, applying make-up and deodorant is still okay.)

Bus rules:
• Stand away from the curb!
• Have your card out before you step into the bus.
• Hold the back door when you exit so it doesn't slam in the next person's face.
• Between 10 pm and 5 am, you can ask the bus driver to make stops at non-bus stop places along the route, provided he/she can safely do it. Good luck with that endeavor!

In some cities, using a bike to get around means you're a broke-ass failure, but here it's something to aspire to, and you'll be in good company. It's generally safer to bike in Brooklyn than in Manhattan, but be careful. Ditch the headphones, bike with the traffic, stay off the sidewalks, use a white headlight and red taillight at night, and if we catch you without a helmet, there'll be hell to pay. You'd also be smart to invest in the best chain you can find. Prospect Park is fantastic for cycling, or try following Ocean Parkway down to Coney Island. Biking through Brooklyn down to the beach at Fort Tilden is another good route, though that's actually in Queens. The Shore Parkway Greenway covers much of Brooklyn's shoreline, featuring a dedicated bike path and remarkable views. If you want to get political, ride down Bedford Avenue through the Hasidic part of Williamsburg. Hasidic residents had the bike lane removed because it posed a "religious hazard," especially with young ladies riding in short skirts. Neighborhood cyclists protested, and although some outlaws repainted the bike lane under the cover of darkness, Bedford Avenue currently has no official bike lane (though it is a "recommended on-street route" and there's a proper bike lane along Driggs). For an organized event, try the 40-mile Brooklyn Waterfront Epic Ride, the annual Tour de Brooklyn (the 21.5-mile route changes every year), Critical Mass (a monthly ride to support non-polluting modes of transportation), and let's not forget the sexiest, bounciest one of all, the World Naked Bike Ride. Skaters welcome. Bicycle rentals are available at Ride Brooklyn or On the Move near Prospect Park, or Mr. C's Cycles near the Shore Parkway Greenway. They even have tandems! And the Citi Bike share program is designed for quick trips around town; annual memberships cost $149 and entitle the user to unlimited trips of up to 45 minutes. One-day and 7-day "Access Passes" are also available.

General Information

Bicycle Defense Fund:
  www.bicycledefensefund.org
Brooklyn Greenway Initiative:
  www.brooklyngreenway.org
  or @BKGreenway
Department of City Planning:
  www.nyc.gov/html/dcp/html/
  transportation/td_projectbicycle.shtml
Department of Parks & Recreation:
  www.nycgovparks.org
Department of Transportation:
  www.nyc.gov/html/dot/html/bicyclists/
  bicyclists.shtml
Five Boro Bicycle Club:
  www.5bbc.org or @5BBC
New York Bicycle Coalition:
  www.nybc.net or @BikeNYBC
NYC Bike Share:
  www.citibikenyc.com or @CitibikeNYC
Time's Up! Bicycle Advocacy Group:
  www.times-up.org or @nyctimesup
Transportation Alternatives:
  www.transalt.org or @transalt

A Few Bike Shops

Affinity Cycles:
  616 Grand St, 718-384-5181, Map 2
Bay Ridge Bicycle World:
  8916 3rd Ave, 718-238-1118, Map 14
Bicycle Station:
  717 Park Ave, 718-638-0300, Map 6
Bravo's Bike Repair:
  187 Wilson Ave, 718-602-5150, Map 4
Bushwick Bike Shop:
  1342 Dekalb Ave, 347-405-7966, Map 4
Dixon's Bike Shop:
  792 Union St, 718-636-0067, Map 9
Ferrara Cycle Shop:
  6304 20th Ave, 718-232-6716, Map 12
Recycle-A-Bicycle:
  35 Pearl St, 718-858-2972, Map 5
Ride Brooklyn:
  468 Bergen St, 347-599-1340, Map 9

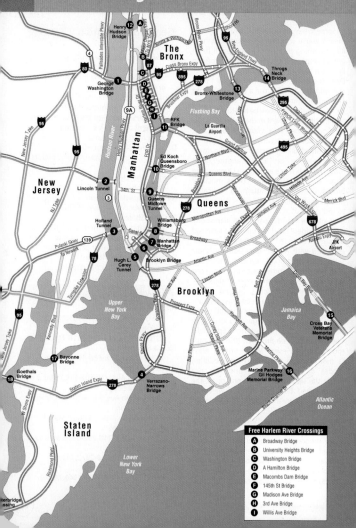

Free Harlem River Crossings

- Ⓐ Broadway Bridge
- Ⓑ University Heights Bridge
- Ⓒ Washington Bridge
- Ⓓ A Hamilton Bridge
- Ⓔ Macombs Dam Bridge
- Ⓕ 145th St Bridge
- Ⓖ Madison Ave Bridge
- Ⓗ 3rd Ave Bridge
- Ⓘ Willis Ave Bridge

By Foot or Bike

Each day, thousands of cyclists cross the Brooklyn, Manhattan, and Williamsburg bridges. There's really no more convenient or scenic way to commute to work (or colder, in winter). Each bridge is distinct, with its own unique structure, aesthetic, and demographic.

Brooklyn Bridge
The most famous of them all, and the most easily recognizable, it is New York's Golden Gate. Separate bicycle and pedestrian lanes run down the center, with the bicycle lane on the north side and the pedestrian lane on the south. Because of the bridge's landmark appeal, both lanes are often clogged by picture-taking tourists, so cyclists need to stay alert. Rollerbladers and skateboarders must watch themselves over some of the bumpy wooden planks. For the most part, the bridge is level, and the ride is smooth and enjoyable.

Brooklyn Access: Ramp at Adams St & Tillary St or stairs at Cadman Plz E & Prospect St in DUMBO
Manhattan Access: Chambers St & Centre St

Manhattan Bridge
The last of the three bridges to have bike and pedestrian paths installed. The bicycle lane is on the north side of the bridge, and the pedestrian lane is on the south side. The enforced separation allows cyclists to pedal worry-free, with no dawdling walkers in sight. Pedestrians, in return, don't have to stress about getting run over. One annoyance, which affects only those on foot, is the entrance on the Brooklyn side. To access this, one must climb a steep set of stairs, which is particularly hard on those with strollers or suitcases. Bikers, however, have no stairs to contend with, and can enter and leave Brooklyn without a care.

Brooklyn Access: Jay St & Sands St
Manhattan Access: Bike Lane—Canal St & Forsyth St; Pedestrian Lane—Bowery, just south of Canal St

Williamsburg Bridge
The bridge of the chosen people (Jews and well-off hipsters), with the biggest bike/pedestrian path of all three. The northern lane is 12 feet wide and the southern lane is 8 feet wide, and both are shared by cyclists and pedestrians. Usually, only one of the paths is open at any given time. When entering or exiting the bridge on both sides, the gradient is quite steep. Going up can be a workout, and going down can either be exhilarating or fear inducing.

Brooklyn Access: North Entrance—Driggs Ave, right by the Washington Plz; South Entrance—Bedford Ave b/w S 5th & S 6th Sts
Manhattan Access: Delancey St & Clinton St/Suffolk St

Driving Across the Bridges

Rush-hour traffic is notoriously awful on all of these bridges. Listen to 1010 WINS or Newsradio 880 for the latest updates.

Brooklyn Bridge
No commercial vehicles are allowed (including your U-Haul rental van, newbie!). With the fewest amount of traffic lanes (6), delays are sometimes unavoidable. If you're coming into Manhattan, you've got easy access to the FDR Drive north, but reaching the BQE on the reverse route is a pain in the ass. And then the NYPD thinks it's interesting to block one lane of traffic in either direction during rush hour for "security" reasons.

Manhattan Bridge
Commercial vehicles are permitted. Seven lanes of traffic allow for a reasonable commute. The lower roadway provides three extra lanes into Manhattan and back into Brooklyn between 5 am and 3 pm. A lane for high-occupancy vehicles (it pays to bring a friend!) has been established for upper roadway drivers between 6 and 10 am on weekdays. The bridge places you directly onto major streets in Manhattan (Canal) and Brooklyn (Flatbush). However, connecting to speedier thoroughfares on both sides, including the FDR and BQE, is far from convenient.

Williamsburg Bridge
Commercial vehicles are permitted across the Williamsburg Bridge, and the eight traffic lanes are generally fast-flowing. Reaching the Queens-bound BQE on the Brooklyn side is smooth like butter. On the Manhattan side, you'll end up on the traffic mess that is Delancey Street. Good luck.

Hugh L. Carey Tunnel
Gridlock can be intense, and you have to pay a toll, but isn't it worth it to ride the longest underwater vehicular tunnel in North America? It's also damn convenient. On the Manhattan side you'll end up directly on the West Side Highway (with an option to immediately make a left so you can loop under Battery Park and be on the FDR in seconds), and on the Brooklyn side you'll find yourself smack dab on the BQE. Take the tunnel if you need to go to Coney Island, the Verrazano Bridge, JFK, or various big box stores.

Verrazano Bridge
Giovanni da Verrazano, the first European to enter New York Harbor, would probably turn over in his grave if he knew his name was associated with a bridge that's best known for its traffic and for charging an extortionate fee to enter Staten Island (it's at least free going back to Brooklyn). But the efficiency factor is high, especially if you're looking to head to the Jersey Shore, Washington DC, Colonial Williamsburg, and other points south.

Getting to Brooklyn

It is a decision fraught with peril: Manhattan Bridge vs. Brooklyn Bridge? Brooklyn Bridge vs. Hugh L. Carey Tunnel? Verrazano Bridge vs. well, nothing?

Consequently, listening to traffic updates (such as 1010 WINS) is the way to go. Because traffic is usually fairly heavy, stations are lax about mentioning buildup on the East River crossings. But if there's a major accident or bridge closure and you tune in, you can be sailing over an alternate bridge with a big smile on your face.

Most of the time, we do think it's paying the toll (unless you're driving back and forth four times a day) to take the Hugh L. Carey Tunnel. The tunnel gives you instant access to both the West Side Highway and FDR Drive in Manhattan, or the Gowanus Expressway and the Carroll Gardens/ Park Slope/Sunset Park area in Brooklyn.

As for the bridges, the Williamsburg heading into Brooklyn will only give you direct access to the BQE heading towards Queens—for south Brooklyn-bound access to the BQE, you'll encounter some annoying traffic lights. The same southbound BQE access problem exists from both the Manhattan and Brooklyn bridges.

Getting around Brooklyn

With no highway that actually runs through Brooklyn, you've simply got to suck it up if you're heading to Canarsie or the Rockaways. Pick your poison: The Belt Parkway, a route with innumerable slowdowns that takes you 15 miles out of your way but avoids surface roads with traffic lights, or Flatbush Avenue, a direct line from the Manhattan Bridge with one lane for traffic and one lane for double-parked cars and many, many traffic lights.

The same dilemma exists for getting out to eastern Brooklyn and southern Nassau County. The alternative to the Belt Parkway is Atlantic Avenue, which moves more fluidly than Flatbush, especially once you get out past Utica Avenue. You'll experience slowdowns on the Belt Parkway around the Verrazano Bridge, Coney Island, JFK, and other random locations, but it is still usually the fastest, albeit longest, route.

For trips to northwestern Brooklyn, the best options are the BQE north to Williamsburg or

Greenpoint or the "coastal route" of Flushing to Kent to Franklin. The route you choose will depend on whether you'd like to drive through Hasidic Williamsburg where pedestrian rules be damned, or whether you'd like to enjoy river views from the possibly bumper-to-bumper BQE, south of the Kosciuszko Bridge.

The strange thing is that even with the hassle of driving in Brooklyn, it's often much easier than trying to train or bus it when traveling throughout the borough. A straphanger from the Slope has to take an Odyssean journey into the city and back again just to get to Williamsburg a mere 5 miles away—so if you have access to a car, it's probably worth it. Remember that driving in Brooklyn is all about attitude. Keep your wits about you, look out for unparking cars and psychotic livery drivers, and rediscover the true use of your horn—as an additional appendage.

A Few Tips

Most of these tips are probably not worth a damn, but they seem to work for us…
• For northwestern Brooklyn, Kent Street is a good way to save time if you don't want to deal with the BQE.
• Fourth Avenue is a good alternative north/ south between Bay Ridge and Park Slope/ Carroll Gardens/Atlantic Avenue.
• 9th Street is a quick through-street east over the Gowanus Canal from Carroll Gardens to Park Slope.
• Don't ask us to choose between McDonald Avenue, Ocean Parkway, Coney Island Avenue, and Ocean Avenue when traveling north/ south between Prospect Park and Coney Island/Brighton Beach—they can all suck.
• Metropolitan Avenue is a wonderfully scenic way to get to central Queens if you're not in a hurry.
• Traffic on the Gowanus heading towards the Hugh L. Carey Tunnel always looks like a nightmare, but most of it is not tunnel traffic— get in the far left lane as early as possible to avoid BQE traffic.
• The Pulaski Bridge is a much better way to cross between Queens and Brooklyn than the Kosciuszko Bridge, but where does that get you?
• If you're going from Brooklyn to New Jersey, take the Verrazano Bridge and go through Staten Island; it's not worth it to slog through Manhattan.

Parking in Brooklyn is pretty straightforward—most folks just park on the street, unless they're lucky enough to have their own garage. Street parking is relatively easy in places like Clinton Hill and Greenpoint, and maddening in more densely populated areas like Park Slope, where the only solution is to become one of those parallel-parking ninjas who can shrink their cars to fit any available spot. Here's a tip: When leaving your car overnight, try to avoid parking alongside a park, as these secluded areas seem to invite break-ins (of course, that's why you can usually find a spot there).

If you live in North Brooklyn, there's an absolute wealth of free parking under the elevated BQE.

The chief nemesis of street parking is street cleaning: The city will tow your car or slap you with a nasty ticket if you're in the wrong place at the wrong time. Posted signs will alert you to street cleaning times. During these times, the alternate side parking rules dictate that you may double park along the opposite side of the street (e.g. If there is no parking on the north side of the street 11–2 on Thursdays, then during that time it is permissible to double park along the south side of that same street). You'll get the hang of this slightly confusing yet strangely graceful system soon if you haven't already. But just in case, you can always check www.nyc.gov/dot/asprules or @NYCASP for rules, exceptions, and suspensions.

Downtown Parking Lots / Garages

The only area where parking is truly a grind is downtown. Unofficially, you can try the lot at the Brooklyn Bridge Marriott, which sometimes accommodates non-guests. Below is a list of some of the key parking lots/garages in the downtown area:

- Sands Parking · 66 Sands St
- Central Parking · 9 Metrotech Center
- Central Parking · 15 Hoyt St
- Central Parking · 71 Schermerhorn St
- Central Parking · 75 Henry St
- Central Parking · 85 Livingston St
- Central Parking · 333 Adams St
- Central Parking · 350 Jay St
- Edison Parkfast · 71 Smith St
- Edison Parkfast · 160 Livingston St
- Edison Parkfast · 203 Jay St
- Flatbridge Car Park · 120 Concord St
- One Pierrepont Plaza Garage · 300 Cadman Plaza W
- Willoughby Street Parking · 120 Willoughby St

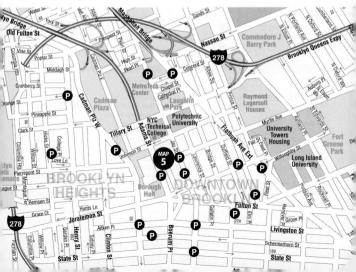

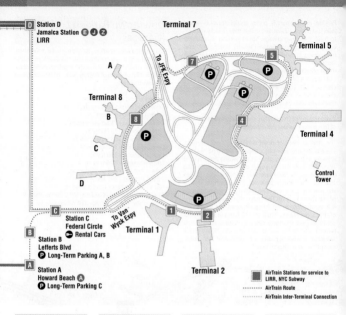

Station D
Jamaica Station 🄴 🄹 🄩
LIRR

Terminal 7

Terminal 5

A

Terminal 8

B

C

D

Station C
Federal Circle
🚗 Rental Cars
Terminal 1

Station B
Lefferts Blvd
🅿 Long-Term Parking A, B

Station A
Howard Beach 🄰
🅿 Long-Term Parking C

To JFK Expy

To Van Wyck Expy

Terminal 4

Control Tower

Terminal 2

🔲 AirTrain Stations for service to LIRR, NYC Subway
········· AirTrain Route
········· AirTrain Inter-Terminal Connection

Airline/Terminal	Airline/Terminal	Airline/Terminal	Airline/Terminal
Aer Lingus: 5	Avianca: 4	Icelandair: 7	Qantas: 7
Aeroflot: 1	British Airways: 7	Interjet: 1	Qatar: 8
Aerolineas Argentinas: 7	Caribbean: 4	Japan Airlines: 1	Royal Air Maroc: 1
Aero Mexico: 1	Cathay Pacific: 7	JetBlue: 5 (some	Royal Jordanian: 8
Air Berlin: 8	Cayman Airways: 1	international flights	Saudi Arabian Airlines: 1
Air Canada: 7	China Airlines: 4	arrive at Terminal 4)	Singapore: 4
Air China: 1	China Eastern: 1	KLM: 4	South African: 4
Air Europa: 4	Copa Airlines: 4	Korean Air: 1	Sun Country: 4
Air France: 1	Czech Airlines: 4	Kuwait Airways: 4	Swiss: 4
Air India: 4	Delta: 3	Lan Chile: 8	TAM: 8
Air Jamaica: 4	Delta International: 4	Lan Ecuador: 8	TAME: 1
AirPlus Comet: 1	Egyptair: 4	Lan Peru: 8	Transaero Airlines: 4
Air Tahiti Nui: 4	El Al: 4	LOT: 1	Turkish: 1
Alitalia: 1	Emirates: 4	Lufthansa: 1	United Airlines: 7
Allegro (seasonal): 4	Etihad: 4	Meridiana Fly: 1	US Airways: 8
American: 8	EVA Airways: 1	Miami Air (charter): 4	Uzbekistan: 1
American Eagle: 8	Finnair: 8	North American: 4	Virgin America: 4
ANA: 7	Fly Jamaica Airways: 1	Norwegian Air Shuttle: 1	Virgin Atlantic: 4
Asiana: 4	Hawaiian Airlines: 5	Open Skies: 7	XL Airways: 4
Austrian Airlines: 1	Iberia: 7	Pakistan: 4	

General Information

Address: JFK Expy Jamaica, NY 11430
Phone: 718-244-4444
Lost & Found: 718-244-4225 or jfklostandfound@panynj.gov
Website: www.kennedyairport.com
AirTrain: www.airtrainjfk.com
AirTrain Phone: 877-535-2478
Ground Transportation: 800-AIR-RIDE (247-7433)
Long Island Rail Road: www.mta.info/lirr
Port Authority Police: 718-244-4335
Twitter: @NY_NJairports

Overview

JFK, once known as Idlewild Airport, is the nation's leading international gateway, so Brooklynites enjoy easy access to the world and lower plane fares. JFK itself is huge, serving more than 49 million passengers per year, but with some practice it's manageable. Getting there is easier with the AirTrain, especially when compared to LaGuardia, which has no train access, and Newark, which for Brooklynites is just a royal pain in the ass.

JetBlue's Terminal 5 rises just behind the landmark TWA building, which you should check out if you have time to kill after getting up an hour earlier. Its bubblicious curves make this 1960s gem a glam spaceship aptly prepared to handle any swanky NY soiree. Top that, Newark.

Rental Cars (On-Airport)

The rental car offices are all located along the Van Wyck Expressway near the entrance to the airport. Just follow the signs.

Avis: 718-244-5406 or 800-230-4898
Budget: 718-656-1890 or 800-527-0700
Dollar: 800-800-4000
Enterprise: 718-553-7013 or 800-736-8222
Hertz: 718-656-7600 or 800-654-3131
National: 718-632-8300 or 888-826-6890

Car Services, Shared Rides & Taxis

Taxis in Brooklyn to and from the airport do not cost a flat fee like they do to Manhattan. The meter is turned on and you pray that the driver knows the shortest and quickest route (usually Atlantic Avenue to Conduit Boulevard). As a result, the fare can and shall vary greatly depending on where your trip originates in Brooklyn. However, catching a yellow cab in Brooklyn can be tricky, and the majority of Brooklynites rely on car services. Most car services charge around $30 to $35 for a ride from Brooklyn to JFK. But there are some deals out there, so calling around may save you some hard-earned cash. Be sure to agree on a price ahead of time.

How to Get There—Driving

You can take the corroded pave of the Belt Parkway or the Van Wyck. Stay at home if 'round rush hour—you'll be squandering hours of your life. If the brake-wearing bliss of stop-and-go highway traffic irks you, you might entertain an alternate route using local roads, like Atlantic Avenue in Brooklyn, and drive east until you hit Conduit Avenue. Follow this straight to JFK—it's direct and fairly simple. Tune into 1630AM for general airport information en route to your next flight. It might save you a headache.

How to Get There—Mass Transit

This is your chance to finish *War and Peace*. A one-seat connection to the airport—any of them—is still a far-off dream, but the AirTrain works fairly well. AirTrain runs 24 hours a day between JFK and two off-site stations, one connecting with the A train at Howard Beach and the other connecting with the E, J, and Z trains at the Sutphin/Archer Ave-Jamaica Station stop. The ride takes around 15–25 minutes, depending on which airport terminal you need.

A one-way ride on the AirTrain is $5, so a ride on the subway and then hopping the AirTrain will cost $7.50 combined. If you're anywhere near Atlantic Terminal and your time is valuable, the LIRR to Jamaica will cost you $9.50 during peak times ($7 off-peak and $4 on weekends using a MTA CityTicket). The AirTrain portion of the trip will still cost you an additional $5 and round out your travel time to less than an hour.

If you want to give your MetroCard a workout, and ridiculously long bus journeys don't make you completely insane—or if you're just a connoisseur of mass transit—you can take the 3 train to New Lots Avenue, where you can transfer to the B15 bus to JFK.

Parking

Daily rates for the Central Terminal Area lots cost $4 for the first half-hour, $8 for up to one hour, $4 for every half-hour after that, up to $33 per 24-hour period. Long-term parking costs $18 for the first 24-hours, then $6 in each 8-hour increment thereafter. The Port Authority website features real-time updates on parking availability, showing what percent of each lot is occupied. Online reservations are available for $5, and EZ-Pass holders can use the tag to pay for parking.

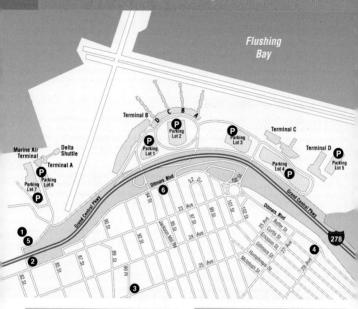

Airline	Terminal
Air Canada:	Terminal B – Concourse A
Air Tran:	Terminal B – Concourse B
American:	Terminal B – Concourse D
American Eagle:	Terminal B – Concourse C
Delta:	Terminals C and D
Delta Connection:	Terminal D
Delta Shuttle:	Terminal A
Frontier:	Terminal B – Concourse B
JetBlue:	Terminal B – Concourses A and B
Southwest:	Terminal B – Concourse B
Spirit:	Terminal B – Concourse B
United:	Terminal B – Concourses A and C
United Express:	Terminal B – Concourses A and C
US Airways:	Terminal C
US Airways Express:	Terminal C
US Airways Shuttle:	Terminal C
WestJet:	Terminal C

General Information

Address:	LaGuardia Airport, Flushing, NY 11371
Phone:	718-533-3400
Lost & Found:	718-533-3988
	lgalostandfound@panynj.gov
Website:	www.laguardiaairport.com
Ground Transportation:	800-AIR-RIDE (247-7433)
Police:	718-533-3900
Twitter:	@NY_NJairports

Overview

Welcome to Queens' other airport. It is so tiny compared to JFK, it feels like a glorified bus station. The best thing we can say about LaGuardia is that it's named for a most excellent former New York City mayor, Fiorello LaGuardia. Although LaGuardia has improved in recent years, it still has a long way to go before it can hold its own against the nation's other airports. Although LaGuardia remains inconvenient to public transportation, especially from Brooklyn, it's still closer than Newark and much easier to navigate than JFK.

How to Get There—Driving

If it is not jammed, take the BQE to Grand Central Parkway right to the airport. Alternatively, you can take the BQE to Exit 38/Northern Blvd, then follow Northern Boulevard to 94th Street, where you take a left. This will lead directly to the airport.

How to Get There—Mass Transit

For those Brooklynites dependent on their Metrocard, getting to LaGuardia is a long haul. From Brooklyn, take the G train to Court Square and transfer to the E, which connects to the 7-E-F-M-R Jackson Heights/Roosevelt Avenue/74th Street stop in Queens where you can transfer to the Q70 limited-stop bus which gets you to LaGuardia in 8-10 minutes. Another option is the M60 bus, which runs across 125th Street and the RFK Bridge to the airport, connecting with the N and Q at Astoria Blvd.

How to Get There—Really

Two words: Car service. Call them, they'll pick you up at your door and drop you at the terminal. If you have the extra cash, it is certainly worth it. Most trips from Brooklyn are in the $40 range.

Parking

Daily parking rates at LaGuardia cost $4 for the first half-hour, $8 for up to one hour, $4 for every hour thereafter, up to $33 per 24-hour period. Long-term parking is $33 per day for the first two 24-hour periods, and $6 for each subsequent 8 hour period. (though only in Lot 3). The Port Authority website features real-time updates on parking availability, showing what percent of each lot is occupied. Online reservations are available for $5, and EZ-Pass holders can use the tag to pay for parking.

Several off-site parking lots serve LaGuardia, including LaGuardia Plaza Hotel (104-04 Ditmars Blvd, 718-457-6300 x295), Clarion Airport Parking (Ditmars Blvd & 94th St, 718-335-2423) and The Parking Spot (23rd Ave & 90th St, 718-507-8162). Each runs its own shuttle from the lots, and they usually charge $14–$25 per day. If all the parking garages onsite are full, follow the "P" signs to the airport exit and park in one of the off-airport locations.

Rental Cars

1 Avis: LGA; 718-507-3600 or 800-230-4898
2 Budget: 83-34 23rd Ave; 718 639-6400
3 Dollar: 95-05 25th Ave; 800-800-4000
4 Enterprise: 104-04 Ditmars Blvd; 718-457-2900 or 800-736-8222
5 Hertz: LGA; 718-478-5300 or 800-654-3131
6 National: Ditmars Blvd & 95th St; 718-429-5893 or 888-826-6890

Map 1 • Greenpoint

America United	718-349-5900
Java Car Service	718-383-5600
Malone Car Service	718-383-1500
McGuinness Car Service	718-383-6556

Map 2 • Williamsburg

Brooklyn Car Service	718-384-7070
MetroLine Car Service	718-388-1111
Mobil Car Service	718-383-8300
The New Brooklyn Car Service	718-388-2828
Northside Car Service	718-387-2222

Map 3 • East Williamsburg

#1 Mexicali Car Service	718-456-4444
Bushwick Car Service	718-386-5002
New Eastern Car & Limousine Service	718-387-0222

Map 4 • Bushwick

Freedom Limousine & Car Service	718-452-5400
New Ridgewood Car Service	718-456-0777
New York Limo & Car Service	718-455-1010

Map 5 • Brooklyn Heights / DUMBO / Downtown

Clinton Car & Limo Service	718-522-4474
Promenade Car Service	718-858-6666
Prominent Car & Limo Service	718-855-7900
River Car & Limousine Service	718-852-3333

Map 6 • Fort Greene / Clinton Hill

New Bell Car Service	718-230-4499
Pratt Car Service	718-789-4900

Map 7 • Bedford-Stuyvesant

Brown & Brown	718-574-4900
United Express Car & Limo Service	718-452-4000

Map 8 • BoCoCa / Red Hook

Avion Luxury Cars	718-797-0777
Cobble Hill Car Service	718-643-1113
Court Express	718-237-8888
Golden Express Car Service	718-797-0777
Jerusalem Car Service	718-522-2111
Trans Union Car Service	718-858-8889

Map 9 • Park Slope / Prospect Heights / Windsor Terrace

Arecibo Car Service	718-783-6465
Castle Car Service	718-499-9333
Continental Car Service	718-499-0909
Eastern Car Service	718-499-6227
Express 11 Car Service	718-499-3800
Family Car Service	718-596-0664
International Car Service	718-230-0808
Legends Car & Limousine Service	718-643-6635
Monaco Car Service	718-230-0202
Pacific Express Car Service	718-488-0000
Seventh Avenue Car Service	718-965-4242

Map 10 • Prospect-Lefferts Gardens / Crown Heights

Bedstar Car Service	718-771-2299
Econo Express Car Service	718-493-1133
Transportation Unlimited Car Service	718-363-1000

Map 11 • Sunset Park / Green-Wood Heights

Bell Car Service	718-833-2929
Elegant Car Service	718-833-6262
Mega Car Service Corporation	718-633-2020
Puebla Express Car Service	718-633-4400

Map 12 • Borough Park

Aemunah Car Service	718-633-3135
Aviv-Express Car & Limousine Service	718-338-8888
Church Avenue Car Service	718-633-4444
Empire Car and Limousine Service	718-972-7212
Jay's Car Service	718-236-5900
Keshet Car Service	718-854-8200
Khageirekh Car Service	718-438-5400
Munkacs Car Service	718-854-4700

Map 13 • Kensington / Ditmas Park

California Car Service	718-282-4444
Five Star Car Service	718-940-0044
Hummingbird Car Service	718-856-6155
Marlboro Car Service	718-434-4141
Mex Express Car Service	718-941-5200
New American Car & Limousine Service	718-972-7979
On Your Way Car Service	718-675-3333
Ontime Car Service	718-891-2600
Rachel's Car Service	718-972-2223
US Express Car & Limousine Service	718-633-4800

Map 14 • Bay Ridge

3rd Ave Express	718-836-8200
Alexandria Limo & Car Service	718-491-3111
Dyker	718-833-3838
Dyker Car Service	718-745-0900
Harbor View Car Service	718-680-2500
Marine Limousine & Car Service	718-680-0003
Max Car & Limousine Service	718-921-3399
Ridge Car Service	718-748-4444
Your Car Service	718-680-2900

Map 15 • Dyker Heights / Bensonhurst

18th Avenue Private Car Service	718-256-2190
AR & Limo	718-236-8881
Car Service 69	718-234-6666
My Way Car Service	718-232-2435
Strictly Car Service	718-256-4225

Map 16 • Midwood

Best Way Car Service	718-252-6363
ELAT Car & Limousine Service	718-339-5111
Jaffa Car Service	718-376-6400
Jilly's Car Service	718-859-8300
Monte's Car Service	718-258-2880
Rechev Car Service	718-338-2003
TOV (Too) Car & Limousine Service	718-375-8877

January

New Year's Eve Fireworks: Prospect Park; Fireworks in the park.
New Year's Day Dip: Coney Island; The Polar Bears come out and play.
Lunar New Year Celebration: Sunset Park; An annual celebration featuring singing, dancing, and fireworks (Jan–Feb).

March

St Patrick's Day Parade: Park Slope; Irish Pride (brooklynstpatricksparade.com).
Central Brooklyn Jazz Festival: Various locations; Event is hosted by the Central Brooklyn Jazz Consortium and musicians from all over the country attend (www.centralbrooklynjazzconsortium.org) (March–April).

April

Opening Day in Prospect Park: Prospect Park; Family-friendly celebration of spring, when the park "opens" for the season.
Earth Day Weekend Celebration: Prospect Park; Various events in Prospect Park honoring Baby Blue.
Sakura Matsuri: Brooklyn Botanic Gardens; Celebrate Japanese culture in a sea of cherry blossoms (bbg.org).
Brooklyn Zine Fest: Hundreds of zines, those who publish them, and panel discussions (brooklynzinefest.com).

May

Norwegian-American Parade: Bay Ridge; Even the Vikings get their own parade around May 17 (www.may17paradeny.com).
SONYA Art Studio Stroll: Various locations; The South of the Navy Yard Artists hold an annual event to show artist studios (www.sonyaonline.org) (May–June).
BayFest/Blessing of the Fleet: Sheepshead Bay; Celebrating the working fishing village of the neighborhood (bigbayfest.org) (May–June).
BWAC Pier Show: Red Hook; Contemporary art exhibit featuring work by Brooklyn artists (www.bwac.org) (May–June).

June

Celebrate Brooklyn: Prospect Park; Brooklyn's long-running, outdoor, summer-long performing arts festival (www.celebratebrooklyn.org) (all summer).
Rooftop Films: Various locations; Snuggle up on the romantic rooftops of Brooklyn and beyond.
Brooklyn Cyclones Opening Day: MCU Park; Brooklyn's own start another season (www.brooklyncyclones.com).
Brooklyn Pride Parade & Festival: Park Slope; Celebrate gay pride (www.brooklynpride.org).
Mermaid Parade: Coney Island; Slap on your fins and celebrate summer (www.coneyisland.com).
Smith Street Funday: Carroll Gardens; Smith Street vendors sell their wares at reduced rates.
Northside Festival: Greenpoint/Williamsburg; Art, music, film (www.northsidefestival.com).
Brooklyn Film Festival: Brooklyn Museum; International, competitive festival for and by independent film makers (www.wbff.org).

July

International African Arts Festival: Commodore Barry Park; Outdoor cultural festival with live performances, marketplace, and kids events (www.iaafestival.org) (July 4th wknd).

Nathan's Hot Dog Eating Contest: Coney Island; Of course we're celebrating international gluttony on the Fourth of July.

The Feast of Giglio: Williamsburg; Italian festival with parades, food and a 80-foot Giglio lifted high in the air (www.olmcfeast.com).

Brooklyn Hip Hop Festival: Various locations; Grammy winners and local acts alike, seminars as well as concerts (www.bkhiphopfestival.com).

Martin Luther King Jr. Concert Series: Wingate Field; R&B, Gospel, and Carriban music (July–August).

Seaside Summer Concert Series: Coney Island; Classic Rock, Oldies, and "Salsa by the Sea" (July–August).

August

Brighton Jubilee: Brighton Beach; A sea of crafts and food.

September

Brooklyn Book Festival: Two of Brooklyn's favorite things: Books and Brooklyn (www.brooklynbookfestival.org).

Great Irish Fair: Coney Island; Family-friendly with music, dancing, food, games, and crafts (www.gifnyc.com).

Williamsburg International Film Festival: Williamsburg; Indie films and indie bands (www.willifest.com).

Flatbush Frolic: Flatbush; Street fair with loads of local vendors and kid-friendly activities (flatbushfrolic.org).

West Indian American Day Carnival: Eastern Parkway; Labor Day weekend, West Indian parade—lots of good food (wiadcacarnival.org).

DUMBO Arts Festival: DUMBO; Art all over the place (dumboartsfestival.com).

Ragamuffin Parade: Bay Ridge; Watch the kiddies parade in their costumes (ragamuffinparadeny.com).

October

Atlantic Antic: Atlantic Avenue; Huge, totally awesome street fair (www.atlanticave.org).

Narrows Botanical Gardens Harvest Festival: Bay Ridge; Craft fair, pumpkin patch and canine costume contest (www.narrowsbg.org).

Gowanus Open Studio Tour: Carroll Gardens; Check out lots of cool art for free (artsgowanus.org).

Halloween Tours: Green-Wood Cemetery; Get spooked (www.green-wood.com).

Brooklyn Timeline

1609: Henry Hudson explores Coney Island.
1646: Town of Breuckelen chartered by Dutch West India Company.
1776: The Battle of Brooklyn results in British victory.
1814: Steamboat service begins from DUMBO to Manhattan.
1834: City of Brooklyn is chartered.
1849: The Great Cholera Epidemic begins and Brooklyn Borough Hall opens.
1855: Walt Whitman publishes *Leaves of Grass*.
1868: Prospect Park completed.
1871: East River freezes and thousands stream across to Manhattan for the day.
1883: Brooklyn Bridge opens with a one-cent toll.
1887: Peter Luger launches New York's best steakhouse.
1890: Brooklyn candy store owner invents the egg cream, which contains neither egg nor cream.
1896: The borough's first free library begins service at Pratt Institute, with an interior designed by Tiffany's.
1898: In a close vote, residents approve a merger with the City of Greater New York
(a.k.a. "Great Mistake of 1898").
1899: Brooklyn Children's Museum opens to become world's first museum dedicated to kids.
1902: Air conditioner invented by Willis Carrier, thereby allowing future elderly Brooklynites to flee to Florida.
1913: Subway deal completed that will extend lines to outer Brooklyn and spur massive development.
1914: Topless bathing at Coney Island leads to arrest of 50 men.
1916: Nathan's sells its first nickel hot dog.
1928: Brooklyn Paramount Theatre opens as world's first cinema dedicated to talking pictures.
1930: Brooklyn residential population surpasses Manhattan's.
1933: G line begins service between Brooklyn and Queens. The first train should be pulling in shortly.
1939: Brooklynite Alex Steinweiss designs the first-ever album cover.
1947: Jackie Robinson bravely joins the Dodgers, breaking the MLB's color barrier.
1954: The BQE rips apart Brooklyn, but offers sweeping views of Manhattan to truck drivers
(Thank you again, Mr. Moses).
1955: Dodgers win the World Series against the Yankees, setting off the biggest street party in Brooklyn's history.
1957: Dodgers run off to LA. Depression/nostalgia engulfs Brooklyn to this day.
1960: Airplane crashes in Park Slope, killing 90.
1964: Verrazano-Narrows Bridge crowned longest suspension bridge in the world.
1968: Brooklynite Shirley Chisholm becomes the first black woman elected to Congress.
1969: First annual West Indian Carnival.
1973: Park Slope Food Co-op founded.
1976: Rheingold and Schaefer breweries shut down in Brooklyn.
1983: Next Wave festival debuts at Brooklyn Academy of Music.
1987: MetroTech Center finishes development in downtown Brooklyn.
1988: Coney Island's Cyclone, the iconic roller coaster, named an official NYC landmark.
1991: Crown Heights riots rage for three days.
1995: Brooklyn Brewery starts producing tasty microbrews.
2001: Brooklyn Metropolitan Detention Center holds numerous immigrants indefinitely after 9/11.
2002: Nation's first urban Audubon center opens in Prospect Park.
2004: NFT Brooklyn published to joy of new Brooklynites looking for an ATM and liquor store in their new 'hood.
2005: "Leaving Brooklyn – Oy Vey!" sign erected on Williamsburg Bridge.
2007: Legendary pizzeria DiFara's shut down temporarily by the DOH.
2009: The battle of the Bedford Avenue bike lane.
2012: Hurricane Sandy causes widespread damage to low-lying areas along Brooklyn's waterfront.
2012: The Brooklyn Nets play their first game in the brand new Barclays Center.

Websites

brooklynian.com · More message boards than anyone needs
brooklynbased.net · Guide to life in Brooklyn.
brooklyn-usa.org · Website of the Brooklyn Borough President with tons of info.
brooklyneagle.com · Daily newspaper devoted to Brooklyn.
brooklynheightsblog.com · Chronicling America's first suburbs.
brooklynhistory.org · Website of the Brooklyn Historical Society.
brooklynpaper.com · Fun, sometimes irreverent local coverage.
brooklynparrots.com · Blog dedicated to Brooklyn's wild monk parrots.
brooklynvegan.com · Music, photos, and news from a vegan. In Brooklyn.
brownstoner.com · An unhealthy obsession with historic Brooklyn brownstones.
freewilliamsburg.com · Essential guide to this Brooklyn place you keep hearing about.
newyorkshitty.com All things Greenpoint and beyond.

Essential Brooklyn Books

Leaves of Grass, Walt Whitman, 1855
A Tree Grows in Brooklyn, Betty Smith, 1943
The Assistant, Bernard Malamud, 1957
Last Exit to Brooklyn, Hubert Selby, 1964
The Chosen, Chaim Potok, 1967
Boys of Summer, Roger Kahn, 1972
The Gift, Pete Hamill, 1973
The Great Bridge, David McCullough, 1983
Brooklyn's Finest, Jay-Z, 1996
The Neighborhoods of Brooklyn, Kenneth Jackson and John Manbeck, 1998
Motherless Brooklyn, Jonathan Lethem, 1999
Brooklyn Babies, RZA, 2001
Brooklyn Dreams, J. M. DeMatteis and Glenn Barr, 2003
Brooklyn Noir, Tim McLoughlin, 2004
Dew Breaker, Edwidge Danticat, 2004
The Fortress of Solitude, Jonathan Lethem, 2004
The Brooklyn Follies, Paul Auster, 2005
Brooklyn Was Mine, 2008
Brooklyn, Colm Toibin, 2009

Essential Brooklyn Songs

"Brooklyn Bridge," Frank Sinatra, 1946
"The Bridge," Sonny Rollins, 1962
"Brooklyn Roads," Neil Diamond, 1970
"No Sleep 'Till Brooklyn," The Beastie Boys, 1986
"Brooklyn Blues," Barry Manilow, 1987
"Brooklyn," Mos Def, 1999

Essential Brooklyn Movies

Arsenic and Old Lace (1944)
The Kid From Brooklyn (1946)
It Happened in Brooklyn (1947)
Bela Lugosi Meets a Brooklyn Gorilla (1952)
A View from the Bridge (1961)
The Landlord (1970)
The Gang that Couldn't Shoot Straight (1971)
The French Connection (1971)
Education of Sonny Carson (1974)
The Super Cops (1974)
The Lords of Flatbush (1975)
Dog Day Afternoon (1975)
Saturday Night Fever (1977)
The Sentinel (1977)
Nunzio (1978)
The Warriors (1979)
Turk 182! (1985)
Brighton Beach Memoirs (1986)
Moonstruck (1987)
Do the Right Thing (1989)
Last Exit to Brooklyn (1989)
Goodfellas (1990)
Straight Out Of Brooklyn (1991)
Crooklyn (1994)
Little Odessa (1994)
Smoke/Blue in the Face (1995)
Someone Else's America (1995)
Vampire in Brooklyn (1995)
The Search For One-Eyed Jimmy (1996)
Soul in the Hole (1997)
Pi (1998)
Girlfight (2000)
Requiem for a Dream (2000)
Everyday People (2004)
The Squid and the Whale (2005)
Block Party (2005)
Half Nelson (2006)
Life Support (2007)
We Own the Night (2007)
Brooklyn's Finest (2009)
Red Hook Summer (2012)

Emergency Rooms

	Address	Phone	Map
Woodhull	760 Broadway St	718-963-8000	3
Wyckoff Heights Medical Center	374 Stockholm St	718-963-7272	4
Brooklyn Hospital Center	121 DeKalb Ave	718-250-8000	6
Interfaith Medical Center	1545 Atlantic Ave	718-613-4000	7
New York Methodist Hospital	506 6th St	718-780-3000	9
Kings County	451 Clarkson Ave	718-245-3131	10
SUNY Downstate Medical Center	450 Clarkson Ave	718-270-1000	10
Lutheran HealthCare	150 55th St	718-630-7000	11
Maimonides Medical Center	4802 Tenth Ave	718-283-6000	12
Victory Memorial	699 92nd St	718-567-1234	15
Brookdale Hospital Medical Center	1 Brookdale Plaza	718-240-5000	n/a
Kingsbrook Jewish Medical Center	585 Schenectady Ave	718-604-5000	n/a

Other Hospitals

	Address	Phone	Map
VA NY Harbor Healthcare System	800 Poly Pl	718-836-6600	15
Beth Israel Medical Center	3201 Kings Hwy	718-252-3000	n/a

Police

	Address	Phone	Map
94th Precinct	100 Meserole Ave	718-383-3879	1
90th Precinct	211 Union Ave	718-963-5311	2
Police Service Area 3	25 Central Ave	718-386-5357	3
81st Precinct	30 Ralph Ave	718-574-0411	4
83rd Precinct	480 Knickerbocker Ave	718-574-1605	4
84th Precinct	301 Gold St	718-875-6811	5
88th Precinct	298 Classon Ave	718-636-6511	6
79th Precinct	263 Tompkins Ave	718-636-6611	7
76th Precinct	191 Union St	718-834-3211	8
78th Precinct	65 Sixth Ave	718-636-6411	9
71st Precinct	421 Empire Blvd	718-735-0511	10
72nd Precinct	830 Fourth Ave	718-965-6311	11
66th Precinct	5822 16th Ave	718-851-5611	12
67th Precinct	2820 Snyder Ave	718-287-3211	13
70th Precinct	154 Lawrence Ave	718-851-5511	13
68th Precinct	333 65th St	718-439-4211	14
62nd Precinct	1925 Bath Ave	718-236-2611	15
61st Precinct	2575 Coney Island Ave	718-627-6611	n/a
63rd Precinct	1844 Brooklyn Ave	718-258-4411	n/a
77th Precinct	127 Utica Ave	718-735-0611	n/a

Public Libraries

		Phone	Map
Brooklyn Public	107 Norman Ave	718-349-8504	1
Brooklyn Public	81 Devoe St	718-486-3365	2
Brooklyn Public	240 Division Ave	718-302-3485	2
Brooklyn Public	340 Bushwick Ave	718-602-1348	3
Brooklyn Public	790 Bushwick Ave	718-455-3898	4
Brooklyn Public	360 Irving Ave	718-628-8378	4
Brooklyn Public	8 Thomas S Boyland St	718-573-5224	4
Brooklyn Public	280 Cadman Plz W	718-623-7100	5
Brooklyn Public	93 St Edwards St	718-935-0244	5
Brooklyn Public	380 Washington Ave	718-398-8713	6
Brooklyn Public	617 DeKalb Ave	718-935-0032	7
Brooklyn Public	496 Franklin Ave	718-623-0012	7
Brooklyn Public	361 Lewis Ave Macon Branch	718-573-5606	7
Brooklyn Public	396 Clinton St	718-596-6972	8
Brooklyn Public	7 Wolcott St	718-935-0203	8
Brooklyn Public	25 4th Ave	718-638-1531	9
Brooklyn Public	431 6th Ave	718-832-1853	9
Brooklyn Public	10 Grand Army Plz	718-230-2100	9

		Address	Phone	Map
NY Methodist Hospital Health	506 6th St		718-780-5197	9
Brooklyn Public	560 New York Ave		718-773-1180	10
Brooklyn Public	725 St Marks Ave		718-773-7208	10
Brooklyn Public	5108 4th Ave		718-567-2806	11
Brooklyn Public	1265 43rd St		718-437-4085	12
Brooklyn Public	1702 60th St		718-256-2117	12
Brooklyn Public	1305 Cortelyou Rd		718-693-7763	13
Brooklyn Public	410 Ditmas Ave		718-435-9431	13
Brooklyn Public	160 E 5th St		718-686-9707	13
Brooklyn Public	22 Linden Blvd		718-856-0813	13
Brooklyn Public	2035 Nostrand Ave		718-421-1159	13
Brooklyn Public	9424 4h Ave		718-748-6919	14
Brooklyn Public	7223 Ridge Blvd		718-748-5709	14
Brooklyn Public	8202 13th Ave		718-748-6261	15
Brooklyn Public	1743 86th St		718-236-4086	15
Brooklyn Public	6802 Fort Hamilton Pkwy		718-748-8001	15
Brooklyn Public	975 E 16th St		718-252-0967	16

Other Libraries

	Address	Phone	Map
Brooklyn Bar Association Foundation	123 Remsen St	718-624-0875	5
Brooklyn Law Library	250 Joralemon St	718-780-7973	5
Brooklyn Supreme Court Law Library	360 Adams St	347-296-1144	5
Brooklyn Hospital Medical	121 DeKalb Ave	718-250-6944	6

Map 1 · Greenpoint

	Address	Phone	Price
Marzili Hostel	66 Clay St	347-551-0480	$
YMCA	99 Meserole Ave	718-389-3700	$

Map 2 · Williamsburg

Hotel Le Jolie	253 Meeker Ave	718-625-2100	$$$
King & Grove	160 N 12th St	718-218-7500	$$$$
Loftstel	112 N 6th St	347-565-5638	$
Williamsburg HostL	318 Bedford Ave	212-464-7748	$
Wythe Hotel	80 Wythe Ave	718-460-8001	$$$
ZIP112	112 N 6th St	347-403-0577	$

Map 3 · East Williamsburg

Bushwick Hotel	171 Bushwick Ave	718-386-1801	$$
New York Loft Hostel	249 Varet St	718-366-1351	$

Map 4 · Bushwick

Kings Hotel Apartments	1078 Bushwick Ave	718-452-9743	$$
Red Carpet Inn	980 Wyckoff Ave	718-417-4111	$$

Map 5 · Brooklyn Heights / DUMBO / Downtown

3B	136 Lawrence St	347-762-2632	$$
Brooklyn Suites	331 State St	718-643-0472	$$
New York Marriott at the Brooklyn Bridge	333 Adams St	718-246-7000	$$$
Nu Hotel	85 Smith St	347-694-5822	$$$
Princess Hotel	211 Schermerhorn St	718-468-3565	$

Map 6 · Fort Greene / Clinton Hill

Regina's New York Bed & Breakfast	16 Ft Greene Pl	718-834-9253	$$
Saddle Down Bed & Breakfast	266 Washington Ave	718-399-7913	$$
Washington Hotel	400 Washington Ave	718-783-9545	$$

Map 7 · Bedford-Stuyvesant

Akwaaba Mansion Bed & Breakfast	347 Macdonough St	718-455-5958	$$
Best Western PLUS Arena Hotel	1324 Atlantic Ave	718-604-7300	$$
Loftstel	1094 Bedford Ave	347-240-5826	$
Loftstel	580 Greene Ave	347-787-1395	$
Prince Lefferts Hotel	127 Lefferts Pl	718-377-4444	$

General Information · **Hotels**

Map 8 · BoCoCa / Red Hook

	Address	Phone	Price
Brooklyn Motor Inn	140 Hamilton Ave	718-875-2500	$$
Holiday Inn Express Downtown Brooklyn	279 Butler St	718-855-9600	$$
Union Street Bed & Breakfast	405 Union St	718-852-8406	$$$

Map 9 · Park Slope / Prospect Heights / Windsor Terrace

Garden Green Bed & Breakfast	641 Carlton Ave	718-783-5717	$$
Holiday Inn Express Brooklyn	625 Union St	718-797-1133	$$
Hotel Le Bleu	370 4th Ave	718-625-1500	$$$
Little Princess Hotel	250 12th st	718-377-4444	$
Park Slope Inn	359 6th Ave	917-627-8047	$$
The Sofia Inn	288 Park Pl	917-865-7428	$$

Map 10 · Prospect-Lefferts Gardens / Crown Heights

Lefferts Manor Bed and Breakfast	80 Rutland Rd	347-351-9065	$$
Serenity at Home Guest House	57 Rutland Rd	347-414-5536	$$

Map 11 · Sunset Park / Green-Wood Heights

Days Inn Brooklyn	437 39th St	718-853-4141	$$
Hotel BPM	139 33rd St	718-305-4182	$$$
Kings Hotel	820 39th St	718-851-8188	$$

Map 12 · Borough Park

Avenue Plaza Hotel	4624 13th Ave	718-552-3200	$$
Park House Hotel	1206 48th St	718-871-8100	$$

Map 13 · Kensington / Ditmas Park

Bibi's Garden B&B	762 Westminster Rd	718-434-3119	$$
Dekoven Suites	30 Dekoven Ct	718-421-1052	$$
Honey's B&B	770 Westminster Rd	718-434-7628	$$
Strange Dog Inn	51 Dekoven Ct	718-338-7051	$$$

Map 14 · Bay Ridge

Best Western Gregory Hotel	8315 Fourth Ave	718-238-3737	$$
Prince Hotel	315 93rd St	718-748-8995	$

Map 16 · Midwood

Midwood Suites	1078 E 15th St	718-253-9535	$$
Royal Rentals	1510 Ocean Pkwy	718-554-3991	$$

They may not make the itinerary of the casual tourist, but Brooklyn is still home to some stupendous destinations. You often simply look up and realize that you are standing at the oldest, biggest, or first…something. Amazing and unique sights around every corner define a native's Brooklyn. And many of the families that built these landmarks still live amongst them. Take that, Manhattan!

Best Views

One of the best things about Brooklyn is how underrated it is. Try the **Beard Street Pier (Map 8)** in Red Hook for a stunning view of the Statue of Liberty and Lower Manhattan, sans crowds no matter what the season. **Brooklyn Bridge Park (Map 5)**, located along the water in DUMBO below Brooklyn Heights, leads to a bevy of scenic vistas, and it has great spots to escape it all to boot. The **Brooklyn Heights Promenade (Map 5)** has gazillion-dollar views of Lower Manhattan and the harbor beyond, and makes for a lovely sunset stroll. The pedestrian pathway across the **Manhattan Bridge (Map 5)** is another destination often overshadowed by its more famous neighbor. The views of the river and the shimmering Financial District are just as good as those from the **Brooklyn Bridge (Map 5)**, and you can also see the **Jetsons Building (Map 5)** on the Brooklyn side, variously lit depending on the whims of its owners. The **Williamsburg Bridge (Map 2)** also offers exciting views of the city. Heading toward Queens on the BQE you'll have to cross the Kosciusko Bridge, named for the Polish general who fought alongside America in the Revolutionary War. While keeping your eyes on the road, take a quick glimpse toward Midtown from one of the borough's highest points.

Architecture

Brooklyn has its own "Arc de Triomphe" at **Grand Army Plaza (Map 9)**, formally named the Soldiers' and Sailors' Arch. It, too, clogs traffic around its gigantic rotary, and marks the way to both the **Brooklyn Museum (Map 10)** and the **Brooklyn Botanic Garden (Map 9)**, two venerable architectural marvels. Both have an antique air about them, though the museum steps have been renovated in a somewhat futuristic fashion. The arch also houses the must-see **New York Puppet Library (Map 9)**, open only on Saturdays in the summer. Even Paris can't top that. Prospect Park West runs along the most expensive side of the park where turn-of-the-century homes that might redefine some people's concept of Brooklyn still stand. In north Brooklyn, the **Williamsburgh Savings Bank Building (Map 6)** with its gigantic golden dome is similarly opulent while the gently curving weathered-steel facade of the **Barclays Center (Map 9)** nices up a fairly standard multi-purpose arena.

Historical

In Bed-Stuy, the **Akwaaba Mansion (Map 7)** is an example of the area's early glory, and many of the surrounding brownstones follow in its stylistic footsteps. Back in Walt Whitman's old neighborhood in Fort Greene is the Pratt Institute where university buildings include a former shoe factory, several original sealed subway tunnels, and a working **Power Plant (Map 6)**. Litchfield Villa (see Prospect Park) is an Italian-style castle just across 5th Street in Prospect Park. Some historic farmhouses worth visiting include the Lefferts House (see Prospect Park) in the "Children's Corner" of Prospect Park and the Lott House (Eastern Brooklyn) on E 36th Street in Marine Park. Both were built in the 18th century and now look slightly odd in their respective neighborhoods, having remained wholly untouched for years. Meanwhile, **Green-Wood Cemetery (Map 11)** in Sunset Park has more famous graves than you can shake a stick at, and hosts many very much live events.

See Also...

Junior's Restaurant (Map 5) is a mecca for those wishing to visit rap star Notorious B.I.G.'s old stomping ground. The cheesecake is world–famous as well, so no matter what motivates you, you'll be satisfied. If you find yourself suddenly in need of more underground mix tapes or perhaps some fresh new kicks, then it's off to the **Fulton Street Mall (Map 5)** for these and other urban necessities. The **Brooklyn Brewery (Map 2)** is also a great place to sample some of the best Brooklyn has to offer, in the form of its delicious lagers and ales.

Arts & Entertainment · **Art Galleries**

Overview

The major players in Brooklyn are located in Williamsburg and DUMBO, but Bushwick now has more than a dozen upstarts and there are notable galleries in Greenpoint, Fort Greene, Carroll Gardens, and Red Hook as well. Wagmag (wagmag. org) is the best place to find up-to-date show listings and keep track of openings. The **Brooklyn Arts Council (Map 5)** (brooklynartscouncil.org) supports local artists in addition to having its own art gallery, film festival, seminars, education programs, and other events.

DUMBO

The DUMBO Arts Festival brings 200,000 visitors to check out work by over 500 artists for three very busy days each fall. Permanent galleries with regular exhibitions include the **DUMBO Arts Center (Map 5)**, the group of second-floor galleries at 111 Front Street, and the always interesting **Jan Larsen Gallery (Map 5)**.

Williamsburg and Greenpoint

Many galleries stay open late on the second Friday of the month (every2nd.org), and the people-watching is as good as the art gazing (or better). Huge spaces like **House of Yes (Map 3)** attract a following with visual art, performances, and high-concept parties.

Other Areas

The **Brooklyn Waterfront Artists Coalition (Map 8)** is largest artist-run, not-for-profit art organization in the borough with over 500 artists involved and a giant exhibition space in Red Hook (bwac.org). The Gowanus Open Studios Tour happens every October, a great chance to see just how the artsy sausage is made (artsgowanus.org). In Clinton Hill, Russell Simmons and his brothers founded the **Corridor Gallery (Map 6)** to showcase local artists.

Map 1 • Greenpoint

Axis Gallery	50 Dobbin St	212-741-2582
Dabora Gallery	1080 Manhattan Ave	917-656-2106
Janet Kurnatowski Gallery	205 Norman Ave	718-383-9380
Rawson Projects	223 Franklin St	718-388-2706

Map 2 • Williamsburg

AG Gallery	107 N 3rd St	718-599-3044
Art 101	101 Grand St	718-302-2242
Black & White	483 Driggs Ave	718-599-8775
Cave	58 Grand St	718-388-6780
Capricious Space	285 N 6th St	718-384-1208
Causey Contemporary	293 Grand St	718-218-8939
Cave	58 Gradn St	347-838-4677
Cinders	103 Havemeyer St	718-388-2311
Espeis Archetype Gallery	90 Wythe Ave	718-388-4049
Eyelevel BQE	364 Leonard St	917-660-4650
Figureworks	168 N 6th St	718-486-7021
The Front Room Gallery	147 Roebling St	718-782-2556
Gitana Rosa	19 Hope St	718-387-0015
Holland Tunnel	61 S 3rd St	718-384-5738
Momenta Art	359 Bedford Ave	718-218-8058
Parker's Box	193 Grand St	718-388-2882
Pierogi Brooklyn	177 N 9th St	718-599-2144
Sideshow	319 Bedford Ave	718-486-8180
Slate Gallery	136 Wythe Ave	718-387-3921
Southfirst	60 N 6th St	718-599-4884
Williamsburg Art & Historical Society	135 Broadway	718-486-7372

Map 3 · East Williamsburg

Brooklyn Fire Proof	119 Ingraham St	718-456-7570
C.C.C.P. Gallery	56 Bogart St	718-821-2180
Chez Bushwick	304 Boerum St	718-418-4405
Eastern District	43 Bogart St	718-628-0400
English Kills	114 Forrest St	718-366-7323
Grace Space	840 Broadway	646-578-3402
House of Yes	408 Jefferson St	
NutureArt	910 Grand St	718-782-7755
NurtureArt Gallery	56 Bogart St	718-782-7755
The Parlour Bushwick	791 Bushwick Ave	718-360-3218

Map 4 · Bushwick

Norte Maar	83 Wyckoff Ave	646-361-8512

Map 5 · Brooklyn Heights / DUMBO / Downtown

5+5 Gallery	111 Front St	718-624-6048
BAC Gallery	111 Front St	718-625-0080
BRIC Rotunda Gallery	33 Clinton St	718-683-5604
DUMBO Arts Center	30 Washington St	718-694-0831
Gloria Kennedy Gallery	111 Front St	718-858-5254
Henry Gregg Gallery	111 Front St	718-408-1090
JLA Studios	63 Pearl St	718-797-2557
Jubilee	117 Henry St	718-596-1499
powerHouse Arena	37 Main St	718-666-3049
Salena Gallery	1 University Plz	718-488-1051
Spring	126 Front St	718-222-1054

Map 6 · Fort Greene / Clinton Hill

Corridor Gallery	334 Grand Ave	718-230-5002
Ex Gallery	872 Kent Ave	718-783-0060
The Rubelle and Norman Schafler Gallery	200 Willoughby Ave	718-636-3517
Underbridge Pictures	181 St James Pl	917-656-5513

Map 7 · Bedford-Stuyvesant

A Space Gallery	1138 Broadway	917-776-0772
Brooklynite Gallery	334 Malcolm X Blvd	347-405-5976

Map 8 · BoCoCa / Red Hook

Brooklyn Waterfront Artists Coalition	499 Van Brunt St	718-596-2507
The Invisible Dog	51 Bergen St	347-560-3641
Kentler International Drawing Space	353 Van Brunt St	718-875-2098
Metal & Thread	398 Van Brunt St	718-414-9651
MF Gallery	213 Bond St	917-446-8681
Micro Museum	123 Smith St	718-797-3116
Observatory	543 Union St	http://observatoryroom.org/
Proteus Gowanus	543 Union St	718-427-2200
Space 414	414 Van Brunt St	718-408-1643
UrbanGlass	126 13th St	718-625-3685

Map 9 · Park Slope / Prospect Heights / Windsor Terrace

440 Gallery	440 Sixth Ave	718-499-3844
Brooklyn Artist Gym	168 7th St	718-858-9069
JK Flynn	471 Sixth Ave	718-369-8934

Map 11 · Sunset Park / Green-Wood Heights

Tabla Rasa Gallery	224 48th St	718-833-9100

Arts & Entertainment • **Bookstores**

Though there are far fewer bookstores in Brooklyn than there are writers, most neighborhoods have at least a few options. Williamsburg's elegant **Spoonbill & Sugartown (Map 2)** is a standout. In Cobble Hill/Carroll Gardens, there's the beloved independent **BookCourt (Map 8)** and funky **Freebird Books (Map 8)** with the perfect combo of used titles and great coffee. Park Slopers head to **Community Book Store (Map 9)**, a cozy neighborhood meeting place complete with a cafe and garden. Small shops like **Unnameable Books (Map 9)** still cram in a fine selection of used and new. Fort Greene's **Greenlight Bookstore (Map 6)** is expertly curated. Head to Borough Park and Brighton Beach for dizzying selections of Jewish and Russian bookstores, respectively.

Map 1 • Greenpoint

Word	126 Franklin St	718-383-0096	Literary fiction, non-fiction, and kids' books.

Map 2 • Williamsburg

Desert Island	540 Metropolitan Ave	718-388-5087	Comics, visual arts books, zines, and consignment finds.
Idlewild Books	218 Bedford Ave	212-414-8888	Extensive foreign-language offerings and language classes.
Open Air Modern	489 Lorimer St	718-383-6465	Old and rare books and furniture.
Spoonbill & Sugartown	218 Bedford Ave	718-387-7322	Art, architecture, design, philosophy, and literature. New and used.

Map 5 • Brooklyn Heights / DUMBO / Downtown

Barnes & Noble	106 Court St	718-246-4996	Chain bookstore.
powerHouse Arena	37 Main St	718-666-3049	One of our favorite gallery/bookstores.
Brooklyn Historical Society	128 Pierrepont St	718-222-4111	Fun gift shop with all manner of Brooklyn-themed merch.

Map 6 • Fort Greene / Clinton Hill

Greenlight Bookstore	686 Fulton St	718-246-0200	Ft. Greene's newest and immediately best bookstore.

Map 8 · BoCoCa / Red Hook

Book Court	163 Court St	718-875-3677	Classic Cobble Hill bookstore w/ great readings, selection, etc.
Community Book Store	212 Court St	718-834-9494	General interest.
Freebird Books	123 Columbia St	718-643-8484	Used.
Idlewild Books	249 Warren St	718-403-9600	Extensive foreign-language offerings and language classes.

Map 9 · Park Slope / Prospect Heights / Windsor Terrace

Brooklyn Museum	200 Eastern Pkwy	718-638-5000	Usual art-related offerings plus fun Brooklyn-made items.
Community Book Store	143 Seventh Ave	718-783-3075	General books.
Terrace Books	242 Prospect Park W	718-788-3475	Used & new.
Unnameable Books	600 Vanderbilt Ave	718-789-1534	General new and used.

Map 12 · Borough Park

Bulletproof Comics	4507 Ft Hamilton Pkwy	718-854-3367	Comics. If you're into that sort of thing.
Eichler's	5004 13th Ave	718-633-1505	Borough Park Judaica superstore.

Map 13 · Kensington / Ditmas Park

Shakespeare & Co	150 Campus Rd	718-434-5326	Brooklyn outpost of Manhattan mini-chain.

Map 14 · Bay Ridge

The Bookmark Shoppe	8415 Third Ave	718-833-5115	Mostly bestsellers and children's.

Map 15 · Dyker Heights / Bensonhurst

International Bookstore	1914 86th St	718-236-1090	Russian books.

Map 16 · Midwood

Here's A Book Store	1964 Coney Island Ave	718-645-6675	Quaint and impressive, rare finds, new and used, knowledgeable staff.

Arts & Entertainment • **Movie Theaters**

This place used to be teeming with hundreds of grand movie theaters. Unfortunately, almost all of the neighborhood movie palaces have been lost to the bulldozer or recycled into 99-cent stores. Despite its huge population, today Brooklyn offers very few theaters and even fewer decent ones. Nonetheless, for those who resist the urge to hop a subway to Manhattan, there are some worthwhile options.

What neighborhood cinemas may lack in sound quality or screen size, they make up for in grit and charm. **Cobble Hill Cinemas (Map 8)** shows first-run and independent films and offers cheap tickets on Tuesdays and Thursdays. The **Kent Triplex (Map 16)** in Midwood could use a major renovation, but it's the place if you're into Russian films and they offer reduced-rate tickets on Wednesdays.

Movie buffs who are especially interested in independent and experimental films will be happy to know that Brooklyn has the most vibrant scene in the city. **Nitehawk Cinema (Map 2)** not only puts good things on screen, they serve cocktails and dinner too. But the gem for the true cinephile is **BAM Rose Cinemas (Map 6)**. It boasts a gorgeously appointed space with tasty popcorn, pleasant service, and an exceptional choice of art house and foreign films. The theaters are rarely overcrowded and it is always clean and inviting, unique to the New York moviegoing experience. Manhattanites have even been known to make the colossal effort to leave their sacred island every so often to attend movies there! Specifically worth checking out is BAMcinématek, which hosts retrospectives, special screenings, and appearances by directors and actors.

Some of the hippest cinema in Brooklyn happens a bit under the radar. At the top of the list is **Rooftop Films** (www.rooftopfilms.com; 718-417-7362) which mixes independent cinema with fresh air on roofs around town during the warmer months. The gang at **BBQ Films** (bbqfilms.com) tends to show classic films in bars with some food and drink options to match. And don't forget the Brooklyn Public Library, which has the best deal in the borough with regular free screenings.

And then of course there are your soulless multiplexes showing typical Hollywood fare, complete with stale popcorn and annoying commercials…

Movie Theaters	Address	Phone		Map
Indie Screen	285 Kent Ave	347-512-6422	Dinner and an art house movie under one roof.	2
Nitehawk Cinema	136 Metropolitan Ave	718-384-3980	Dinner, cocktails and craft beer while you watch indie flicks.	2
Brooklyn Heights Cinema	70 Henry St	718-596-5095	Intimate, classy, and just about perfect.	5
Regal Court Street Stadium 12	108 Court St	718-246-7995	Audience-participation-friendly megaplex.	5
BAM Rose Cinemas	BAM, 30 Lafayette Ave	718-636-4100	Great seating and mix of first runs and revivals.	6
Cobble Hill Cinemas	265 Court St	718-596-9113	Great indie destination, though theaters are small.	8
Pavilion Movie Theatres	188 Prospect Park W	718-369-0838	Nice mix of stuff right across from Propsect Park.	9
Kent Triplex	1170 Coney Island Ave	718-338-3371	Moron blockbuster destination.	16
Rooftop Films	various locations	718-417-7362	Summer rooftop series—check website for locations!	n/a

Museums

The main attraction is the **Brooklyn Museum (Map 10)** with an extensive permanent collection that includes both Rodin sculptures and Egyptian mummies and the occasional major touring show. Loads of people turn out for "First Saturdays" to dance, explore, mingle, and admire the cutting-edge architecture (a transparent, space-age exterior fronting an old-world, Romanesque facade). History aficionados will enjoy the **Brooklyn Historical Society (Map 5)**, housed in a four-story Queen Anne-style building downtown. The nearby **New York Transit Museum (Map 5)** is a must for trainspotters. Williamsburg's funky and fascinating **City Reliquary (Map 2)** exhibits the historic treasures of everyday New Yorkers. Kids and adults alike shouldn't miss the touchy-feely exhibits at the **Brooklyn Children's Museum (Map 10)**, which is regarded as the best of its kind in New York.

Museums	Address	Phone	Map
City Reliquary	370 Metropolitan Ave	718-782-4842	2
Brooklyn Historical Society	128 Pierrepont St	718-222-4111	5
New York Transit Museum	Boerum Pl & Schermerhorn St	718-694-1600	5
The Toy Museum of NY	157 Montague St	718-243-0820	5
Museum of Contemporary African Diasporan Arts	80 Hanson Pl	718-230-0492	6
Waterfront Museum	290 Conover St	718-624-4719	8
Brooklyn Museum	200 Eastern Pkwy	718-638-5000	9
Morbid Anatomy Museum	424 3rd Ave	347-799-1017	9
The Old Stone House	336 3rd St	718-768-3195	9
Brooklyn Children's Museum	145 Brooklyn Ave	718-735-4400	10
The Living Torah Museum	1601 41st St	718-686-8174	12
Harbor Defense Museum	230 Sheridan Loop	718-630-4349	15
Coney Island Museum	1208 Surf Ave	718-372-5159	n/a
New York Aquarium	Surf Ave & West 8th	718-265-3474	n/a
Weeksville Heritage Center	158 Buffalo Ave	718-756-5250	n/a
Wyckoff Farmhouse Museum	5816 Clarendon Rd	718-629-5400	n/a

Theaters

Broadway and Lincoln Center may have the big bucks and the well-known stars, but Brooklyn has many firmly rooted theater, dance, and music companies and seems to welcome new ones every year. The Brooklyn Academy of Music (just call it BAM) serves as the centerpiece for performing arts in Kings County. Consisting of the gorgeous, Beaux-Arts **Harvey Lichtenstein Theater (Map 6)**, the **Howard Gilman Opera House (Map 6)**, Rose Cinemas, and BAMcafé, it's a popular stopping point for an assortment of international, national, and local theater, dance, and classical music companies. BAM supplies a healthy mix of the traditional, contemporary, and experimental and serves as home to the illustrious and very hip Brooklyn Philharmonic.

For classical recitals in a casual setting, you can't get less formal than **Bargemusic (Map 5)**, moored at the Fulton Ferry landing. Concerts (some free) are presented year round, but with a romantic view of the Manhattan skyline it's especially popular on date nights during the warmer months.

For opera lovers on a budget who don't want to stand in the nosebleed section of the Metropolitan Opera House, where you can't tell a mezzo from a countertenor, the **Regina Opera Company** (reginaopera.org) gives you all the classics within the confines of a Catholic school auditorium in Sunset Park. Production values are modest, but do you really need live horses to do La Boheme?

The **Galapagos Arts Space (Map 5)** and **St. Ann's Warehouse (Map 5)** encourage artists to experiment with music and performance. St. Ann's productions have been known to move to Broadway. Galapagos regularly hosts a new breed of retro-yet-feminist-approved burlesque shows, where mixed gender audiences cheer on female striptease dancers whose routines are so funny and bizarre you'll probably forget to become aroused. The **Brooklyn Lyceum (Map 9)** has a regular hodgepodge of vaudeville and theater shorts.

Is your iPod loaded up with Rodgers and Hammerstein? Can't get enough of those Neil Simon comedies and Arthur Miller dramas? **The Heights Players (Map 5)** have been entertaining Brooklynites with popular favorites and recent Broadway and Off-Broadway hits since the days when Tennessee Williams was a fresh new voice. The slightly younger **Gallery Players Theater (Map 9)** lean more toward off-beat works by the likes of Terrence McNally and Stephen Sondheim, often mounting the first New York revivals of recently closed plays and musicals.

Theaters	Address	Phone	Map
Brick Theatre	575 Metropolitan Ave	718-907-6189	2
Charlie Pineapple Theater Company	208 N 8th St	718-907-0577	2
Bargemusic	Fulton Ferry Landing	718-624-2083	5
BRIC Studio	647 Fulton St	718-855-7882	5
Brooklyn Arts Council	55 Washington St	718-625-0080	5
Galapagos Art Space	16 Main St	718-222-8500	5
The Heights Players	26 Willow Pl	718-237-2752	5
Issue Project Room	22 Boerum Pl	718-330-0313	5 tavern
St Ann's Warehouse	38 Water St	718-254-8779	5
651 Arts	651 Fulton St	718-636-4181	6
Harvey Lichtenstein Theater	651 Fulton St	718-636-4100	6
Howard Gilman Opera House	30 Lafayette Ave	718-636-4100	6
Paul Robeson Theatre	54 Greene Ave	718-783-9794	6
The Billie Holiday Theater	1368 Fulton St	718-636-0918	7
Jalopy Tavern	315 Columbia St	718-395-3214	8
Brooklyn Arts Exchange	421 Fifth Ave	718-832-0018	9
Brooklyn Conservatory of Music	58 Seventh Ave	718-622-3300	9
Brooklyn Family Theatre	1012 Eighth Ave	718-670-7205	9
Brooklyn Lyceum	227 Fourth Ave	718-857-4816	9
Douglass Street Music Collective	295 Douglass St		9
Gallery Players Theater	199 14th St	718-595-0547	9
Puppetworks	338 Sixth Ave	718-965-3391	9
Regina Opera Company	5902 6th Ave	718-232-3555	11
Gershwin Theater	2900 Bedford Ave	718-961-5666	13
Walt Whitman Theatre, Brooklyn Center for the Performing Arts	2900 Campus Rd	718-951-4500	13
Goldstein Performing Arts Center Kingsborough Community College	2001 Oriental Blvd	718-368-5000	n/a
Harry Warren Theater	2545 Bath Ave	718-996-4800	n/a

In terms of nightlife, it's no longer about whether Brooklyn can match up to Manhattan. Those days are long past, dear friends—the question now is: why bother to go into Manhattan at all? The live music scene in Brooklyn is better, the drinks are cheaper, and you have to deal with far fewer tourists, fratboys, and suits (although you will have to deal with far more hipsters, so maybe that one's a push). There are now even more bowling alleys in Brooklyn than Manhattan—crazy, right? Well, below are some of our favorite sports to listen, drink, groove, or simply hang. Enjoy!

Live Music

Brooklyn is enough of a tastemaker to now demand the attention of touring acts. The largest venues, **Warsaw (Map 1)**, **Music Hall of Williamsburg (Map 2)**, **The Bell House (Map 9)** and **Knitting Factory (Map 2)**, book rock, hip-hop, and experimental music for panting droves of audiophiles. For a more intimate feel, and an emphasis on folk music, check out **Pete's Candy Store (Map 2)** or **Jalopy (Map 8)**. **Barbes (Map 9)** is the spot for world music, including great African gigs every Wednesday night, and jazz is also alive and well there.

Hipster Bars

If you're not sure whether you've stumbled into a hipster enclave, look for board games and quiz-night emcees and a swarm of oddly dressed folks trying their damnedest not to enjoy themselves. Of course, hipsters aren't all bad. At least they know how to pick bars. They've made several their own, including **Buttermilk (Map 9)** in Park Slope, **Enid's (Map 1)** in Greenpoint, and **Union Pool (Map 2)** in Williamsburg.

Atmosphere

This is a subjective category to be sure, but there are just certain bars that you go to for more than simply the beer selection or the drink specials. You go there because the ambience is interesting and inviting. **Iona (Map 2)** in Williamsburg, with its backyard patio and fire pits, is a case in point, as is secret-entrance **Larry Lawrence (Map 2)**. Since 1890, **Sunny's (Map 8)** has been the bar in Red Hook. It once took in patrons on a pay-what-you-wish basis, but Red Hook's rise has given them reason to actually charge for the alcohol served in this charming hideaway. And if you just want to go somewhere to relive the glory days of your teen years (but with legal drinking), rush over to **Barcade (Map 2)**, which is filled with '80s video games including NFT fave Q*bert.

Jukebox

If the DJ won't take requests and the bartender is only interested enough to put an iPod on shuffle, then you've got to go for the jukebox. For pure eclecticism, you can't beat **Daddy's (Map 2)** in Williamsburg. Indie rock fans should visit **Commonwealth (Map 9)** in Park Slope. For classic rock, new wave, and everything in-between, check out **Boat Bar (Map 8)** in Carroll Gardens. **The Levee (Map 2)** also has a stellar jukebox.

Arts & Entertainment • Nightlife

The Great Outdoors

For about eight months of the year, outdoor drinking is fun. One perennially popular spot is **Gowanus Yacht Club (Map 8)** in Carroll Gardens. Bushwick's **The Narrows (Map 3)** has a patio bigger than the bar itself. Locals love **Franklin Park (Map 10)** in Crown Heights and **Soda (Map 9)** in Prospect Heights. Williamsburg's **Nita Nita (Map 2)** and **East River Bar (Map 2)** cater to a trendy crowd. Even outer borough-averse Manhattanites will make the trek to the neighborhood for a chance to gaze back at their island while sipping swank cocktails at **The Ides Bar at Wythe Hotel (Map 2)** or on the more laid-back rooftop of **Berry Park (Map 2)**.

Dive Bars

Truly grimy old bars are either closing shop or they're becoming stylized versions of truly grimy old bars. Bucking the trend right in the heart of irony-drenched Williamsburg is **Turkey's Nest (Map 2)**: no hipster joint pretending to be seedy, it's a certified craphole. If you want something a little more tame, try **Greenpoint Tavern (Map 2)** for long-time locals and newbie hipsters all drinking cold Bud in disposable cups together. **Tommy's Tavern (Map 1)** and **Palace Café (Map 1)** in Greenpoint also host a mix of boozehounds young and old, and on the weekends Tommy's has live music in the back room that is surprisingly good. For those in need of a brewski in Midwood, the perfectly dingy atmosphere of **Nitecaps (Map 16)** will treat you right. Bay Ridge's best bet is the cluttered confines of **JJ Bubbles (Map 14)**.

Best All Around

Certain bars, for whatever reason, simply rule. If you like a strong drink with no attitude and a touch of history, saddle up to the ancient bar at **The Brooklyn Inn (Map 8)**. This is an excellent watering hole for locals to chat and drink up among friends. Plus, they get major bonus points for being one of the few TV-free bars left in the city. For Manhattan quality cocktails at Brooklyn prices, check out **Brooklyn Social (Map 8)** in Carroll Gardens. Their old-fashioned mixology makes it worth dealing with the crowds. **Red Hook Bait & Tackle (Map 8)** is a perfect place to pass a lazy Sunday afternoon or a lively Friday night. The place has everything going for itâ€"pinball, funky décor, nice bartenders, stiff drinks, and a great soundtrack. **Spuyten Duyvil (Map 2)** in Williamsburg is usually bursting with patrons due to its cultish following, but it's worth weaving through the hordes to sample over 80 international beers that will blow your mind. Luckily, the warm, knowledgeable staff will help you decipher the menu. Nearby **Barcade (Map 2)** runs a close second in beer geekery and has more space to handle a crowd. For the ideal modern Brooklyn bar, you can't do better than **Sycamore (Map 13)**. Approachable bartenders, a nice back patio, and a chill vibe add up to one of the best places to down a drink with friends. Plus, what other bar anywhere has a flower shop in the front room?

To eat in Brooklyn—it's anything you want it to be…

You Got Ya Two Kinds of Italian Places—

The old ones and the new ones. With a few exceptions, the new ones come out on top. The exceptions? **Ferdinando's (Map 8)** for killer Sicilian, no pun intended, **Queen (Map 5)** for classic white-linen Italian, and **Joe's of Avenue U (Eastern Brooklyn)** for buffet-style. But for 21st-century Italian, almost every nabe in BK has it goin' on—so check out **Acqua Santa (Map 2)** in Williamsburg, **Locanda Vini & Olii (Map 6)** in Clinton Hill, **Al Di La (Map 9)** in Park Slope, **Frankie's 457 (Map 8)** in Carroll Gardens, **The Good Fork (Map 8)** in Red Hook, **Bocca Lupo (Map 8)** in Cobble Hill, **Scopello (Map 6)** in Fort Greene, and **Tuscany Grill (Map 14)** in Bay Ridge. Trust us—any one of these "new"joints will take you back to the old country.

Wait, What About Pizza?! Relax, Pizza Gets Its Own Category

The champions include **Grimaldi's (Map 5)** in Brooklyn Heights, always top-rated by Zagat, the utterly fresh and brilliant **Franny's (Map 9)** on the Prospect Heights border, **Totonno** on Coney Island, the thinnest thin-crust of them all, **Di Fara (Map 16)** in Midwood, see Dominic DeMarco take the pizzas out of the oven with his bare hands, **Lucali (Map 8)** in Carroll Gardens, worth the considerable wait, and the furthest out there of them all, **L&B Spumoni Gardens (Eastern Brooklyn)** in Bensonhurst, get the Sicilian. Other favorites include hip **Roberta's (Map 3)** on the Bushwick border and **Grandma Rose's (Map 1)** under the BQE just shy of Greenpoint.

Globally, We're Just Getting Started

They say Queens is the most diverse of the five boroughs, but let's not forget, Brooklyn has impressive variety. We love the Mexican at **Alma (Map 8)** and **Tacos Matamoros (Map 11)**, but we're already in the Americas, we can get more far-flung than that. Try the simple and unpretentious Middle Eastern at **Bedouin Tent (Map 8)**, Michelin-starred **Ki Sushi (Map 8)**, South African at **Madiba (Map 6)**, Polish at **Lomzynianka (Map 1)**, Georgian at **Tbilisi (Map 16)**, Portuguese at **Convivium Osteria (Map 9)**, Malaysian at **Nyonya (Map 11)**, banquet-style Chinese dim sum at **Pacificana (Map 11)**, and more than Australian meat pies at **Sheep Station (Map 8)**.

Hip, Chic, Nouvelle Cuisine

Consult this section when your Manhattan friends, who are paralyzed with fear of the Z train, deign to visit Brooklyn. In Williamsburg, find the camouflaged door for **Zenkichi (Map 2)** or try **Diner (Map 2)**. In Bushwick, **Northeast Kingdom (Map 4)**. In Vinegar Hill, the **Vinegar Hill House (Map 5)**. In Brooklyn Heights, **Jack the Horse Tavern (Map 5)**. In BoCoCa, **Char No. 4 (Map 7)** and **Buttermilk Channel (Map 7)**. In Fort Greene, **The General Greene (Map 6)** and **No. 7 (Map 6)**. In Clinton Hill, **Locanda Vini & Olii (Map 6)**. And in Park Slope, **Flatbush Farm (Map 9)** and our perennial favorite **Blue Ribbon (Map 9)**. Or don't take your Manhattan friends, let them have their flavorless, over-priced UWS brunches.

Real, Affordable Comfort Food

The antidote to hip, in the form of burgers at **Bonnie's Grill (Map 9)**, pierogis at **Christina's (Map 1)**, breakfast at **The Usual (Map 9)**, decent BBQ at **Mable's (Map 2)** or **The Smoke Joint (Map 6)**, and tacos at **Tortilleria Los Hermanos (Map 4)** or **Mexico 2000 (Map 2)**.

Where Everyone Knows Your Name

This is by no means an exhaustive list, but these are just cool, friendly places to go to. **The Hope & Anchor (Map 8)** is close to the top of the list, followed by **Tom's (Map 9)** in Prospect Heights, **The Richardson (Map 2)** for small plates in East Williamsburg by the BQE, and **Northeast Kingdom (Map 4)** in Bushwick. Insert your own here:_____.

Our Favorite Restaurants

Again, impossible to make a definitive list, but here we go: **Applewood (Map 9)**—Brooklyn slow food, **Blue Ribbon (Map 9)**—surely you didn't think we'd forget, **Stone Park Café (Map 9)**—any place with marrow is a friend of ours, **Pates et Traditions (Map 2**—easily the finest savory/sweet crepes in the borough on an unassuming corner, **Convivium Osteria (Map 9)**—one of the best interiors (especially the basement) this side of the Atlantic, **Henry's End (Map 5)**—Elk Chops + Samuel Smith's Nut Brown Ale = Bliss, **Anella (Map 1)**—impeccable seasonal Italian and delicious bread baked in flowerpots, **Vinegar Hill House (Map 5)**—possibly the best cast-iron chicken on the planet, and last but not least, **Peter Luger (Map 2)**—this steak will change your life, if you don't die from the unadulterated pleasure.

Brooklyn has been called the world's largest small town, and we feel this most strongly when strolling down charming streets lined with fruit stands, cheese shops, butchers, bargain basements, bookstores, clothing boutiques, and other essentials. You can find everything you need without ever leaving the borough. Most of the good stuff is concentrated in Williamsburg, BoCoCa, and Park Slope, but every neighborhood has something to offer.

Food

For anything and everything Italian, get thee to Bensonhurst or to Carroll Gardens. In the former, **Villabate (Map 15)** will make you quiver with sweet delights while **Frank and Sal Prime Meats (Map 15)** can supply you with top notch mozzarella and sopressata for life. In the latter, it's **Mazzola (Map 8)** for lard bread, **Caputo's (Map 8)** for imported goods and home-made mozzarella, and **G. Esposito & Sons (Map 8)** for killer sopressata. Williamsburg's **Bedford Cheese Shop (Map 2)** is at the top of its game, though **Stinky (Map 8)** in BoCoCa is also a contender. While in that area check out the specialty dry goods at **Sahadi's (Map 8)**, fresh ground coffee at **D'Amico Foods (Map 8)**, and one of the city's best meat selections at **Staubitz (Map 8)**. **Marlow & Daughters (Map 2)** in Williamsburg also has a lot to offer a carnivore (especially one with a retro mustache). In Fort Greene, **Greene Grape Provisions (Map 6)** and **Choice Greene (Map 6)** stock all manner of gourmet groceries with an emphasis on local products. A similar option in Park Slope is **Bklyn Larder (Map 9)**. For god's gift to man (re: chocolate), **Jacques Torres Chocolate (Map 5)** in DUMBO can't be beat. The chocolate chip cookies alone are worth a trip.

Vino

In Greenpoint, **Dandelion Wine (Map 1)** stands out from the Polish vodka-filled crowd. Williamsburg's **The Natural Wine Company (Map 2)**, **Uva (Map 2)**, and **Blue Angel (Map 3)** are great. Fort Greene drinkers love **Gnarly Vines (Map 6)**, **The Greene Grape (Map 6)**, **Olivino (Map 6)**, and **Thirst (Map 6)**. In BoCoCa, **Smith & Vine (Map 8)** will never lead you wrong.

Clothing

Unique boutiques are everywhere: head to Smith and Court Streets in Carroll Gardens, Fifth Avenue in Park Slope, Franklin Avenue in Greenpoint, and just about any commercial strip in Williamsburg. You can treasure hunt in vast vintage warehouses like **Beacon's Closet (Map 2, 9)** or score deep discounts on last season's designer dresses at **Century 21 (Map 14)**. For jewelry, **Swallow (Map 8)** and **The Clay Pot (Map 9)** are excellent choices. Toppers can be found at Fort Greene's **Malchijah Hats (Map 6)** and Borough Park's **Kova Quality Hatters (Map 12)**. Nearby **Underworld Plaza (Map 12)** sells underwear, not mafia accoutrements. If uniqueness is not what you seek, the **Atlantic Terminal Mall (Map 6)** provides a comfortably bland home to Victoria's Secret, Old Navy, Children's Place, and other familiar bargain chains.

Home

All the basics can be found at **Target (Map 6)**, **IKEA (Map 8)**, and **Costco (Map 11)**. More interesting (and expensive) furnishings are on offer in DUMBO at places like **West Elm (Map 5)**. You'll find antiques in Brooklyn Heights and Cobble Hill, and mid-century modern wares at Williamsburg's **Two Jakes (Map 2)**, Fort Greene's **Yu Interiors (Map 6)** or Park Slope's **Trailer Park (Map 9)**.

Miscellaneous

Who the hell still buys records? Ask the clerks at **Earwax (Map 2)**, **Academy Annex (Map 2)**, or **Rough Trade (Map 2)**, all in Williamsburg (duh). **Bierkraft (Map 9)** is among the best places in the city to buy brews, and **Blue Marble (Map 8)** does the same for ice cream. McSweeney's shop/tutoring center, **Brooklyn Superhero Supply (Map 9)**, is a fun place to buy gifts. The local appetite for handmade jewelry, vintage clothes, twee knick-knacks, and irresistibly hip baby clothes gives rise to many a pop-up market throughout the year. The **Renegade Craft Fair** (www.renegadecraft.com) is one of the biggest and best. The ever-expanding **Brooklyn Flea (Map 6)** runs all year round, indoor in cold months and outdoors in warm, with its foodie extension Smorgasburg now popular enough to have spinoff locations all its own. And don't forget humble stoop sales: you may even make a new friend while buying a gently used Cuisinart for $10.

Street Index

Street	Map	Grid
E 65th St		
(1300-2199)	*	F5
(2400-2649)	*	G6
(2650-2799)	*	G5
66th St		
(400-849)	14	A2
(850-2171)	15	A1/A2
(2172-2178)	*	G3
E 66th St		
(1200-2099)	*	F5
(2136-2328)	*	F6
(2329-2662)	*	G6
(2663-2799)	*	G5
67th St		
(100-849)	14	A1/A2
(850-2049)	15	A1/A2
E 67th St	*	F5
68th St		
(1-654)	14	A1/A2
(1517-2049)	15	A2
(2100-2199)	*	G3
E 68th St	*	F5
E 69th St		
(1200-2049)	*	F5
(2050-2499)	*	F6
70th St		
(1-849)	14	A1/A2
(850-1999)	15	A1/A2
(2000-2099)	*	F6
(2100-2199)	*	G3
E 70th St		
(1200-1999)	*	F5
(2000-2499)	*	F6
71st St		
(1-849)	14	A1/A2
(850-1999)	15	A1/A2
(2100-2199)	*	G3
E 71st St	*	F6
72nd Ct	14	A1
72nd St		
(1-849)	14	A1/A2
(850-1999)	15	A1/A2
(2050-2199)	*	G3
E 72nd St		
(1-1999)	*	F5
(2000-2499)	*	F6
73rd St		
(1-849)	14	A1/A2
(850-1999)	15	A1/A2
(2050-2199)	*	G3
E 73rd St		
(1-1999)	*	F5
(2000-2499)	*	F6
74th St		
(1-662)	14	A1/A2
(900-1999)	15	A1/A2
(2050-2199)	*	G3
E 74th St	*	F6
76th St		
(31-661)	14	A1/A2
(950-2199)	15	A1/A2
E 76th St		
(600-949)	*	E5
(950-999)	*	F5
77th St		
(1-661)	14	A1/A2
(1000-2999)	15	A1/A2
E 77th St		
(600-949)	*	E5
(900-999)	*	F5
78th St		
(1-660)	14	A1/A2
(1000-2099)	15	A1/A2
(2100-2299)	*	G3
E 78th St	*	E5
79th St		
(1-653)	14	A1/A2
(1000-2099)	15	A1/A2
(2100-2399)	*	G3
E 79th St	*	E5
80th St		
(20-643)	14	A1/A2
(900-2049)	15	A1/A2
(2050-2249)	*	G2
(2250-2399)	*	G3
E 80th St		
(1-899)	*	E5
(1000-1099)	*	F5
(1117-1499)	*	F6
81st St		
(61-635)	14	A2/B1
(674-2049)	15	A1/A2
(2050-2249)	*	G2
(2250-2399)	*	G3
E 81st St		
(501-999)	*	E5
(1100-1199)	*	F6
82nd St		
(1-634)	14	A2/B1
(667-2049)	15	A1/A2
(2050-2499)	*	G2
(2250-2499)	*	G3
E 82nd St		
(501-999)	*	E5
(1100-1299)	*	F6
83rd St		
(1-619)	14	B1/B2
(600-2049)	15	A1/A2
(2050-2249)	*	G2
(2250-2499)	*	G3
E 83rd St		
(250-999)	*	E5
(1100-1449)	*	F6
84th St		
(150-599)	14	B2
(645-2049)	15	A1/A2
(2050-2349)	*	G2
(2350-2598)	*	G3
E 84th St		
(100-899)	*	E5
(1000-1099)	*	E6
(1200-1499)	*	F6
85th St		
(34-640)	14	B1/B2
(637-2049)	15	A1/A2
(2050-2349)	*	G2
(2350-2599)	*	G3
E 85th St		
(501-899)	*	E5
(1000-1099)	*	E6
(1200-1499)	*	F6
86th St		
(1-633)	14	B1/B2
(600-2015)	15	A1/A2
(2016-2379)	*	G2
(2380-2875)	*	G3
(2874-2966)	*	H3
E 86th St		
(100-899)	*	E5
(900-1099)	*	E6
(1150-1499)	*	F6
87th St	14	B1/B2
E 87th St		
(100-749)	*	E5
(750-1199)	*	E6
(1194-1499)	*	F6
88th St		
(1-580)	14	B1/B2
(622-799)	15	B1
E 88th St		
(1-699)	*	E5
(800-1249)	*	E6
(1250-1499)	*	F6
89th St	14	B1/B2
E 89th St		
(1-663)	*	E5
(664-1249)	*	E6
(1250-1499)	*	F6
90th St		
(200-583)	14	B2
(601-699)	15	B1
91st St	14	B1/B2
E 91st St		
(1-465)	*	D5
(466-860)	*	E5
(1163-1509)	*	E6
(1510-1813)	*	F6
92nd St		
(1-599)	14	B1/B2
(600-715)	15	B1
E 92nd St		
(1-445)	*	D5
(476-960)	*	E5
(961-1599)	*	E6
(1600-1826)	*	F6
93rd St	14	B2
E 93rd St		
(1-485)	*	D5
(486-916)	*	E5
(917-1506)	*	E6
(1601-1808)	*	F6
94th St	14	B2
E 94th St		
(3-434)	*	D5
(548-884)	*	E5
(885-1565)	*	E6
(1566-1664)	*	F6
95th Ave	*	C7
95th St	14	B2
E 95th St		
(1-536)	*	D5
(537-849)	*	E5
(850-1616)	*	E6
(1617-1708)	*	F6
96th St	14	B2
E 96th St		
(1-550)	*	D5
(551-786)	*	E5
(787-1613)	*	E6
(1614-2099)	*	F6
97th St	14	B2
98th St	14	B2
E 98th St		
(1-626)	*	D5
(628-715)	*	E5
(716-1620)	*	E6
99th St	14	B2
E 99th St	*	E6
100th St	14	B2
E 100th St	*	E6
101st St	14	B2
E 101st St	*	E6
E 102nd St	*	E6
E 103rd St	*	E6
E 104th St	*	E6

Street Index

Street	Map	Grid
Cleveland St		
(83-380)	*	C6
(381-698)	*	D6
(699-1076)	*	D7
Clifford Pl	1	B1
Clifton Pl		
(1-278)	6	A2/B2
(279-410)	7	A1
Clinton Ave	6	A1/B1/B2
Clinton St		
(1-185)	5	B1
(181-799)	8	A1/B2
Clove Rd	10	B2
Clymer St		
(36-173)	2	B1
(174-204)	*	H3
Cobek Ct	*	H3
Coffey St	8	B1
Colby Ct	*	H3
Coleman St		
(1500-1949)	*	F5
(1950-2299)	*	G5
Coleridge St	*	H4
Coles St	8	B1
Colin Pl	16	B1
College Pl	5	B1
Colonial Ct	14	B1
Colonial Rd	14	A1/B1
Colonial Gdns	14	B1
Columbia Pl	5	B1
Columbia St	5	A1/B1
Columbia Heights	5	A1/B1
Columbus Pl	*	C5
Commerce St	8	B1
Commercial St	1	A1
Commercial Wharf	8	A1/B1
Concord St	5	A2/B2
N Conduit Blvd		
(301-667)	*	C7
(668-769)	*	D7
S Conduit Blvd		
(442-622)	*	C7
(623-762)	*	D7
Coney Island Ave		
(300-1102)	13	A1/B1
(1103-2404)	16	A1/B1
(2405-2654)	*	G4
(2655-3308)	*	H4
Congress St	8	A1
Conklin Ave	*	E6
Conover St	8	A1/B1
Conselyea St		
(1-142)	2	A2
(143-245)	3	A1
Conway St	*	C6
Cook St	3	B1/B2
Cooke Ct	*	C6
Cooper St		
(1-283)	4	B2
(284-314)	13	B1
Corbin Ct	13	B1
Corbin Pl	*	H4
Cornelia St	4	A2/B2
Corso Ct	*	G3
Cortelyou Rd		
(1-149)	12	A2
(150-3049)	13	A2/B1/B2
(3050-4667)	*	E4
(4400-4999)	*	E5
Court Sq	5	B2
Court St		
(3-121)	5	B1
(122-764)	8	A1/A2/B2
Cove Ln	*	F5
Coventry Rd	*	E5
Covert St	4	A2/B2
Cox Pl	*	C7
Coyle St		
(1962-2199)	*	G4
(2400-2549)	*	G5
(2550-2852)	*	H5
Cozine Ave		
(1-169)	*	E6
(168-999)	*	D7
Cranberry St	5	B1
Crawford Ave		
(600-849)	*	G3
(850-1046)	*	G4
Creamer St	8	B1/B2
Crescent St		
(1-476)	*	C7
(477-1099)	*	D7
Crooke Ave	13	A2
Cropsey Ave		
(1-2015)	15	B1/B2
(2016-2538)	*	G2
(2539-2713)	*	H2
(2714-3131)	*	H3
Crosby Ave	*	C6
Cross St	5	A2
Croton Loop	*	E6
Crown St		
(1-640)	10	A1/A2
(641-863)	*	D5
Crystal St		
(1-124)	*	C7
(125-246)	*	D7
Cumberland St	6	A1/B1
Cumberland Walk	6	A1/B1
Cypress Ave		
(2-65)	*	B5
(66-274)	4	A1/A2
(3700-3999)	*	H2
Cypress Ct	*	C7
Cyrus Ave	*	H5
(953-1402)	*	F3
(1399-1799)	*	H5
Dahill Rd	12	A1/A2/B2
Dahl Ct	12	B2
Dahlgreen Pl	15	B1
Dakota Pl	*	G6
Danforth St	*	C7
Dank Ct	*	H3
Dare Ct	*	H5
De Sales Pl	*	C6
(19-281)	8	A2
(282-894)	9	A1/A2
(895-1566)	10	A1/A2
(1567-1772)	*	C5
(1773-2381)	*	D5
Dean St	*	D6
Dearborn Ct	10	A1
Debevoise Ave		
(1-91)	3	A1
(91-142)	*	A4
Debevoise St	3	B1
Decatur Ave	*	H5
Decatur St		
(1-431)	7	B1/B2
(424-675)	*	C5
(676-1356)	4	B2
(1357-1399)	8	A1
Degraw St		
(45-553)	8	A1/A2
(554-726)	9	A1
Dekalb Ave		
(1-56)	5	B2
(57-650)	6	A2/B1/B2
(651-1151)	7	A1/A2
(213-1735)	4	A1/B1
Dekoven Ct	13	B1
Delavan St	8	B1
Delmar Loop	*	E6
Delmonico Pl	3	B1
Dennett Pl	8	B2
Denton Pl	9	A1
Desmond Ct	*	H4
Devoe St		
(1-106)	2	A2
(107-376)	3	A1
Devon Ave	*	G5
Dewey Pl	*	C5
Dewitt Ave	*	D6
Diamond St	1	B2
Dictum Ct	*	G5
Dikeman St	8	B1
Dinsmore Pl	*	C7
Ditmars St	3	B2
Ditmas Ave		
(1-2240)	13	B1/B2
(5700-9749)	*	E5
(9750-9898)	*	E6
Division Ave	2	B1/B2
Division Pl	*	A4
Dobbin St	1	B1/B2
Dock Ave	5	A2
Dodworth St	3	B2
Dooley St	*	H4
Doone Ct	*	H4
Dorchester Rd	13	B1/B2
Dorset St	*	E5
Doscher St		
(1-61)	*	C7
(62-168)	*	D7
Doughty St	5	A1
Douglass St		
(1-256)	8	A2
(257-417)	9	A1
Dover St	*	H4
Downing St	6	B2
Drew St		
(412-609)	*	C7
(610-1299)	*	D7
Driggs Ave		
(1-70)	*	A4
(71-296)	1	B2
(297-919)	2	A1/A2/B1
Duffield St	5	B2
Dumont Ave		
(12-301)	*	D5
(302-979)	*	D6
(980-1620)	*	D7
Dunham Pl	2	B1
Dunne Ct	*	H4
Dunne Pl	*	H4
Dupont St	1	A1
Durland Pl	*	E6
Duryea Ct	15	A2
Duryea Pl	13	A2

Street Index

Street		
Linden Blvd		
(2-293)	13	A2
(294-470)	10	B2
(471-614)	*	E4
(615-1377)	*	E5
(1378-1459)	*	E6
(1460-2166)	*	D6
(2167-2898)	*	D7
Linden St	4	A2/B1
Linwood St		
(75-402)	*	C6
(403-496)	*	D6
(497-1130)	*	D7
Little St	5	A2
Little Nassau St	6	
A2**Livingston St**		
(25-303)	5	B1/B2
(304-376)	6	B1
(230-915)	*	D6
Livonia Ave		
(1-933)	*	D5
Llama Ct	*	G3
Lloyd Ct	*	G3
Lloyd St	13	A2
Locust Ave	16	A1
Locust St	3	B2
Logan St		
(1-437)	*	C7
(438-1077)	*	D7
Lois Ave	*	H5
Lombardy St		
(1-150)	*	A4
(151-323)	*	A5
(35-440)	3	B1
Lorimer St		
(1-869)	2	A2
(870-1131)	1	B1/B2
Loring Ave	*	D7
Lorraine St	8	B1/B2
Losee Ter	*	H4
Lott Ave		
(1-125)	*	D5
(126-352)	*	D6
Lott Pl	*	F5
Lott St	13	A2
Lotts Ln	*	F4
Louis Pl	*	C5
Louisa St	12	A1
Louise Ter	14	A1
Louisiana Ave		
(1-262)	*	D6
(263-875)	*	E6
Love Ln	5	B1
Ludlam Pl	10	B1
Luquer St	8	B1/B2
Lyme Ave	*	H2
Lynch St		
(2-167)	2	B2
(168-265)	3	B1
MacDonough St		
(3-543)	7	A2/B1/B2
(544-678)	*	C5
(679-822)	4	B2
MacKay Pl	14	A1
MacKenzie St	*	H4
MacArthur Rd	15	B1
MacDougal St		
(1-265)	*	C5
(266-353)	*	C6
Macon St		
(1-658)	7	A2/B1/B2
(659-799)	*	C5
(800-915)	4	B2
Madeline Ct	14	A1
Madison Pl		
(1501-1550)	14	A1
(1551-1899)	*	G4
Madison St		
(1-70)	6	B2
(69-912)	7	A2/B1/B2
(873-1407)	4	A2/B2
Madoc Ave	*	H5
Main St	5	A1
Malbone St	10	B2
Malcolm X Blvd	7	A2/B2
Malta St		
(1-251)	*	D6
(252-402)	*	E6
Manhattan Ave		
(1-314)	3	A1/B1
(315-591)	2	A2
(592-1299)	1	A1/B1/B2
(4000-4348)	*	H2
Manhattan Ct	*	H3
Manor Ct	*	H4
Maple Ave	*	H2
Maple St		
(1-586)	10	B1/B2
(2350-743)	*	D4
(744-850)	*	D5
Marconi Pl	*	C5
Marcus Garvey Blvd		
(1-56)	3	B1
(57-505)	7	A1/A2/B2
Marcy Ave		
(2-392)	2	A2/B2
(393-461)	3	B1
(462-580)	6	A2
(581-968)	7	A1/B1
Margaret Ct	*	H4
Marginal St	11	H4
Marginal St E	*	C6
Marginal St W	*	C6
Marine Ave	14	B1/B2
Marine Pky		
(1501-1649)	16	B2
(1650-1899)	*	G4
Marion St		
(1-70)	7	B2
(71-516)	*	C5
Market St	6	A1
N Market St	*	E5
S Market St	*	E5
Marlborough Ct	13	B1
Marlborough Rd	13	A1/B1
Marshall Dr	15	B1
Marshall St	5	A1/A2
Martense Ct	13	A2
Martense St		
(1-294)	13	A2
(295-368)	*	E4
Martin Luther King Pl	6	A2
Maspeth Ave	3	A1
Matthews Pl	13	B1
Maujer St		
(2-72)	2	A2
(73-379)	3	A1
Mayfair Dr N		
(1-137)	*	G5
(101-341)	*	G6
Mayfair Dr S		
(334-536)	*	G6
(537-630)	*	G5
McDonough Ave	5	A2
McGuinness Blvd	1	A1/B1/B2
McGuinness Blvd S	1	B2
McKeever Pl	10	B1
McKenny St	5	A1
McClancy Pl	*	D6
McDonald Ave		
(1-710)	12	A1/A2
(711-1034)	13	B1
(1035-2082)	16	A1/B1
(2083-2598)	*	G3
McKibben St	3	B1/B2
McKibbin Ct	3	B1
McKibbin St	3	B1
McKinley Ave	*	C7
Meadow St	3	A1/A2
Meeker Ave		
(150-527)	2	A2
(527-840)	*	A4
(841-1016)	*	A5
Melba St	*	H5
Melrose St	3	A2/B2
Menahan St	4	A1/A2/B1
Merit Ct	*	H5
Mermaid Ave		
(1400-2349)	*	H3
(2350-3799)	*	H2
Mersereau Ct	*	H4
Meserole Ave	1	A2/B1/B2
Meserole St	3	A1/A2/B1
Metropolitan Ave		
(1-663)	2	A1/A2
(3-1340)	3	A1/A2
Metrotech	5	B2
Metrotech Ctr	5	B2
Miami Ct	10	B2
Micieli Pl	12	A1
Middagh St	5	B1
Middleton St		
(1-136)	2	B2
(137-231)	3	B1
Midwood St		
(1-584)	10	B1/B2
(585-710)	*	D4
(780-872)	*	D5
Milford St		
(1-175)	*	C7
(176-796)	*	D7
Mill Ave		
(1401-2249)	*	F5
(2250-2799)	*	G5
Mill Ln	*	F5
Mill Rd	*	H3
Mill St	8	B1/B2
Miller Ave		
(1-223)	*	C6
(224-826)	*	D6
Miller Pl	*	C6
Milton St	1	B1
Minna St	12	A1
Moffat St		
(1-345)	4	B2
(346-398)	*	C5
Monaco Pl	*	C5
Monitor St		
(1-93)	*	A4
(94-300)	1	A2/B2
Monroe Pl	5	B1

Street Index